SCOTA'S
HARP

SCOTA'S HARP

MICHELE BUCHANAN

Scota's Harp

Copyright ©2015 Michele Buchanan

ISBN: 978-1-940769-46-2

Publisher: Mercury HeartLink

Albuquerque, New Mexico

Printed in the United States of America

Front cover design: August Hall

Contact the author at *tmbuchs@gmail.com*

Mercury HeartLink
www.heartlink.com

Acknowledgements

Michele would like to thank the many voices that helped in writing this novel: her husband Tom, who is supportive in all things, and special help from her daughter Megan, a writer in her own right. Help came from a long list of many friends, many from the Wordwright Group, and others that just listened to Scota's story. Special thanks to Stewart Warren who helped with publication, and August Hall who composed the beautiful art work for the cover. And, thanks to the ancient Celts, who kept their oral history alive through the ages.

*This book is dedicated
to my daughter, Megan,
and all those who treasure mythic histories,
may they never be forgotten.*

FOREWORD

University of New Mexico, Tuesday, April 16, 2013

Student backpacks cluttered aisles as people scrambled for seats in the sold-out auditorium. It was another popular lecture sponsored by UNM's "Institute of Medieval Studies," Spring Lecture Series, and featured a Harvard professor of Irish Studies.

A standing ovation greeted the bantamweight Irishman. His grey Harris tweed was perfectly tailored to his slight frame, making him look like a whimsical, jovial elf. Albuquerque in April was already hot and the auditorium was full of sweaty people, who laughed at his spicy jokes and anecdotes of his Irish childhood. His lecture smoothly coursed over ancient origin legends of Ireland, converging into the "Lebor Gabala Eirenn," the "Book of the Taking of Ireland" commonly known as the "Book of Invasions."

The distinguished professor described the Celtic gods, and the "Tuatha de Danann," the fifth group of invaders of the leprechaun's homeland. He made derisive jokes about "shape shifters" and Finn McCool, and had the audience laughing at the things ancient people held as reality.

"Even in this day and age, my very own mother told me that we are Milesians!"

The professor assured the audience that the ancient oral history of Ireland had absolutely no basis in fact. With his thorough academic research into Irish narrative mythology he showed how the "thematic content and structure of Irish mythos supports the politico-religious ideology of Ireland today." Academic prestige had trumped any value for believing ancient oral legend.

I was not convinced. Furthermore, I was saddened by his refutation of even the possibility that myths could be based on actual people.

No. Ireland was really invaded by the Milesians. Who then was Scota?

౭౦ ౭౦ ౭౦

Please refer to the Glossary for foreign words and idiomatic phrases.

ONE

Scota's Harp 343BCE

I awake in the dark to the stirring of birds
a murmur in the trees, a flutter of wings
It is the morning of my birth, the first of many,
the past lies knotted in its sheets, asleep.

Freedom is the night. Great Goddess Nut arches her body over all creation, and the stars, my sisters, blink their distant cold light. Only then is there freedom for me, Princess of Kemet. The huge palace sail fans begin to slow, the rowers sleep on their oars, and all is still. The air in this *praA*, this "great house," is heavy with sharp incense. I part my gauze curtains and step onto the cool, pink granite floor. Flower petals, now mostly dry, rustle beneath my bare feet, but give up their scent as I pass. Sher-Ri, my body servant, stirs.

"My lady?"

"No, nothing is needed," I whisper. With my *lahaf* covering my fiery red hair, I step noiselessly to the servant doorway. Miew, my small grey cat, winds through my steps to follow. "Stay here!" I plead, and she turns back to the pallet, watching me with yellow rebuffed eyes. My practiced feet know the way even with my eyes closed. Silently I count the steps for each turn. Soon I will be out into the night air where my breath can come freely.

Common people, the *nekhyt*, could not know the oppression of these palace walls. Outside, at night, all is still, even the dogs have quit their barking. Their owners may think of the palace as a great golden pinnacle of wealth and power, but for me it is a prison, where criminals live holding secrets. Outside, the thick darkness only reminds me that my future is unclear, caught in tangles like a tiny fish in slimy swamp roots. Starlight frames the doorway, and the smell of the sea gives direction to my feet.

No one really guards this passageway. The doorman is old and frail, sleeping off his beer as usual in a back corner. He would be shocked to see me! It's been easy to slip out, no lamps are lit here. Palace walls keep out foreigners, for guards are not needed to keep out the *nekhyt*. Commoners value their future spiritual lives greatly, thus order is established. Public artwork of Maat's scales, with Anubis the judge, supply strict morals for daily life. I feel safer outside of the palace walls, for the danger to me is within those walls, danger from those who would relish my death. I slip into my sandals now, and whisper, "Oh Ankh straps, tie me to mortality and guide my steps safely, this night."

My feet are too tender for going barefoot these days. As I sat in the starlight, memories came unbidden like maidens dancing. When I was a child, life was freedom at my feet, toughened on palace stone. We princesses played games and splashed in lotus scented pools. Palace rooms echoed with childish laughter. My uncle, who long ago made the journey by camel caravan with Mother, would often take me to the marshes. We poled through reeds and cattails on the raft, laden with sweet delicacies. Those days became treasured, carefree memories. My childhood friends would play hide and seek among the papyrus reeds. Sometimes Uncle would let me pole the boat through the rushes and other times he would spear a fish or frog, and teach me the ways of the marsh. There were great herons, and of course the red ibis, but those we would not hunt. We listened to their mating songs, and watched their beaks dip into the roots for bugs. It was a green forest of reeds, a green memory for my happy heart.

"Look, Scota, there is a covey of ducks... pick one, breathe slowly. Slide the string to the nock. Place your arrow in one smooth movement, feathers to your cheekbone. Hold your breath. Aim. Release!" And the arrow flew with a little whispering sound. I had my duck! My bow, a greenish recurve, had bull-horn nocks in the shape of duck heads, and strong sinew for the string. Its curves, designed by tribal people, gave it the strength of a war bow, yet the design was so different from the straight stick bows of the Medes or Persians. Perhaps the leather grip, tooled with talismans on each side, added magic to my aims. And my golden yellow fletches were easy to find in the tendrils of verdant green. Thus, I became well acquainted with hunting in the marshes, and learned to hide from quarry.

In those days my bow was raised at squabs or lesser birds, or a fat duck. I carried only bird points, while Uncle was fully armed with deadly arrows, for crocodiles or worse. With the sun on high we would find a cove, take out the small brazier, and have a secluded meal. We never saw the great grey water beasts whose pendulous bellies promised fertility through Hapi-Ta-uarit, nor were there fearsome crocodiles in this shallow water. No one would presume to follow us. We felt safe as in a dream, where the confinement of palace walls dissolved into green colonnades of papyrus stalks.

So very often these excursions were my education about the nature of things, the life cycle of creation. Uncle's tales of the old ways. Being here, in Rhakoti, should provide all that I could ever want. But I am not content just to take a river trip to Bubastis, or grow old inside these palace walls. Kemet is a great green embroidery between two deserts, but that is not the world. Cataracts to the south, and visits to the great monuments and temples all along our river are denied me. The safety of the palace binds my spirit, and Uncle knows this well.

Life seemed like a trip on a boat, as if the future was laid out along a river. "Is all that is to happen already decided?" I asked Uncle as he steered the boat to a quiet inlet.

"What do you mean?"

"Many days I feel caught in a snare. As if the palace walls want to keep me confined, and keep me as a child. Without you, and my harp, I would be totally miserable. Is it my destiny to live there always?"

"Scota, people of Kemet believe their lives are already written by their gods. You may study this when you are older."

"I want to make my own choices. It seems plain to me that Mother did not have a choice about coming to Kemet, or did she?"

"Why do you think that she did not have a choice? We were very proud of her to become the Queen of Kemet! Scota, you surprise me...what is bothering you?"

"If Mother wanted this life in Kemet, then why does she keep to her couch all day long? Why does she not visit the city, or come with us to the marsh? She closes herself up like an invalid. Even her servants who play Senet in some corner are told to "Hush!" She does not even want my harp music, tells me to leave. She is not happy."

Uncle did not need to hear more, just nodded, and quietly watched the dragonflies. They darted among the papyrus as if their zig-zag path was planned, but it was just evasion from frogs and birds. Their jeweled wings glistened, their bodies buzzed around my head, as if they too waited for answers to these life questions. Finally Uncle spoke.

"Listen to your spirit, Scota. Be quiet, and your mind will always make the best choice for you. Life presents many obstacles and pathways, just as the reeds part here, and there. Which path you take is not already decided, but if you are thoughtful, your feet will go the correct way. Our lives are not planned already. You are a princess, which was not your choice, but your station in life is just the framework for your spirit. Beyond that, your destiny is yours alone to choose."

"Then I will listen. Thank you for your teaching this day, Uncle."

A distant noise, perhaps of a bottle dropped, was far off down a crooked street. And I was once again into the present cool darkness. But what of other lands? Mother would be angry to know the things Uncle has taught me, I'm sure, for she does not understand my discontent. Perhaps she wishes to forget her homeland, and has replaced those memories with palace luxury. She would scold Uncle for this teaching, for spoiling my acceptance of life in Kemet. Uncle teaches me my peoples' tongue, called Tocharian...simple conversation really. There is no written language for mother's tribal people, but the sounds roll easily off my lips. Even so, I want to learn all I can from him, as I may need foreign alliances, someday. And I have the *neb* to pay for them.

As I continued quietly in the dark, the farther I went from the palace, those happy times seemed to be the life of some other child. As if they weren't my memories, but someone else's. Carefree days had come to an end on my twelfth birthday, as it does for all children, it seems. But how I would like to forget that summons to Mother's couch that day! She did not even sit up to talk to me, she was so deep into smokey incense and in thrall to the blue lotus blossoms near her lips. She bade me lie beside her, and stroked my hair as if to smooth the sharp edges of her words. Mother was the Queen, the God's Wife.

I did not see her often, and rarely did I see her away from her palace pallet covered in fine silks and soft goose down pillows. So that day didn't seem unusual at first. She was often absent even on major feast days or special processionals with Father Phar'o, for he could have other wives accompany him if he so chose. But then quietly, she spoke.

"Daughter, you are my pride. You are the only one in my life worth living for, and I am most thankful for you," she whispered. Words came haltingly, slurred through the haze of sedation. "Your beauty, and your true nature shines from your beautiful blue-green eyes. You are destined to be Queen of Kemet, when you reach the age of sixteen." She smiled, as if I knew the meaning of her words.

"What are you saying Mother? You are the Queen." I watched her face, now wrinkled and deeply lined by years of lotus blossoms at her mouth.

"You are the first-born Princess to your Father, and unless a son is born, you will ascend the Throne as Father's wife on your sixteenth birthday."

Momentarily stunned, I choked violently on the meaning of her words. I forgot to breathe. This is what she wanted to explain to me? As if my future was some unspoken secret I should already know? The palace became a PRISON that day. My carefree days would become nothing but a myth in a child's memory.

"Mother! Surely there is another way?" I moaned as a dead sound rose in my throat. Thoughts hung in my head like a long, dissonant harp chord. "Bribe some other mother to give you her son, and present him to Father! It would not take much gold to buy such a baby! Surely Father could be fooled?" My thoughts searched through a maze of alternatives, like a mouse in a trap.

"Lies and conspiracy will not take my honor! Your Father will have his way, or lives will be forfeited. It is only because of the alliance with Karkissa that I am still alive...There is much you do not know, and things I have not told you, to protect you." Tears welled up in her eyes, and the black kohl made ugly tracks down her wet cheeks.

"Don't you know why I am the Wife?" she continued. "Doesn't Uncle tell you of our homeland, and the long caravan and voyage to Kemet?" Mother's eyes widened, betraying distant memories of her lost family. "I have protected you as long as I can, and your solution of a stolen boy-child is a fantasy!" Grasping my cheeks, Mother said, "Do not ever think you can evade or fool this great man! His power is beyond imagining, and he *will* have his way in all things.!"

"I do not believe Father is the incarnation of Ra!" I blurted out this heresy. "A God should not be cruel. I think he has been ill-tempered since the day he was weaned! I keep my distance hoping he will forget I exist! How did he ever come to be Phar'o?"

Mother's startled mouth formed words. "Those are secrets...but perhaps you can understand his power." Then she softened. "It is true that he bought the Spartans for 250 talents of gold, and turned them away from Djedhor, the former Phar'o of Kemet. Djedhor was weak! He found refuge in Sidon's palace. Your father was a great general! And with Father's help, the king of Macedon was able to overthrow Thessaly, Illyria, and Epirus. Surely you see the evidence of bloody battles on his wound-writ face, scarred body, and crooked leg. He complains to the palace physicians about continual pain."

"But is he hateful to you?"

"Your's is not to question this Scota!" Mother is shaken by my persistence. In anger, her fists struck the pillows, as she realized I was no longer a silly child. "Your Father is the Great God Incarnate, and his power of his name is beyond question!"

"I know this Mother! He calls himself Nekhtenebef. I do not call him anything!"

"You are only twelve."Then in a calmer voice, mother said, "there is time for you to understand your responsibility as Princess of Kemet. You should fear your father, for though he does not seem to concern himself with your presence, he is told of your behavior. His piercing dark eyes see more than the surface of people. I know you never meet his gaze, although that is allowed. Just understand that he is to be obeyed."

"But Mother, when I look at him, even from the side his mouth is cruel. His lips turn down at the corners. When he first took you as his wife, was he handsome?"

Still she did not speak, only looked at me as if questioning how to explain the responsibilities she shouldered. Again I asked, feeling that this was my best opportunity to understand this once proud woman. My words tumbled out in a torrent of rebellion.

"Why do you keep to your bed and leave all the palace routines to servants? Is he so cruel to you? Is it only the lack of a son...or that you are barren? He does have half part in this!" My voice was raising into a scream. "You are *nibit pi*, mistress of the house, and yet you lie here in silence?"

To this day, I will never forget Mother's shock at my insolence. My words hung in the air like some unending chant, waiting for her answers. Time stood still while Mother formed words.

"You know times are unsettled. You know your father's power. You have seen his temper flare, seen servants, even an emissary disappear. He will have a son from you, or lose the throne. And that he will not lose." Her words were measured, her voice dry as sand. But then she turned to face me fully.

"My daughter, there is one choice I can offer you, and if you take this, another will become Father's wife." Her voice slowed again, with emphasis on each word. "But if this should be so, I will not remain within these walls."

"What choice? What of the alliance? Surely Father must keep you safe!"

"There is no safety except with my honor as First Wife. Without that, or your body continuing his line, there will be oblivion. "People *do* disappear, you know."

After a long silence, Mother turned to face me. "Here is a thing to consider: Become the Great Phar'o's daughter-wife, or become a priestess virgin. Live a cloistered life of prayer to Neith." She smiled a small perverse smile. "Service is required in life. You have this choice I give you. You have until your sixteenth birthday to decide."

I pushed away from her in shock! Composure fled from me. "Mother, is there no other path?" In truth, I should have been thankful to be given any choice for my future. I should have thanked Mother for preparing me at age twelve, instead of delaying. Perhaps I should have known all along that I was to be Phar'o's next wife. It should be an honor to bear the son he needs to continue his dynasty. An honor to couple with my Father and sit with him in processionals and feast days. But to give my supple sweet flesh to this terrifying man, so ruthless and dark? A choice of no choice! I lay on the floor, sobbing, not able to appreciate this gift of choice.

Presently she rose from her couch and cradled me in her arms. "You have some years to decide. Make the best of these years. Learn the ways of the priesthood. Find a place for your spirit to soar. Do not despair, for the future is not open to us, except in the steps our feet make." And then, with a precise wave of her hand, I was dismissed without another word. Outside, the cicadas sawed through the humid air in unison. They had purpose, but no choice.

TWO

Father's other wives had given him only daughters, and Mother was barren after my birth. The palace physicians told Father our bloodline was too foreign for more children. Even when she thought she might be pregnant again, the old wives' test failed. For when the urine was placed on two saucers, one of emmer wheat and the other barley, neither grain would sprout. And the emmer saucer, which would predict a male child, would putrefy and stink. Even though she tried every magical spell known to Kemet...a trip to Dendera, many magical potions, prayers to Ta-uarit, Apet, and every other goddess of fertility, she still failed to conceive. There were potions made with male foreskins, and special foods prescribed, and Father himself cast spells. But no more babies issued from her womb, as if it were cursed.

I have heard whisperings about his abilities with spells. But I have seen firsthand that he can bend time. At least the sunlight advanced on the floor without our moving, and the day's tasks did not get done. Father's *heka* is so strong, he can be in two places at once! He is able to fly great distances with his *qarina*, this body double, to see the far reaches of his kingdom. He has plenty of spies though, and if this ability is true, perhaps his body of flesh travels while leaving a spirit double on the throne. I have hidden in private chambers where there is a great golden bowl filled with thick wine, or perhaps blood. I have seen him staring into its scarlet ripples as if watching dancers spin. He puts little wax soldiers on little wax boats on opposite sides of the bowl. Concealing his face under a black cowl, he uses an ebony rod, swirls the water, and calls upon unseen entities. I dare not repeat the names I heard. Little ships advance, some sink, and he sees the battle outcome. Air is swirling, his cloak flaps violently, and shadows move over the ceiling. Suddenly, all is quiet. I think this is not soothsaying from an oracle as he tells it, but dark powers over enemies. If he controls the winds and seas, it is only this distraction that he did not perceive my presence there, hidden in his chambers. For Father is never to be approached without permission, even by me. I fear him for good reason.

Could Father's power extend to the stars? His astronomers read the stars as if life and futures are plainly written in their cold light. Add to this the many eyes of many mages, who report these star messages. I know the names of some stars, but sadly, they do not talk to me.

Other stories, of how he ascended the throne itself, are dismissed as heresy! Instead, fantastic accounts of heroism in battle are carved on walls and stelae throughout the kingdom. The palace *TAty*, a great bald eunuch named Hariesis, slinks in shadows, watching always...another trusted spy that strengthens Father's rule. His eyes are dark pits of hatred, seeking always to further his own plans, by controlling the palace for Father. To the people of Kemet, Father is the incarnation of RA. None raise their eyes to him, nor turn their backs. His power as Phar'o of the Double Crowns extends from the Great Green Sea to the ends of the Great River, and beyond.

Father's short, barked orders are never repeated. I never knew this man as a loving father, or anything more than a gilded king behind a cruel mouth. This is the way of Power. Being the God Incarnate, the risen Osiris, gives him all the authority over the world and our people. But not of me.

Father's mother died long ago, but no one talks of her lineage. His father, Teha-hap-imou, must have met disgrace, for he is not spoken of, nor did I ever meet him. Nor have I ever heard of other family members in his line. There are no names inscribed in the great hall. Yet, twenty years ago Father became the high general for the armies of Kemet. I do not know if he is related somehow to Phar'O Nekhthorheb I, the "falcon." I have never dared to ask him. Some say that man was Father's uncle. But there is one I can always ask, my Uncle.

"Your mother's marriage, at sixteen, was fulfillment of a pact between nations," said Uncle. "Kemet needed warriors, needed armies of foreigners to defend this green strip of land. Kemet's people are artisans, farmers, priests, physicians, and chemists. They do not take up arms."

"But I have seen paintings of wonderful chariots, with kings in battle. And great monuments of glorious past victories. And I know there are garrisons of men, parade marches, and glorious campaigns to Nubia and Punt."

"That is past history," said Uncle. "Few soldiers are natives of Kemet. Only the upper ranks, those who control the armies and direct their deaths, are native sons of this strange land. Great battles lead by Phar'o's of the past are just glyphs on our walls. Here citizens feel no shame in hiding to avoid the recruiters, nor is it awkward for the family to pay the prescribed fee to avoid service. Kemet has long been a country of mercenaries, and great fighters are well paid. Our warriors from Karkissa earn their gold. Kemet has granaries that feed the world, physicians that heal, and medicines of great worth. Your heritage, Scota, is warrior strong. I will not let you forget that."

Mother's people were a roving tribe, great swordsmen and seafarers. Some called them Karkissans, but their true name is hidden in their strange language. Mother's father, brother to Mausoleus, King of Karkissa, is a leader reputed for courage. These warriors are fearless in battle, with strong shields, recurve bows, and slings that can kill at a hundred paces. Their ships are seafaring cities, which bring wonderful trade goods to Kemet and other ports. Uncle says their seamen are unafraid of the worst storms, even at great distances from land.

"Scota, there is nothing to be feared in death but parting breath. This life is but a step into the next one. The more glorious the death, the better fortunes for the next life. No mortuary temples are needed, only a new birth in a new mother's belly. This is not the way of Kemet, but it is your blood heritage."

"You know your mother was a princess of our nation, and because our women are also warriors, her value brought enormous litters of gold to our tribe. We would not accept payment in loaves of bread, which is the custom here in Kemet. Nor would our warriors accept a papyrus tally of payment, even as honor would permit. No, it had to be gold, and not by some god or goddesses effigy or statue. Long ago Phar'o Nakhthorheb I directed his goldsmiths to strike out the first coins of Kemet with his name and face. Your father continues this coinage, pretending it is *his* face. Your mother as Great Wife, bought a great army. Do not ever doubt her value to Kemet."

All the civilized world hated the hordes from the east, those armies of men who wore dresses in battle, and prayed to some bloodthirsty eater of children. If this war were lost, civilization itself would fall, and with it, the world economy, the trading routes, and the progress and inventions of all people would surely be lost. Kemet, with the help of other civilized peoples across the Great Green Sea, formed alliances with the Sea Peoples to defend the world from this heresy from the east. And Kemet could afford the gold.

As I slipped quietly through the dark streets, I felt the small bag of coins hidden in my girdle. These I would take to my rendezvous, where they will be given in secret. My best friend could be trusted about my nightly forays, even so, I do not tell her of my real plans, for her safety and mine. She knows I am able to evade the palace at night, but Sher-Ri does not worry about me. She knows better than to ask what I'm doing. A true friend like that is full of trust and acceptance. I think of her as a true sister, or my dark twin, as she is just one month older than I. Sher-Ri is a much better sister than any of those from Father's loins. My wet nurse, Nabanna, is her mother, who came long ago from the south. Nubia, it is called. Her skin is dark as dates, warm and inviting, and Nabanna is the happiest of mothers.

Perhaps that is where Sher-Ri gets her joy of living. She is a dancer, and she seems to be continually dancing, moving with unheard rhythm. When Sher-Ri was twelve, she received patterns of scarification that look like a beaded collar around her upper chest. She did not even whimper, but joyfully accepted whatever was being done. That is Sher-Ri, who never questions the future or the past. So if I tell her I am going out at night, she smiles, and understands my need for freedom. It is something she has already inside. I would like to have that sense of security that we had at her mother's breasts, with the warm sweet milk dripping down our chins. But I am not Sher-Ri. Nor is my *shay* set in stone.

When I appear daily at the Temple of Neith for my training, the priestesses never suspect I had been out most of the night. Images of Neith, with her great bow and arrows, decorate the walls, as if protecting my secrets. The symbolism of the huntress speaks to me. How fitting that we are veiled, and secret, and skilled as the huntress! The inscription on the lintel reads:

> I am What Is and That Which will be,
> and That Which has been.
> No one has lifted the veil which covers me,
> and the fruit I have brought forth is the Sun."

My secrets are my own, hidden. But if Mother asks, the servant girls would bring news of my studies to her, for I make myself known to all at the temple. If sometimes I fall asleep during chanting, who is the wiser? Only another friend nearby, named Kenti-Sur. She lets me sleep, but pokes me if I begin to snore. In this way we care for each other, she with my sleep, and me with her calligraphy.

Afternoons were filled with other studies. My tribal harp was never brought to the temple, perhaps they thought it too shabby next to the various harps of Kemet. Those are tall, bowed at the bottom, and highly decorated with glyphs and gold plating. They are covered with magical phrases, but their sound is shrill. My harp, with its secret name, is less than my height, and played while seated. The curved wood rests on my breast, where I feel the song inside my heart. The strings do not have the high tension of the temple harps, and instead give a mellow, rich tone. I can play them both easily. In official presentations, along with drums and sistrums, I only play the gilded things. I stand behind it, swaying with the music. Our gossamer gowns shimmer in the temple oil lamps. The rooms fill with incense, and the sweet smells and beautiful sounds we make mesmerize even the most stoic listener.

I have never asked others what they think of my harp. After all, it is used differently by the tribal people. Tribal harps are used for storytelling, for accompaniment to retelling glorious battles, or odes to heroes. Harpers have high tribal position, as they are the historians for the clan. All stories are memorized, put to verse, and recalled at the chieftain's request. I know some of these stories, told to me by Uncle, but those I play only in my rooms. Once I took my harp to the Queen's chambers, to play those histories for my mother. Too soon, tears would streak down her face, and she would turn her face again to the blue lotus.

As I arrive at the Temple at first light, I stow my ragged *lahaf* behind a stone niche where offerings are laid. Sometimes I just tuck the cloth under my mantle, but it depends whether there are other eyes that might see. Passersby do not recognize me as the princess, as there are other red-haired people in our city. Lately, there are many foreigners trading and laboring, so it is not unusual to see many shades of hair color on the streets. My blue-green eyes, however, are to be hidden. As a novitiate I do not wear any jewelry or painted eye designs. I am good at blending in, so far.

My first task is to arrange trays of food, just flat bread with braised onions and green herbs. I set out some fish scraps for the temple cats, and I bring the feather of ash to light with a few quick breaths. We do not eat any flesh in the temple, only dates and bread, and an occasional honey cake. Other girls will be arriving soon, as only the temple priestesses reside here overnight. Deliveries of food, offerings, and prayer requests appear on the front steps, so these too, I bring inside. Water jugs are refreshed, and I am charged with opening new wine each week. I sniff the jugs of beer, and those few leftover drops that have soured are poured into a drain that leads away from the temple walls. Outside, small birds find this a treat.

When water has boiled for tea and all is ready, I call "*onkhou, ouza, sonbou.*" Everyone performs "*ouabou,*" a purifying ritual wash, with rose and hibiscus-petal perfumed water. Sweet smells fill the air. But this is one too many mornings for me, and I am obviously tired.

Distracted by my tasks, I did not realize that Sha'Bet, our head priestess, was standing there. "Bentreyshyt, you do your work well, setting out the morning foods and water. How was your walk to the temple this morning?"

"I am here timely, as usual, my lady. The city sleeps yet." The Head Priestess never calls me "Scota" as it is a foreign name. Instead she refers to me as Bentreyshyt, "harp of joy." But I am not joyful with her constant interrogations and suspicions, however well founded. Unlike others, I am much less interested in young men. She and her priestesses sleep within the temple each night, under virginal lock and key.

"And did you encounter any handsome strangers on your walk this day? Are you keeping to yourself, or do you raise your eyes to the foreigners in the city?" Sha'Bet has a smile on her tight lips. "Remember, you are not to visit with the shopkeepers or anyone on your visit here. As a novitiate, you must be chaste in body and mind." Her words reminded me to be even more vigilant each morning when I come. I bow deeply and look obedient.

I suspect she herself would not be able to walk the streets of Rhakoti without meeting someone's gaze, except for her heavy veils. With a quiet voice, I reply, "My Lady? I do not need either veils or your warnings. I am here to serve our great goddess, and it is my wish to be a virgin priestess some day."

Sha'Bet nods, and says, "We will be preparing for the Feast of Shemu. Make yourself useful! Go now and prepare the trays, for there is much to carry!" She is irked with my impertinence, but I cannot help but smirk at her turned back.

Every day keeps to the same routine, only interrupted by certain feast days. Soon it will be Khameseen, the days for smelling the Zephyr. Our great river Nile will turn to Hapi, and the water table will slowly rise, the water will turn green. All of Kemet will make ready for the inundation to bring life to the fields, and with that, the wind will shift from the north. There will be five happy feast days, where everyone sets off to the harbor with baskets of food, to smell the changes in the wind. Cooked duck eggs are colored brightly with onion skins for the feast of Shemu. There will be dried fish, hard cooked eggs, bundles of lettuce-wrapped honey cakes, and my favorite, cheese stuffed dates. Many people will board boats and have an early morning celebration on the water. People gather at first light, their carts loaded with small children, brightly colored pillows, and provisions for the feast. Those who stay on shore will spread blankets, lie in the soft sun, and have much appreciated rest from the daily stress of work and struggle. Children will play games --- some games of round bao stones which march around depressions in the sand, take much thinking and strategy before the stones are moved or captured. Other games of "hounds and jackals" use carved sticks to march around their wooden board. Groups of men will gamble with dice, or cards of papyrus, and get drunk with beer these days. Even the laborers on the monuments will come to rest.

In past years, I attended Shemu as a carefree child. We princesses formed a gaggle of girls, and with our handmaidens, would have free movement through the crowds. Kenti-Sur and I watched in awe as women of the temple made a special procession through the streets. "I will be with them soon," I said, "under those veils." Kenti-Sur and Sher-Ri now know of my choice, but it was a fond memory to remember those days in the streets.

"Who are those foreigners?" Sher-Ri asked.

"Uncle says those are the Milesians. Their swift boats come from the farthest east shores of the Great Green Sea, and they bring many wonderful trade items to Kemet. Miletus is a huge trading city where you can hear a hundred different languages at their bazaar."

"Oh, what fun it would be to go there!" exclaimed Kenti-Sur. "Oh, to feel the silks and smell exotic fruits. Ask your Father for a trip there someday?"

I stared at her in wonder. "Even if it were possible, this is something I could not ask. Foreigners come when the wind shifts, for sailing the Great Green Sea is very tied to the seasons.

With the wind coming from the north, they can sail from Miletus to Rhodes in a few days, but they cannot go back until the feast of Shemu. Uncle says they circle the Sea, visiting many ports along the way, go west, then finally back to northern shores. Besides, Father will not let me out of Rhakoti."

How naive were my friends in those days past. Now they know why I go to the temple each day. Their futures are not tied to some distant date. Kenti-Sur has chosen to attend the temple of Neith with me, though as one of my handmaidens, she is allowed to choose freely. At the temple we perform our morning prayers before food enters our bodies. The girls here are not poverty stricken, for the priesthood station is above that of the working people. Normally a child will follow parents' footsteps, and remain in the family occupation. But Kenti-Sur is an orphan, given to the palace by relatives long ago. It is well to have her here beside me.

Soon there will be others coming, half-sisters to me, though these other princesses come for an education rather than as novitiates. It is hard for me to imagine Articana in the temple, for even one day. It would be a sight, to see the expected confrontation with Shar'Bet! I giggle with the thought of it. But my duties in the temple have formed a numbing habit.

After first light prayers the common meeting room is filled with girlish chatter, food is eaten and cleared away. There are lessons each day in learning to read glyphs. I carefully roll papyrus, and learn many passages by heart. I would like to be a scribe, but women are not permitted in scriptoriums. Soon I will be admitted to the mysteries, to the beliefs of soul journeys and religious secrets of the priesthood. I can already recite the names of each goddess for the hours of each day and night, and those who have specific honors: those who guard the threshold, or the sleeping pallet, or the harvest. How busy these entities must be, just listening to our missives! But it is not my future to close myself up, both body and spirit, in this temple. Our highest priestess, Sha'Bet, admonishes me to listen to my "inner ear" and develop simplicity of heart and mind. She is always at my elbow.

"Novitiate! You must stop your daydreaming and attend to real meditation. Recite the prayers by memory and stop making so many mistakes!" Her stern voice breaks the calmness like a knife through water. "I can tell you are not listening to your inner ear but only to the noisy birds outside! Attend to Neith!"

"I will try harder, my Lady, and open my mind to inner peace. I will count my breaths and match the cadence." I bow my head even lower; she accepts my subservience and moves on.

Well, there *is* a relationship between Nature and Spirit. Our actions, and all experience, act as a framework to how things come about. How can my daydreaming be sinful? Sha'Bet does not suspect that I am only marking time in her midst. Still, time is no longer on my side. The feast of Shemu will put final plans in motion. My responses at catechism are perfect, my submissiveness is above question, and my adoration of the Goddess is beyond suspicion. I intend to learn every prayer, every spell, and every incantation. Maybe there is heavenly help to guide me, for my prayers are sincere. Let Maat strike me down if my plan is not honorable.

After a small noonday meal there is midday rest. I can catch up on missed sleep as the desert heat swells to its height. The temple is cooled by north facing roof openings which are slanted to bring down cool breezes from the Great Green Sea. Our pallets are raised from the floor, for protection from scorpions, and we have a deserved respite from novitiate duties. As Horus crosses the sky soon it will be time for learning music, poetry and dance. Sometimes the shrill call of a peacock breaks the rhythm, and everyone laughs. Ever present Gods and Goddesses receive messages from Kemet, but where are their responses? There is more power in gold!

Another two hours of recitation and harping, and I am now free to leave. The temple is swept of sand, and everything is put away for another day. I retrieve my hidden hood and it becomes a bundle of left-over foods to be given to beggars on my way home. As I head north into the evening hours, merchants are tallying sales of the day. The bazaar is a cacophony of noise. There is no need to cover my hair in this evening light, nor is there any hurry. I quietly seek out the old stone mason, and slip through the door like a shadow. He is busy with a customer for the moment, as the woman is ordering a new lintel with special glyphs. . . a protection spell against west winds, no doubt. In Rhakoti, everyone has a north facing door, but some close alleyways cause the wind to swirl the dust into invasive sand attacks. She is tired of sweeping out the inexorable sand. I think better to barter for a new reed curtain, as a lintel roll, than to rely on magical glyphs, but belief is stronger than her limp purse. Only the very rich have wooden doors, as wood is too precious for a citizen's home, and still, that would only invite termites. Taxes are high these last few months, due to the massive stone works ordered by Father, and the alliances he has bought.

I make my way to the back recesses of the shop, and when his customer leaves, KhamNasef finds me waiting. This old wizened man seems prosperous for the first time in his life, after a lifetime of working in the quarries. He was an overseer at huge stone millworks, until his eyes could no longer bear the bright sun. His fine sons have taken his place at the quarries, and there are many, many monuments under construction by Father. By raising magnificent monuments at Bubastis, Athiribis, and Sebennytos, Father establishes communion with the Gods for all the populace to see. The first pharaoh of the dynasty commissioned one hundred human headed sphinxes along the avenue at Luxor. Perhaps Father tries to outbuild that man? But the kind faces on those sphinxes are not that of my father. Instead artists have rendered his true likeness, full of power and determination, a mouth with corners bending down into a sneer.

Past pharaohs kept alliances with Sparta, and the other nations across the Great Green Sea, to hold power in balance. People supported the legitimacy of their leaders. Instead, Father has levied the heaviest of taxes on all of Kemet, not only to pay for the mercenaries, but to erect these monuments to certify him as the Great God. He continues to glorify the Bubastis bulls at their necropolis, and makes sacrifices to the great warrior god, Montu. I watched the ceremony at Father's anniversary, as he gave the Blue coronation crown to the Goddess Maat, as if writing in stone makes something the truth. This constant need to establish his identity with the gods seems excessive, and the people have been grumbling. Still, the stonemason's shop is busy.

"Welcome to my lowly shop, my lady," as the old man bows deeply. "Your commission is nearly completed. You shall look here?" The old man lifts several flat stones away, to show me the special marble block. It is dark gray, with tiny golden specks. He has impaled two copper rings into the opposing ends. The stone is too heavy for me to lift, of course, as it is a cubit and a half long and half as thick. But the rings will make it portable. It weighs as much as I do, but with skill, the stonemason slides the stone easily in its sand slurry. I can see each smooth face and the carvings on each side. The bas relief covers the whole stone with glyphs, large enough to read at a distance, though they are not painted or colored. It is curious to me that he is such a fine artisan, but cannot read. He has wielded his cutting tools and made the glyphs I have ordered without knowledge of their meaning.

"Here we have the glyphs you ordered," he says quietly, "are they correct?" Of course he recognizes the glyphs encircled in the rope oval, for this is Father's name, Nakhtenebef. Like all pharaohs, Father has at least five names, in order to align himself with the pantheon of major gods. My stone has room for only one more name, mine, which will suffice.

"And here the other side shows the last glyphs," his voices barely audible. "Your name, my lady?"

The other roped oval encircles my name, "Princess of Kemet, Scota Nefara-Selkis." Other glyphs the mason cannot read, or maybe he knows not to ask.

"I am extremely satisfied with your work, good man, and my father will be very pleased to receive this new stone. But I want it for a surprise, as you know. Here is your payment."

I place a mound of gold coins on the stone. His hand deftly scoops them into his account box. He knows who I am, even without my regal jewelry, but this payment price will close his mouth in secrecy. No matter, the stone could be a gift to my father, as my sixteenth birthday festivities are already on the calendar. I hope that is what he thinks.

"It speaks to you?" The old man sees the admiration on my face, as I finger the glyphs and tooled designs he has made. Some of these are tribal, and foreign to him. Ever so slightly I brushed the hanging oil lamp, causing shadows to move over the stone. The glyphs dance and sway with the light, and seem to come alive in the dimness of his shop.

"Yes, dear Sir, the glyphs speak to me and to all who look upon them. It is a good work that you have done for his majesty and me, and your skill with the *rn's* will give life forever."

The old man nods, with pride in his eyes. It is a talking stone, for there are no portraits that could be chiseled off if I fail.

It tells my name, my royal position, and my birthright as heir to the alliance. For the people of Kemet, one's "Ren" or name, is a necessary component of life, and inscriptions give vigor to the actual body. If lost, there is no immortality.

At the temple I learned that there is the physical body, "khat", the personality, "ba", the spiritual essence called "kA," all of which are connected under the Ren. The heart, "Ib," is the spiritual seat of the soul, kept inside the "ha" the physical form. There is also "Sheut," one's shadow, that can be harmed by evil forces, and a magical double, called the "qarina." And one other part, the "Akh," which we call the "shining, one" joins the stars after death. It is very complicated but all these parts must work together for the person to enter Amina. And my Ren must not be lost.

"My two sons are home from the quarry for the festival," says the old man. "They would be honored to take your stone to the palace. I am pleased that it is ready in time for Shemu!"

"Yes, of course! That would be most pleasing to me," I reply. I smoothed the layer of sand by the stone, and with a finger, drew a sketch of the palace proper. "Here is the special doorway for their entrance, on the west side. I will wait at this doorway for the delivery."

The old man called his sons, and had them wrap the stone in a reed mat, and secured it with ropes. Soon it was hoisted on a pole and carried toward the palace. I slipped away in the lengthening shadows, for I did not want to be seen leading this bundle. No one else need know of my connection to it for now, and I arrived at my doorway unnoticed. When they had stowed it safely in my chambers, I gave them each a small gold coin, to seal their lips.

THREE

Five months will pass until my sixteenth birthday. I refuse to imagine that day. Still, there is little time. Marriage normally comes with a dowry, though I do not expect this as I would not be actually leaving my family. Perhaps the goldsmiths are already working on a special collar to shackle my spirit. It will need to be very heavy to prevent words of rebellion! Here in my chambers, the stone is my "dowry," and it makes a fine pedestal for my cedar-wood chest. Mother brought this huge chest with her on the camel caravan when she left her homeland. If it were empty, I could curl up and fit inside, and let the aromatic cedar diffuse its aroma into my skin. I keep the chest well oiled, inside and out, for the dry desert of Kemet would surely cause it to crack and die.

The craftsman who made it must be a genius, for the wooden hinges close quietly, and the lid becomes a snug fit. On the outside, the oiled planks are smooth and undecorated, belying the value of the treasures inside. What is most remarkable is the wooden lock with bronze pins that keep it secure. Opening it without my key would require an ax, and I keep my key well hidden within my girdle. Even Sher-Ri does not know how to open my wonderful chest. I keep all my precious jewelry, mirrors, and special mementos within it, as it holds my future as well. Most special of all, however, is that it has a double bottom. This fits so snugly, and gives a fist-deep secret level for hidden storage.

From the temple physician I took rolls of linen bandages. These strips I used to wrap gold coins tightly into stacks, just at the height of the secret compartment. They are packed so securely that there is no chance of them shifting, or making any noise if the chest is bumped. This false floor fits so tightly that only a thin strip of linen sticking out at one edge would give it away. It took me many years to fill it; I do not open it anymore.

Above this false floor are layers of beautiful linens, silks, boxes of cosmetics, and storage of my personal things. I have asked for certain garments to be woven, of the sheerest gossamer gauze linen, which have gold threads and beads for decoration. Other linens are the deepest blue-green, that match my faience jewelry. I have a stunning faience *uadjet* necklace with gold beads, another necklace of orange carnelian lotus flowers, and many carved scarabs. There are many gold bracelets and arm bands, cajoled from Father's master goldsmith, Natef-Bak. He lives in the palace also. I danced for him many times as a young girl before I realized he was aroused by my nubile hips. Now I play my harp while he works plating gold strips onto wooden boxes or inlaying electrum and precious stones onto jeweled pieces for the palace.

From his huge box of jewels he has given me the reddest stones, green jasper, and a milky white stone that is polished like the shine of the moon. I have a special bag of yellow stones, which are my favorite, that shine like the sun. All these I keep hidden under the linens.

Natef-Bak is a skilled carver as well as a goldsmith. He has given me ivory figurines carved from elephant tusks, amulets from hippo teeth, and even crocodile leathers shaped into boxes to hold my green stones. Imagination becomes reality under his strong hands. He has mastered secrets of the finest gold granulation, done only with his blowpipe, as if by magic. His face brightens when he sees me come near. Often, I bring my harp to play as he works.

"I have come again, dear sir. I love to visit your workshop. What new beauties are you working on since I last came?'

Silently, Natef-Bak opens a wooden box to show the many small scarabs he has cast for me in faience, engraved with my name in glyphs. "Here are scarabs, molded faience and carved cinnabar. They do not take much time, for your name sings to me." And within another box, he shows me a necklace of scarabs and carnelian beads. There are many little scarabs, "left over" that he has not set yet. "These are useful as votive scarabs," he says.

"How lovely! Thank you, I will be so proud to wear your craftsmanship. All will recognize the maker when I wear them for the feast days. Others will be safe in my cedar chest. But votives? I will save them for a special need, when urgent help is asked. But Natef... do you want to make one for yourself? I could bring a special votive scarab to the temple in the morning."

Natef nods, but does not say what bothers his spirit today. Instead he shows me his workbench, littered with tools and strips of gold.

"Today I am giving this piece a skin of *neb*." His strong hands deftly curve the thin gold strips into place. The thinnest gold is soft, melded together by the push of his curved, copper, spoon-shaped tool. Natrum and other glues are applied. Soon the gold strips hold the stone in place with no apparent seam. Burnished gold glistens in the afternoon sunlight that streams through the high windows. Sometimes when the light comes down just right, it fills his workbench with the brightest beam of light. He says the tears of Ra direct his hands.

"I will play a new song for you today, a song of the sea and a rocking boat." With a few notes in a cadence, my harp sings waves and foam, and sounds like little fish jumping joyfully. My fingers slide over the strings, images of waves crashing soon come to rest as the sound fades into a lull, then quiets. His never idle hands play with a strip of gold wire as he makes another pair of anklets for me. These are connected quickly to woven gold straps for a special pair of sandals.

"It is my pleasure to work for you, my lady, for I love to adorn your beauty." Natef looks suddenly pensive, and says, "But your sister Articana is coming soon, and I must ready myself for her sharp tongue."

"What is she asking of you, good sir? Can I help by staying a bit longer?"

"Perhaps you should not stay. It's just that she yells at me, and cannot be pleased." His head bows, and I suspect there is much more he would like to say, but doesn't. Articana could cause him much suffering, and it is best to be submissive. So I begin to leave.

"Thank you again for a lovely afternoon." I give him a little hug, and turn to leave. It is best to avoid Articana whenever possible. She is the eldest daughter of Father's second wife, and her hatred of me is never hidden. How sad though, her treatment of him. He is just a very kind, silly man, who talks to his tools as he holds his breath to set each piece just so. I am always so pleased with the trinkets he has made for me. But as I leave the room, Articana brushes by me, not recognizing me in her haste.

"Have you finished my commission? Where is it? Show me, this instant! Do not move so slow!" She has screamed into the room like a whirlwind. The old man cowers by his workbench, as if her demands cut his thin dry skin. Her withering glare is intensified by her hands on her hips.

"I want to wear those for the feast days coming,"she yells. "If they are not ready, you shall be lashed!" Articana's red face puckers like a pomegranate, ready to burst. Ugly red pimples on either side of her nose threaten to exude from her anger.

"You will receive more speed with kindness, sister," I say, making myself visible. "Surely your jewelry will be done on time."

Articana turns sharply at my voice, and glowers at me, while the old man produces earrings--- gold earplugs as thick as my little finger. With outstretched hand, he offers them to her, all the time bowing and keeping his eyes downcast. She snatches them from his open hand.

"Good for you that these are done!" Then she stomps out of the workroom, brushing my shoulder again. It is well that she did not push me aside, for I would have put her down to the floor.

Natef-Bak breathes a sigh of relief. "Those earplugs will be too heavy, but it is her order. Her earlobes have stretched already too far to hold the old ones she had. She wants the most gold at her ears." Natef looked at me kindly, and said, "Good that I am old, and will not be here when she looks to punish the person who made her earlobes reach to her chin," he says with a laugh. "Better to have her earlobes connected to a nose ring, than swing loose!" And we both giggle at the thought of Articana in old age with earlobes like bat wings.

∻ ∻ ∻

Back in my rooms, I spend some time alone with my special cedarwood chest. It's aroma fills my room as I open it to stow my latest gold trinkets. The littlest gold bracelets and anklets are so soft and malleable that I can easily straighten them into flat rods. By inserting them into hems of garments, along shoulder seams, or wherever they can slide in easily, they become well hidden. Some of my pillows are less soft, but thus they hold more value than meets the eye. In a separate little box I have finger and toe rings, loose scarabs, and other scraps of gold gleaned from the floor of Natef's workroom. And I have a lovely hand mirror shaped like an ankh, tortoise shell combs, and long gold plaits for weaving into my red hair. There are pouches of gemstones, blue, yellow, orange, and the greenest stones which have swirls of darker green, with "eyes" that remember their mountain home in the east.

I have other carved boxes that hold various unguents, perfumes, and bottled potions. These are some that are dangerous to use. A few drops into the oil lamps, and everyone sleeps soundly. Too many drops, and no one would wake. The recipes and teachings I am learning at the temple are more useful than the priestess suspects, but I am careful to not ask too many questions, or ask for evil spells. Still, many spells and potions require spices and unguents that are easily found in the bazaar. Those that are rare I do not ask about, in order to avoid suspicion. Kemet is the world's eminent medicine source, and the artisans can make glass bottles in any shape, color, or size for export. Perhaps I will become a healer instead of a priestess. Such would be an appropriate choice, if it were offered to me.

Besides the potions and herbs, there are cosmetics: black kohl for the eyes, powdered green malachite for eyelids which protects from maladies of the eye. And there are the reddest unguents for lips. I fully believe that I could disguise my youthful face to such an age that no one would recognize me. Hopefully, that will not be necessary! In years past I have also thought about having the palace physicians give me a skin design, like mother's. Hers is a spiral design, or rather three spirals, that emanate out into a circle the size of a small onion. Mother wears this on her right cheek, as a sign from the ancient goddess of her people. Uncle tells me it is the symbol of birth, death, and rebirth. But it is a symbol of foreigners, and I am a princess of Kemet. Best not to call attention to my face at all. Someday, I may be allowed to be the person on the outside that I am on the inside. These thoughts are locked into my chest, now secure atop my reed-covered Ren stone. Satisfaction is mine, today. Great Goddess, protect me!

I sense excitement in the air, and happy voices echo in the hallways. Uncle has just returned from a hunting expedition in the desert, and servants are busy unpacking and organizing what he has brought. His two great greyhounds, the fastest and smartest of the kennel, have diverted both a gazelle and an antelope for Uncle's arrows.

"We had much success today! A grand hunt!" Uncle was beaming with pride, stroking his well trained dogs. They can outrun and corner the larger animals, but not a rabbit. "How fine it is to watch your grey bodies weave through the tall grasses." He gave them each a well deserved treat, then sent them to their kennel.

"Oh, Scota, had you not been at the temple I would have welcomed your presence on our hunt today. Remember when you were younger, we went on many hunts together. . . but none as successful as today."

"My days of hunting are sadly trapped in the temple. I am thankful for those memories though. Uncle, did you see a band of cheetahs or leopards? They often follow the herds of antelope."

"For truth. They may have been there, but were too far away to be sure. I would not hazard my greys so far off from our party. Cats are keen with tactics. They could have surrounded my jewels."

"Please tell me of your next planned hunt, Uncle," I replied. "For I am in need of your company. I would have loved to loose an arrow or two at the antelope. My days at temple have made my aim less sure, I think. But this new meat will make a welcome feast for the festival."

"My sleek hounds proved their skill today. They cornered a fat antelope. I wish you had been there to see them work together. I know you have other duties now. Just know that my arrow flew straight and true. I have saved this white piece of fur for you, for your cedar chest."

"Thank you so much, Uncle. This piece of soft fur will make good lining for my mirror, and perfume bottles. Thank you for thinking of me."

"There is other news, Scota." Uncle put away his excitement about the hunt. "I have orders from the overseer, Hariesis, about the procession tomorrow. Your mother will ride her litter throne next to Father Phar'o, followed by the other wives in the rear. You will ride with the other young daughters, while the various officials will walk behind. It will be a grand procession."

"It is as I expected," I say, "but sitting with Articana will demand my best control. Perhaps I could sit beside her, rather than opposite her?" Uncle's eyes questioned this. "That way I won't have to see her face, her evil stares, or smirks," I explain. "You do not know of the ill will she harbors for me. I think she hopes I will die soon." Uncle nods, showing that he understands full well our palace intrigues.

"Well, control your breath and body as if you were on a hunt with me," he says. "The whole city will be watching, and it is only one day that you must attend with the other princesses. Other days you may follow behind with the temple priestesses and novitiates."

"I know my responsibilities, Uncle. I will do my best, I promise." With assurance in my voice I say, "I will make you proud of me, and Mother, too. I know it is to be a spectacle of people, soldiers, and citizens, and I must put my best face forward for all to see."

Uncle nods. "Yes, but the surprise and good news is that we will board separate boats. At the harbor we will have various boats, and you will go on your mother's boat. Your Father will board his royal barge. It will be completely decorated, and filled with his ministers, generals, and wealthy citizens. It is a high honor for them, for sure."

"That gives me great ease, not to be with him! So Mother's boat will be decorated with our silk flag? Our boat should be different than the others, is that not so?"

"Yes, all the boats will be decorated with silk flags. The emblems will show their occupants. Your mother's flag will stand out with its blazing red snake upon a brilliant blue background. Do you remember it, Scota?"

"I remember it clearly, Uncle. The snake is not coiled, but stretches up with fangs open, as if seeking to climb and strike. It is easy to see amongst all others, as the flags of Kemet are either red or blue, signifying our two lands of Upper and Lower Kemet. Father's flag is both colors, with the sign of Amen Ra in the center. But my flag is golden yellow, with our red snake. I will be proud to see it wave in our harbor."

Uncle smiles, and gives me a quick hug. "I am glad to be the one to tell you these plans. By your flag I will know where you are in the grand retinue. I will look for you from my barge which will carry my hunters and friends. Still, only a few dignitaries will be honored with being on boats. The rest of the palace people will remain on shore where they can recline and enjoy "the breeze."

"Do you know who else is coming besides the Milesians?" I ask. "I know Father will be having a war council, because I heard gossip in the hallways. According to some scouts, and a goatherd, the Persians are massed at our eastern border."

"Scota, you are not to worry about such things," says Uncle. "Evagoras, the main general, will be giving your Father an accounting of the armies that have amassed for the defense of Kemet. This man comes from a long lineage of kings, and his reputation in forming alliances is proven. I trust that he will be able to form many alliances for Kemet. But this is not your concern!"

"It is my concern, Uncle! I know Evagoras managed an alliance with both the Spartans and the Persians at the same time, to dethrone Djedhor! I how devious and masterful he is. I do not trust his actions." With a lowered voice I whisper, "The assassination of his own father is rumored, yet Father has accepted him for making alliances? Ambition and power are qualities they hold in common. But not trust."

"You are wise beyond your years, Scota. Even so, the alliances will be kept until they are broken by more gold, or other thrones to rule. Evagoras can be trusted as long as Kemet holds the strength of gold. I am much older than you, my dear. It is true that the Persians have controlled Cicilia and Cyprus from time to time, but there is imbalance everywhere and no one can predict the future of wars. Please have faith in our armies, and worry no more."

"How can I not worry, dear Uncle? Who will come to defend our country? Is it not my place to know these things as well? I am no longer the child you taught to shoot!"

As if shocked, Uncle looks at me with new eyes, then silently takes me aside. It is not impertinence that I have shown him, but maturity. There is a more secluded place to sit, a palace alcove, and he motions us there. Air does not stir here, but it feels quiet, safe from unseen ears. Uncle seems old and frail somehow, a different person than when talking about his dogs and his expeditions. He talks differently about nations, and wars, and becomes serious. He chooses his words carefully.

"Tonight the emissaries will gather in the great hall. There will be the Achaeans, Spartans, Hoplites, Mittani, Karkissans, some emissaries from Nubia, and some other tribes. The nine tribes of the Sea Peoples are also in alliance with Kemet, but they cannot enter the palace as they are uncircumcised, and "unclean."

"Will they all be inspected... and will they wear weapons?" I ask. "Surely Father does not trust everyone completely."

"These are only emissaries. Their warriors will not enter the palace. The rumors you heard of the advance of the hated Persians is true. It is perfect timing for Kemet, as the Great Green River will soon begin its transformation into Hapi. If their armies advance next week, Phar'o can be assured of victory, for it is not likely the enemy's chariots could survive the swamp. Only the wisest of our scouts know the height of the deluge to come, as they check the water tables daily and give reports to your father. Evagoras will devise his plans accordingly, and with the legions at his command, he should be able to flank the invaders as they drown in the swamps of the Delta. The emissaries will discuss Father's plans in secret."

I embrace Uncle and say, "Thank you Uncle, my mind is at rest." He nods, and goes off to make preparations for the feast days. I feel more informed, but also thoughtful. I have fleeting thoughts about stowing away on one of their moored ships. But my absence without explanation could cause an alliance to fail, could cause a misunderstood war, or my being sold into slavery or for ransom. No, I cannot chance this, at least without making secret paid arrangements. But, who to trust? Uncle would talk me out of such a foolish plan. Mother would have me kept under guard for this willful idea, I think, though perhaps she does keep some love in her heart for my sake. I am alone, with a wooden chest full of a future that has but little chance.

FOUR

Dusk is falling now, and palace dwellers form family groups for their evening meal. Servants bring forth beer and trays of fruits and cheeses. Mother is not here as usual, so I go to the maiden quarters and find Sher-Ri. Her mother is braiding her heavy black hair into loops, and fastening these with tortoise shell combs. Happiness spreads through our rooms like the sweet fragrance of flowers, as everyone makes preparations for the festival to come. Sher-Ri will be joyfully dancing with the other palace dancers, all the way down to the harbor. Musicians with drums and sistrums will ring out an intricate beat. The ankle bells and armlets on Sher-Ri's waving feet will beat counterpoint to the tiny cymbals on her fingers. Of the twenty or so girls in her troupe, Sher-Ri is the most awesome dancer. Her turns, and flips of her body almost mesmerize all who see her. Perhaps dancing bent over with her head upside down gives her a true vision of the world? I have never seen her upset at simple twists of fate, that so bother me. So fine is her dance ability, she is sure to be chosen as chief of the palace dancers. Father will give her a heavily decorated tomb when her life here is over.

Of course, I should be in the procession with the priestess of the temple. Our dance is mostly light swirling of linen and smooth dipping gestures that are meant to indicate prayers to the Great Goddess Isis. Isis is the Goddess of Motherhood, who gave the great God Osiris his bodily form, which now inhabits Father. He is the physical embodiment of power and majesty. Father's golden litter is like some wonderful gilded house, which will be carried smoothly down to the harbor. There he is to meet the rest of the foreign dignitaries, massed in a swarm of bright colors. A feast of famous proportions will be laid out for their amazement, and huge sums of gold will strengthen the alliances. All the people of the city will have five days of feasting, celebrating, and praying that the temple seers will predict a harvest of plenty.

Everyone is busy with something or other, so I decide to enter Mother's rooms. It is much quieter here, but for once, Mother is sitting up, admiring the garments laid out before her. Evidently she wants to participate in the celebration of Khamseen this year. The tinge of color in her cheeks makes me happy to see her, and a remnant of humor dances around her eyes. She seems to have new purpose, renewed strength, and is once again the strong mother I used to know. She sees me enter, and motions for me to sit by her side. We have not talked for many weeks, nor have I seen her lately in such a good mood.

"Good news, my daughter," she says. "Some of my tribes-people are coming, and will accompany the Milesians." And, clapping her hands, she says, "We will have a lovely short boat trip around the harbor. I will send up my flag with pride."

Giving Mother an embrace, I pretend that I had not heard the news already from Uncle. She is so happy, and looking forward to this festival, that I did not have the heart to mention Uncle's news to me. Let her have this happiness to see my face brighten as well.

"There is some grave news, though, my daughter." Mother's happy mood is broken for a moment. "The leader of the Karkissans has died. And his sister/wife, Artemisia, has become a Satrap of the Persians. They will let her rule her people, but she is really controlled by the east. We women are but pawns, and you must never think you may have your own way in these things, Scota."

"Oh, I wish we could just sail away and never return!" I exclaim. But this meets a scowl.

Mother's happy mood is only paused for a space. Soon she returns to talking about the celebration tomorrow. "We will display a grand regatta of boats, and your Father's power will bring new alliances for our nation's people. He will hold everything together." Her voice is assertive, but we both know there is suffering in her homeland. All the civilized world is fragile where the Persians are concerned. They seem to roll over the land like a thick, fetid carpet.

"I heard that people from Karkissa might establish a small colony in Kemet," I say. "Perhaps this respite will allow them to rebuild their forces and they can then reclaim their mountains." But Mother seems dismissive about this notion, and waves her hands in the air to show her frustration with me. It is as if any thoughts of the future are to be avoided like the sting of a wasp. She will not allow such thoughts to be spoken. I should keep my silence.

After a lull, Mother slips into speaking to me in our tribal language. I am so grateful to Uncle for keeping this language alive with me, as no other than he and Mother in the whole of Kemet could speak it to me. A few words come quietly, like little kitten feet.

"Lie with me here on my pallet. My heart aches to hold my daughter." Suddenly, I feel a mother's love that had been locked away for so many years. "When I was a child, I felt a freedom, and respect from all in our tribe, because I was a valued warrior and princess. There was peace in our land, and beautiful cities, and markets were full of trade goods. It was different from the ways of Kemet, and this palace."

"I understand, Mother. In your homeland, you would not need a food taster."

"It is much more than that. My home was near that of the Queen, my aunt Artemisia, but we did not live in the same house. Nor did we need to be guarded or secluded from our people. Our great houses of wooden beams and pine boughs smelled of cedar forests and hunting birds. How long it has been since I felt the power of my horse between my legs. Mostly, I miss the love of family... and the feeling of safety." Her eyes closed as if she were deep in memories. I could almost smell the leather garments and taste the salt sea in the air as I laid beside her.

"And going on hunts with my bow, sailing, feeling the sea swells under my feet, and visiting trade ports... finding treasures in the bazaars. These things I cannot do as Queen of Kemet." Then Mother began to hum a lullaby that I learned to play on my harp. The whole afternoon was like a wonderful heavenly dream as I lay in her arms and felt my imagination transport us to her homeland. How I wish to have my mother as free and secure, and always open to me as on that blissful afternoon.

The sun began to set below the horizon, the air stilled, and the sail fan beaters began to row. The incense was lit, as were all the oil lamps, and time itself slowed. Am I in a trance? This is so unlike usual time with my mother. I am speechless, just listening to her as she weaves this tapestry of happiness. How could I ever have doubted her love for me? How could I ever have felt so lonely when I was near her? Somehow, something has changed. Finally Mother broke the silence.

"Choose your tribal clothing for the procession tomorrow. Your beaded corset can go over a linen dress. And wear your gold diadem, with your hair dressed in heavy looped braids, and pearls and gold netting. I want you to be seen more like the peoples of Karkissa, as well as a princess of Kemet." Mother's chin is firm. "And I will dress in such a combination also, so that all visitors will recognize our tribal origins."

"This would please me greatly, Mother. And, it might even strengthen the alliances, and let people of Kemet know they do not stand alone against the Persians."

Nodding in agreement, Mother says, "This gold neck ring will add to your heritage appearance, as all warriors wear this symbol." Then, with reverence, she hands me her beautiful solid gold torque. "I do not wear this anymore, and it should be yours to wear with pride." So saying, she slips it onto my neck. Its gold, shining like the sun, is twisted but flexible, and ends with terminals that look like knots. "Bring your harp as well, so that you can play on the boat." Then with another warm embrace she says, "We shall have the best time of our lives together on the boats!"

I can envision our flags flapping in the breeze. When the mooring stakes are removed we will sail farther out from shore to see the other visiting boats and larger ships. My thoughts are tumbling with images. What if I could just swim away? Sadly, people of Kemet do not swim, nor have I learned this skill. Again, I must contain my emotions, and remain in the present. I know Mother has plans for the next days, but she does not explain any further, as if saying anything would spoil her plans. Another embrace, and I get a kiss "goodnight."

My heart is racing as I make my way to my rooms. My feet seem to float over the flower petals, still fresh with their perfume. Sher-Ri is busy in our room, piling linens and silks into various boxes. She has been told to pack things away for the feast tomorrow, to make room for other guests in the palace. Spaces are made for more sleeping pallets! Nabanna has told her that other girls will be visiting from the ships, and it will be like a great harem of girls in our rooms for five days. Much fun! Sher-Ri is flitting around like a dragonfly, twirling and weaving a joyful dance, and she spins me around when she sees me enter.

"How grand it will be to have new faces and new stories!" she laughs. "Gossip from far away places and people!" Sher-Ri is even more excited than I have ever seen her. "We are to dance for all the foreign guests!"

"Yes, there will be a sumptuous feast. And we must put on a superb scene for all the various generals and dignitaries. My mother has told me what to wear, and I am to personify a Princess of Karkissa, as well as Kemet. Look at the gift Mother bestowed on me." Sher-Ri's giddiness came to an abrupt halt when she saw the gold torque at my neck. I stood there with pride. With this gold, there would be no trace of weakness before the generals.

With permission from the leader of the dancers, I am allowed to bring my harp to the main meeting room. I have offered to play some tribal tunes, sing some melodies, and entertain the foreigners. The other palace harpers will arrive later in the evening, when all the food has been cleared, but they will play the typical cascading notes that lull people to sleep. My music is from the tribe, forceful and strong of note, with surprises in cadence and intervals. Sher-Ri loves to dance to my songs, as the music has unexpected quick notes between longer ones. It sounds foreign, dark and strong, and brings visions of far-away mountains and rivers, cascading over sharp rocks, under bright blue skies. Her dance interprets each measure.

Sher-Ri has chosen an especially revealing linen mantle to wear. She is so mischievous tonight that I wonder if she is looking to catch the eye of some worthy foreigner. She admonishes me to wear something equally revealing, but bright blue in color.

"See how the linen swims over my nipples? And my belly swings through these folds? We can play the seductresses tonight while the men are drinking their beer and wine. It will be fun to tease them!" She smirks. I give her only a cautionary shake of my head. Who knows who will ask for us? Sher-Ri is not a slave, nor is her future laid out like mine. Perhaps what I thought was free expression is really a boldness of heart. Kenti-Sur, my other handmaiden, does not have this lack of modesty. Still, we will make a grand entrance. And we will not let this evening be wasted in sleep!

Sher-Ri, Kenti-Sur, and I make our way to the reception room where Sher-Ri quickly blends in with the other palace dancers. Kenti-Sur stays at my side to help with whatever I need. I motion to her, and show her where we will sit. "We can have a good vantage point here," as I direct her to a space by the side wall.

"I will bring cushions," replies Kenti-Sur. "Your harp will sound wonderful here. The notes of the strings will sound off the polished walls and floors." She busies herself with arranging pillows, and my dress flows around the floor in waves. Soon my fingers fill the room with music.   Many strangers are already seated on our gilded chairs and silk pillows, and pipes are lit for their enjoyment. The finest incense is burning in swinging golden censors, and there is wine and beer for all to taste. Each envoy is dressed in their traditional garb, so interesting and delightful to see.

Father is already seated on his golden throne, the center of attention, and is wearing his double crown. His finest golden breastplate, studded with faience lotus petals and carnelian scarabs, has a commanding Eye of Horus in its center. Hariesis stands to his right, glowering as usual, the oil on his bald pate shines dully in the lamplight.

"Look to the man on Father's left," I whisper. Kenti-Sur slowly averts her eyes, trying not to stare. "He must be General Evagoras. Uncle told me he will be in charge of strategy in this war." We watch as this man whispers continuously to Father, mentioning important names and positions of those in attendance. He will announce the dignitaries in order when all are assembled. I cannot tell how old this man might be for his chest and shoulders are covered by a heavy black leather mantle of armor called *kalkus*. Uncle tells me that this leather, boiled and layered, can repel an arrow point. His eyes are small, sunken under heavy eyebrows, and a beard and hair cover his jaw and neck. His arms are covered by black leather braces, and his legs hide behind thick leather armor. He is like a black leather statue. His arms and legs do not move, nor does he turn his head. He only stands and whispers names to Father.

"The Queen's chair is empty," says Kenti-Sur. "Your mother will make a grand entrance, walking in like a mortal person."

"I noticed that too, Kenti-Sur. Father never walks in, but always appears already seated. Mother is the 'God's Wife' and will come in with the other wives and ladies of the court. I think her delay is intentional, to make a grand entrance surrounded by emissaries from Karkissa. She will make the most of that alliance, and make the others wait for their entrance."

"Who are those people so differently dressed?" She gestures to the right.

"I think they are eastern people called 'Mitanni' since they look like depictions I have seen. Other Phar'o's have taken queens from those people." Their main envoy wears a long beaded tunic, a heavily jeweled breast plate, and his jeweled reddish hair hangs loosely down his back. He has so many bracelets and arm guards that he sounds like finger cymbals tinkling when he shifts. He seems nervous and fidgety, constantly pushing his hair in place.

Again I nudge Kenti-Sur to look to the next group. "I think those next to him are more interesting. They are from Miletus. There is a General, and the King's son, at least I think he has the look of a prince by his rich clothes." They are bare-chested, and wear short white pleated kilts, clasped at the waist with gold belts. At their waist, each has a curved ceremonial dagger whose jewels catch the light from the alabaster oil lamps. Their bronze skin and broad shoulders glisten in the lamp light as if they were plated with gold. As I gaze at them, the tall prince figure motions to me, beckoning me to come to them. I am embarrassed as our eyes meet, but enthralled with the urge to come to him. My heart skips a beat. How very bold indeed! I do not avert my eyes, as if ignoring that fleeting glance. Instead, I bend to my harp and begin to play. I will learn his name tomorrow!

With a few notes, even as I touch the strings lightly, the sound fills the room. There is an audible sigh of recognition from another group to my left, as the Karkissans have entered with five warriors and the General of their army. These are my mother's people, and they all turn their faces to me and bow the heads slightly. They are dressed in heavily embroidered sh short woolen kilts, and have metal plates covering their shi shoulders. Their helmets are crested with tall cock feather glisten purple and gold. Each man wears a gold neck ri as a man's finger, decorated with swirls and deep eng metal shoulder armor is decorated with spirals and special significance, and remind me of Mothe have my reddish hair, which falls just past the wear it into a short tail. The servant motio will be seated on pillows. I think they'd wear no undergarments under their ki leather apron called *dutiwa* that ha the pleats down well enough, bu I can see short knives at the man has a sling tucked into in time to my music, in re then, Kenti-Sur distract advancing. Immediately, I stifle the strings with my left hand, just in time, as all eyes shift to her entrance.

Mother quietly moves into the midst of these men, and gives each one a light touch on the shoulder. She smiles to each envoy, and thanks them all silently with her eyes and gestures, before taking her throne next to Father. She is serene, tall and lithe, moving with the grace of a gazelle, and her feet glide over the smooth stone floor, making no sound. She wears her black beaded wig which meets her eyebrows and circles her chin line. Her cheek tattoos seem to weave into the wig. Today she is the ͜ ͜d's Wife, beautiful, regal, and respected.

" is hushed in quiet as Mother moves further into
linen dress is woven with gold strands,
the toes. As she glides closer
d and together they
they are

rts,
s and
s, which
g, as thick
avings. Their
signs that have
s skin art. Many
r neck rings. Some
s to them where they
ather have chairs, as they
s. They do have a pouch or
gs in front, which will hold
for now they remain standing.
op of one boot, and at least one
his belt. They appear to be swaying
ognition of the song I am playing. Just
e from the strings, as she sees Mother

Other envoys are grouped together, though they wear distinct clothing. These must be envoys from Sparta, or other Achaeans, who are generally not in alliance with other nations. Perhaps they are paid unequally, or have long standing rivalries, or territories in dispute. My understanding is so inadequate! I know the Athenians are often their adversary, as are those people of Cicilia. Those city states and small kingdoms rival each other, but must band together against the threat of the Persians. People of Thrace and Samothrace, Rhodes and Ephesus, all share some need for alliance with Kemet, as if the great all-seeing eye of Artaxerxes singles nations out for conquest, one at a time. It is as if the whole of the civilized world is under attack, because if Kemet falls, so shall all of them. *Thanks to the gods for the gold of Kemet!*

Some of the envoys represent mostly raiders of coastal settlements, who plunder and lay waste to cities and towns along the Great Green Sea. The "Sea Peoples" who have the strongest ships, are the best seafarers of the world. Somehow, Father has struck an alliance with them and their envoys have come to our hall. They alone know the routes beyond the Great Green Sea to the west, and the costal settlements to the north beyond the Sea. They can be trusted as long as the payment is agreed to, as they hold their honor above destiny. Once their bond is given, it is unbreakable for generations. Uncle tells me that they have sea battles, throwing fire at other ships. Death in battle is their highest aim.

A hush falls over the palace as the dancers enter. My heart is racing with excitement to see Sher-Ri, one of twenty spinning creatures. They shimmer in gauzy linen. They lift their legs to their chins, spin, and swoop like cranes at mating. The drummers' tempo is fast, then slows, swirls in unison crescendo to a high pitch. Then everything cascades down to a slow heartbeat. The audience is mesmerized, sometimes keeping time with clapping hands, other times silent with eyes fixed on the enticing hand movements of the girls. Finger cymbals cling-clang, and ankle bells chime out their rhythm. The dance raises to its highest pitch, then suddenly stops in mid step, as if the dancers' legs are suspended by threads. The audience roars with delight. Amidst this applause, the dancers dissolve back into the recesses of our great room.

Horns sound, and all eyes turn to the golden throne. Father stands, raises his arms in welcome to his court. He holds the symbols of his office, the Shepherd's Crook and Master's Flail. With a commanding voice he speaks the words all want to hear.

"Allies! We have come together against the invasion of those filthy dress wearers, eaters of children, and immoral god worship. The might and power of Kemet will be victorious against this invasion! Hear me now, Great God Osiris, let all be a witness to our strength!"

Father beckons, and two black robed priests enter, bearing tasseled pillows. They bend to one knee, raise the pillows in an offering of something to Father. He reaches for each item, a red clay tablet, and a sheaf of papyrus. Then Father shows these to the crowd, a special red clay tablet, inscribed with the names of Artaxerxes and his family. He then reads the words written on the sheet of papyrus with an even more forceful tone of voice:

Here is depicted every enemy of Re and every enemy of Pharaoh, dead or alive, and every proscribed deed he might dream of, the names of their father, their mother, and their children—every one of them—being written here with fresh ink on a sheet of gilded papyrus—and their names being written on their chest, they themselves having been made of wax and bound with bonds of black thread; they will be spat upon, they will be trodden with the left foot, they will be struck with a knife and a lance, and they will be thrown into the fire in a blacksmith's furnace! Utterly destroyed for all time!"

As the papyrus drifts from Father's hand, it bursts into flame, and slowly comes to rest at his feet. It has become a pile of ashes as the flames lick out. Father then takes the red clay tablet and crashes it to the floor, breaking it to smithereens. The noise shatters the quiet in the room, and eerie echoes resound against the walls, as if the tablet is being broken repeatedly. Surely, Father's magic is strong, and will itself destroy the enemies of Kemet.

Father lowers his hands, as if smearing out the pieces of clay, without touching them, mixing them into the ashes. Then he speaks again:

"Kemet is the breadbasket of the world. Our physicians and chemists conquer disease and suffering. Our Great God Osiris will bring prosperity to all involved for their service and protection. I invite all gathered here to develop settlements in the Delta. Bring your populace to safety. Bring trade and innovation. I have directed the mapmakers to make plans for such settlements, to establish city quarters and avenues of friendship. This I decree on this day."

Then Father resumes his throne, and motions for Evagoras to speak. The visitors and invited guests had been sitting quietly, without nodding, or apparently understanding his speech. It is apparent that all understood the magical incantations, for all are quiet. Evagoras does not speak long, then motions for the young Milesian prince to approach. As Evagoras speaks, the Milesian repeats the sentences into three other languages, first in Ionian, then in Luwian, and another language I don't even recognize. He rephrases some of Father's speech, so all will fully understand the intent of the incantation. Lastly, he speaks in the language of Kemet.

"My name is Gamal Miledh, of Miletus, fourth son of King Miledh. Our refugees from Miletus have already set up dwellings in the Delta area, provided by Pharaoh Nectanebus. His plan is to have a great trading area close to the harbor, a place of safety and unity for our civilized people of the world. He will have a stela erected there to commemorate this day."

Nearby, a scribe is busily writing all that is said today, in multiple languages. There is some discussion in the crowd, but everyone seems receptive of Father's proposal, as they are now smiling and talking amongst each other, perusing the distributed maps and street layouts.

As these formalities are completed, the visitors mingle with each other, and parades of servants bring in trays of sweets, fruit, and beer. I turn back to my harp, tilting the curved wooden back to my heart, where it nestles in its home between my breasts. I play quietly, not for an audience, but just to provide some musical ambiance for the vast hall. I am engrossed in making the strings sound, a peaceful and happy tune of water cascading over rocks. So, I did not hear his footsteps when Gamal approached, with a smile of recognition on his lips. He began to speak in Kemet's language, but I replied in Tocharian, wondering what he would do.

"I admire your playing, for I have heard none better. You are Princess Scota?"

"Thank you sir, I am pleased to accept your compliment. It is a song taught to me by my Uncle. So, you understand Tocharian?"

"Yes, the bazaars of Miletus have many vendors of tribal people. Those who speak Luwian are now under the control of the

Persians in Karkissa, but not the Tocharians. I see some of your mother's people in this hall."

What should I say? I am suddenly unsure about conversing with this handsome prince. "Tell me about Miletus, good sir. How is it that you have come to Kemet?"

"My skill with languages is useful here, so my father has sent me as special envoy of Miletus. I am his fourth son, and travel often for my nation's cause. These alliances must not fail, and I can sometimes act as diplomat among rivals."

"Yes, I admire your ease with languages. Thank you for helping Kemet." *Try to be ignorant of politics, I think to myself.*

"Your harp contributes much to soothe our feelings, this night," Gamal says. "May I touch it here?" He follows the arch with light fingers, as if feeling the strings' vibrations with his fingertips. "Miletus is a great prosperous city, and holds many harpers. The bazaars are filled with music and dancers always. You would be welcome there."

"My fondest wish would be to visit your great city! How many days is the trip by sea? Have you brought many ships? Will you stay long in Kemet?" Questions tumble out like an upended basket of onions, before he has space to answer anything. Calming myself I say, "I have little knowledge of the outside world. I apologize for so many questions. Please excuse me for my childishness."

In the dimming light, Gamal's bronze chest shines in the lamp light, like some gilded statue in our entry hall. He carries no weapons, but his strength of arm is apparent as his hand moves over my harp. He smiles, nodding with understanding, and seems eager to give me a short education of these things. With a short chuckle, he smiles again.

"My sailors are the best in the world, but the trip is not without some danger. Several squalls delayed our voyage, so we were diverted to camp on shore outside of Rhodes, an island about mid-way to Kemet. But the distance can be crossed within two days when the winds are in our favor. I have my ship, which is the fastest, plus a supply ship and two vessels of warriors from Miletus."

"Is this your first trip to Kemet? How fortunate to have your own ship." *I simply do not know how to make small conversations with such a person.* "Perhaps I could invite you to see our palace grounds, see our gardens and lotus pools. I could explain the many monuments here, if you are interested."

I glance around to see if anyone is watching us. I think no one is noticing our conversations, but all have eyes to see if they looked our way.

"Yes, I am the leader of this expedition. We will stay until business is completed, then sail west from Kemet with our trade goods. We are not rushed for time, at least until the winds shift." Then Gamal gave a short bow, taking his leave, and moved on to other groups around the hall.

Mother is still seated on her throne, but no one talks to her. Father does not pay her any attention either, but seems to be admiring this palace event and the congregation of allies he has amassed. Night is drawing closer as the moon rises, giving its silver light through the high ceiling windows. Soon everyone will disband and retire to their appointed rooms. Tomorrow is the first feast day of Shemu, and everything is prepared for the harbor excursion on the Great Green Sea.

I lower my harp to the floor and stow it close to the wall for safety. No one appears to have had too much beer or *shodou* tonight, and the people are beginning to disperse. Some tempers seem to flare among the Ionians. I see Gamal moving through the group, acting as the mediator. He knows instinctively what to say. "Let us find sleep," I hear him say. Voices are hushed, but I see that emotions are calmed. I begin to rise to leave, and Gamal is again at my side.

"May I take your hand?" He takes my hand, and forearm, and draws me safely up, lifting me smoothly as a feather, as if I have no weight. I imagine him at home in the bazaars, loading boxes and helping others. Perhaps as the fourth in his father's line, there is none of that competition for power that I feel here in Kemet. Nor do I sense the utter laziness of my younger sisters.

"I am here to help in all ways," he says, "though I must soon be back on my ship. You are welcome to sail with me in the morning."

"I am honored with your invitation, kind sir. But that would not be allowed for me. Tomorrow I must go with my Mother, and I have many duties to perform on other days. Thank you, but I cannot go." Again I am divided against myself, for I know immediately where I'd like to be: With Gamal, and far, far, away.

"Of course," he says, "Some other day. But do not deny me the pleasure of showing you my ship."

I nod my head in parting and say, "Goodnight to you, sleep in safety within your ship."

I pick up my harp by its pillar and begin to slip away. Kenti-Sur comes to my side, helping always. She is quiet, but gives a knowing glance about my meeting with the handsome prince. I'm sure she is bursting with questions. I give her a small smile, but soon she will know all.

The guests begin to depart, to find their appointed sleeping spaces. I notice many servants guarding doorways, hallways, and some are positioned outside in the gardens. Evidently the palace guardians will have sleepless duty tonight, safeguarding all envoys, guests, and the palace retinue. Sher-Ri grabs my elbow with exuberance, swinging me around, still so excited to be in such an eventful affair. We practically skip down the halls to our room, and find other girls equally excited. Noisy giggling fills the room, and all the girls seem intent on one thing...making themselves especially alluring to some visitor or other, as if Kemet has no youth worthy of their hand.

"What a grand night! Did you see me dance?" Sher-Ri displays no trace of fatigue, which is amazing in itself after such acrobatic dancing.

"How could I not?" I exclaim. "With your heels to the ceiling I thought you would take off like a bird. One of the soldiers was intensely watching your spinning, as if to catch you in mid-flight!"

"Maybe he thought I might accidentally kick him in the groin!" said Sher-Ri. "I saw that Milesian you speak of."

"No, silly girl," I say, "that man was a Karkissan! I mean the one wearing cock feathers on his helmet. He couldn't take his eyes off you."

"I saw many men watching me," replied Shar-Ri. "And one young man among the Nubians kept the beat with his hips. That's the one I liked best. At least we got their attention. Do you think Phar'o was pleased? Perhaps he will send some extra coin our way. I have been saving, you know."

"You have no concern about your dowry," I replied, giving her a quick hug. "But I'm sure Father was feeling very pleased with the reception Your dancing will be remembered for a long time."

Families in Kemet may be no different than other lands, I do not know. Surely parents will choose marriage partners for their daughters, and the dowry may be the stumbling block for many girls who want a certain young man. Who knows what a foreigner expects from a daughter of Kemet. I wonder if they think we are all dripping with gold. Even so, my girls know I will help them in any possible way to enhance their dowry. On many nightly travels I observed the cruel truth of poverty in the bazaars and a life of burdensome work for the common man. These young dancers have a more hopeful future, and their excitement is contagious.

"I saw you getting a special audience with the prince from Miletus," said Sher-Ri. "He was touching your harp as he would have touched your body. He only had eyes for you, I think."

Kenti-Sur chimed in, "Yes, I think he's a pirate, out to steal you away, Scota."

"My heart is set on another man, one whose skin glows like mine," said Sher-Ri.

"Girls, you make me laugh! What fun you had admiring the visitors," I say.

Then Kenti-Sur said, "Sher-Ri, You danced so close to the dark skinned man... and nearly fell on him! How bold you are Sher-Ri!"

"Yes, but he smiled, and pretended I was attacking him. He opened his arms as if to catch me, but I kept my balance. You know even on one leg I will not fall. But Scota, what is his name? How can I meet him?"

"I wish for your sake that I had the power to arrange such things." And then all the girls in the room looked at me with expectation in their eyes. They would all like me to arrange meetings with the envoys, even the servants who accompanied them.

"Ladies, I am not the matchmaker! But, take heart, for tomorrow we have a grand feast, and you can mingle with the crowds. You will not be herded like geese! Go to sleep now, and wake rested in beauty."

The girls find their pallets, and are soon breathing softly, asleep. Sher-Ri and I, however, lie awake, watching the moonrise framed in a high window. "Do you find sleep?" she asks.

"No," I whisper. Soundlessly we rise together and find our way to the door watched by our faithful servant. Lamps are still burning in the corridors, but all is quiet as we step outside. The moonlight colors all the stones with a beautiful purple light as we find a place to sit on a low stone bench. It is not even cool, this night, for the north breeze will not arrive until dawn at the earliest. I stretch my legs out to embrace the moonlight, as if it could color my skin with its blueish purple tint. We are both startled a bit, for at my feet a large scarab beetle makes its bumbling march across our path.

"Oh, Kheper-Ra, guide our feet. How shall we travel this lifetime?" whispers Sher-Ri. The beetle stops for a moment, then turns back the way he had come. Then he turns north and makes his way into the shadows. His shell glistened purple-black in the moonlight. He knows where he is going, it seems. Sher-Ri and I linger for a few minutes more, then rise to go back to our beds. I will dream of Kheper-Ra tonight. Perhaps an oracle dream will guide my feet tomorrow.

As we enter the servant's entrance, there is a slight odor of foul breath? My skin prickles with awareness of someone watching. Hariesis is here, crouching in shadow! He springs up behind me and swiftly has his arm around my neck, growling in my ear.

"I've caught you this time!" he sneers, and I feel his oily skin as I twist around to confront him. Sher-Ri jumps on his back, biting and scratching like some wild cat, grabbing his hair and digging her fingernails into his cheeks. I manage a knee into his groin and break free, but his foul breath envelops the close space.

"I am Princess Scota! How dare you lay hands on me!" And Sher-Ri drops to a crouch, ready to spring again for his throat.

"I well know who you are, girl! Your Father will hear that I suspect you of treachery. Which foreigners do you conspire with? I will find out, and have you dealt with!"

"Father will hear of what you have done this night, you filthy toad!" Through clenched teeth I hiss a savage curse: "You threaten me? My needs for cool night air are none of your concern. Tell whatever lies you can conjure up, and we'll see what Father does with you for this assault!" With that, Sher-Ri and I push past him. On the floor lies the body of our faithful doorman, crumpled like an old papyrus sheaf, still and lifeless.

"Thank you for your service, old one," I whisper, and we find our way back to our room.

Sher-Ri and I walk in a close embrace, find our beds where all is quiet. I kiss her on the cheek, thanking her for being my friend. Without her, I might not have been able to spurn the overseer's terrible grasp. I think he would have me dead this night. Sleep comes finally, but too soon Great God Ra rises to fill the sky with his golden light.

FIVE

A new day dawns, Ra begins his journey across the sky. In our chambers, girls are rising, stretching their legs which might have stiffness from all the dancing last night. Sher-Ri looks at me, and her eyes ask, "Are you all right?" I nod, and try to ignore my sore shoulders where Harsiesis had his stranglehold. Soon we are dressed, and cleanse our hands and faces. I am to wear my tribal bodice today over my gauze linen. It is dark blue, colored like dark faience, and tiny gold beads swirl around the tribal symbols. The lacing is on the front, sides, and back, and the top curves just under each breast. It extends to below the hips, but it is wonderfully comfortable in its stiffness. When I am in this bodice, I feel a closeness to Mother and her people. It is so different than the loose linens we usually wear. I will wear my uadjet necklace, Mother's torque, and my best earrings. Sher-Ri will help add the pearl netting to my hair.

When my hair is ready, we add my gold diadem. It is a narrow circlet, with a tall feather of Maat at the center front. I have two arm bracelets to wear on my upper arms, which are embossed with the snake of Neith, and my forearms bear my other bracelets that match my collar necklace. Sher-Ri is busy applying scented perfume to my neck and hands, and takes some for her body as well. The visitors will certainly smell us before we are even seen! Sher-Ri has on her sheerest gauze dress, sleeveless, and has oiled her skin decorations so they glisten like black pearls around her chest. Her arms are smooth and move like black serpents as she arranges her hair loops for today's procession. She is barefoot, but I put on my gold sandals with the turned up toes. When we are ready, we go to join the other noisy girls in the main room.

Breakfast has been laid out, just fruits and bread, but there are sweet juices and scented water to moisten our throats. There will be a grand feast at the harbor today, so we partake just lightly, not wanting to spoil our appetites. When we are ready, our instructions are to assemble on the main street that leads to the harbor. All the populace will be there with their children and pets to see our grand procession. Many families have pet dogs, not for hunting, but for companions. Even a pet rabbit, or sometimes a pet duck, can be seen accompanying children and their parents. As we move down the hall, the walls resound with our jubilant voices. It sounds like a flock of herons, with so much giggling and girlish jesting. Dancers are twirling in their dresses and playfully hugging each other.

Suddenly, all are dispersed, like chaff on the wind. Sher-Ri is curled into a ball at my feet, and it seems that all the air has left the room, and taken our voices with it All is suddenly still. I feel a presence to my left, and the back of my neck prickles in attention. No one is aware of his entrance, but Father is standing at my left. He moves closer, soundlessly and purposefully. The girls cower, and cover their eyes.

"This is your mother's girdle," comes his gravelly voice. He touches the lacings on my back. "It is some protection, and sturdy, but it does not extend far enough." His hand runs down my back, grasps my left buttock. I am suddenly off balance, lifted like a piece of meat on a skewer. But I am strong, and do not fall. Nor do I look at him in defiance.

"Today you can be the warrior princess, and tomorrow the priestess. But soon your body will be mine, and then you will no longer have free movement from the palace. Hariesis has informed me of your forays. Your discontent is but a ripple in the flow of my power. Be careful that I am not embarrassed these next days."

He says nothing more. I close my eyes, then peer out and watch him leave. He takes the silent air with him, and the girls collect themselves as if his spell has left as well. But it is not broken. Everyone seems shaken by Phar'o's presence, and his ability to appear so suddenly, and alter the very air we breathe. His power is not beneficent, and everyone's belly is tense for many minutes even after he has left. I do not know what lies Hariesis has told him. No matter, my will is not shaken, and I am not my fragile mother. Instead, I clap my hands.

"Girls, Find your places. All is well!"

Sher-Ri takes her place among the dancers, while Kenti-Sur mingles with the other hand-maidens. We are soon back to being a troupe of lovely gauzy butterflies, excited for the feast day ahead. I go to find Mother. Within minutes we are assembled outside in the morning light. Throngs of visitors are already waiting, forming a grand parade. The air is still, no sand whirls except for that disturbed by the many feet of so many people. All is made ready.

Mother and Father Phar'o are seated on litters at the head of the colorful procession. Mother looks so happy and healthy, her high cheekbones glisten in the bright sunshine. Kohl surrounds her eyes in a great uadjet design, and she wears her black beaded wig and gold crown. Father is seated next to her, but his demeanor is stiff and warlike. He holds the Crook and Flail. No humor graces his face, as if the double crown is a heavy burden. He intends to present himself as the stone-cold warrior that he is, an immensely powerful and protective God of Kemet. Eight Nubian eunuchs will bear this litter. Their chests have been oiled, or maybe it is sweat, but they glisten like bronze shields in the morning sun. Their muscles ripple as with perfect precision they lift the litter in one smooth motion, and wait for the signal to proceed. A nod from Father and the litter moves by such tiny steps that it seems to float, like some magic carpet. I'm sure that at a distance, Father appears to be flying, slowly like some bird of prey.

How I would love to ride my horse in this parade! Instead, with my three half-sisters, I am carried on our litter, behind that of Father's other wives. My sisters are all younger than I, and are dressed in many folds of linen. They each have pretty faience collars, but not much gold. They have just enough decoration to signify their royal station. Articana gives me hateful looks as usual, and repeatedly shifts her body so that we do not touch. Her new heavy earplugs seem to add to her discomfort at having to sit next to me. The abundance of today's feast will only add to her already plump hips, and she has painted her lips pomegranate red. The other two sisters look like lumps of linen, and look even shorter and fatter than Articana. I sit tall and straight, and do not look at her, though I can feel her eyes trying to find an entrance to my soul.

"Everyone is admiring your new earrings. Do they feel very heavy?" I murmur.

Articana does not answer, or nod her head. She is just trying to maintain her posture of looking proud and haughty. The other two sisters opposite us just look, wide-eyed. I smile grandly and begin to wave at the crowds. The people cheer in admiration as we pass.

Fathers's other three wives ahead of us are also decked out in beautiful gold collars and heavy earrings. Each one is certainly attractive by Kemet's standards, but somehow to me they are empty-headed creatures. Their only function is to bear a boy child, and until that happens, none of them has any real status. They sit like statues with entwined arms, a sister-hood of wombs. They are small light-weight creatures, carried easily by the servants, as if they were mere paintings on the palace wall.

Behind my litter, Uncle rides on horseback with those from Karkissa who were at the feast last night. A woolen cloak woven with the colors of the tribe, is clasped at his left shoulder. Orange flowers are woven into the horse's mane, and Uncle's great greyhounds match steps with the horse. Other envoys either walk or ride, and a long line of foreign visitors make up the length of the procession. Behind these dignitaries come the priests and priestesses of our many temples, other city officials, and other important people in Father's employ. But I do not see Natef-Bak the goldsmith. Perhaps he is too infirm to walk this distance. The common people line the parade route, wave and cheer to us as we pass. Everyone is jubilant, as if something wonderful has already happened.

But it is only the cool north breeze. This is not the breeze that signifies the rise of our Great River which will bring nutrients to the fields. When we get to the harbor, Father will make more speeches and decrees. The people will listen obediently while waiting for gifts. They know that Father will have colored hard-boiled eggs distributed, and a few "lucky" loaves of bread will have a coin inside. Some years there were many hidden coins, but all clammer for the chance to improve their lot. Such is Father's hold on the people.

This great throng of excited happy people line the streets of Rhakoti, praising their Phar'o as the parade passes. "Come to the harbor, come to the harbor," sing the people. The godlike figures in the first litter do not wave at the populace, nor do they turn their heads. But we mortals are thrilled by the exuberance of the crowd, we smile and wave. The musicians are trumpeting their horns as the Karkissans advance, and Sher-Ri and her troupe are swirling and swooping to the beat of gigantic drums. Children are running and jumping around their mothers' skirts. We are followed down to the harbor by this multitude of Kemet. The litters are lowered, and I see Father stand. He raises his arms to speak.

"Greatest of tidings to Kemet!" His voice booms over the now still crowd. "Moonbeams have entered a virgin cow. A new Apis Bull has been discovered!"

A cheer rises out of the crowd like a tornado, hands are raised raised to adore Ra. Arms swirled en masse, in jubilation of the wonderful news.

"One hundred talents of gold to the farmer who has discovered our new Hapi-Ankh! The Incarnation will board a barge from Beheira today, for the procession down our Great River to Memphis. I decree that He will be here tomorrow, so that all women wanting his fecundity may raise skirts to Him, and honor Osiris incarnate."

The crowd raises another thundering cheer. Husbands are embracing their wives, young girls are blushing, and Mother is staring at me....*What? What are you telling me*, I wonder. But no words form on her lips, nor does her stony face melt into a smile. She is just staring at me, standing mute. The other princesses are hugging each other, but not me. The other wives raise their arms and wave at Father, as if reminding him to visit their rooms, one by one.

From my vantage point, I see the envoys smiling with the news, although they may not understand what has been announced. They assume a great victory? Or another alliance? Or perhaps the Persians have retreated? I am curious to know what they think. All of Kemet is resounding with Father's announcement, for it portends abundance from the River, and surely victory in battle. As the noise begins to subside, the entourage begins to board the boats, and a grand flotilla is arranged. The harbor water, smooth and cool, licks small waves at the quay. Musicians play soothing tunes to Hapi. There is a slight, perceptible breeze from the south, bringing delicious smells of food on braziers, and everyone settles into their feasting.

On Mother's barge there is a space reserved next to her for me to sit. The other wives and princesses are there as well, and their servants and handmaidens. I feel caught in this hive of buzzing bees, the boisterous noise of women fills my ears. Mother stares straight ahead, eyes focused on nothing, as if she is in another world. I want to touch her, shake her awake, but her eyes are distant. The waves swell slightly under our feet. She is lost in a reverie of a long ago voyage.

Central to the flotilla is Father's barge, radiant with gold and hundreds of lotus blossoms. Father and his generals are celebrating with beer while Hariesis glowers at the prow. The barges are so close in the calm water that revelers could easily step from one barge to another. In the deeper water float the larger ships of the Sea Peoples, like cities of warriors. Tall masts and colorful sails are supported by thickest planks of hardest wood that no arrow could pierce. The boats of the Karkissans are nearby also, boats made with hardened leather skins from animals I can only imagine. Their central mast supports square sails, dyed in many colors. They must be able to catch twice the wind of Kemet's triangular sails, and they ride high in the water. Farther out I can see even larger ships, holding many oars, and flags of the Milesians and Ionians. Somehow they move carefully, like pieces on a game board, like a grand dance of boats. As they maneuver closer, the Karkissan boat comes alongside. I see that Uncle is with them.

"Mother, they are calling to you...come to the railings." Taking her hand I slowly lift her, and guide her like a sleepwalker to the railing. Finally her face brightens, color returns to her cheeks, and she waves to them. I am relieved to see her finally engage with the festival.

"Are we allowed to change boats?" I ask.

"You are allowed, Scota, but I may not," comes the answer.

Strong arms lift me into their boat while Mother is content, happily talking over the space between the boats. And I am thrilled to meet some very handsome young sailors indeed! As I cross over, someone hands over my pennant. "Take your pennant, my lady, so your mother will not lose track of you," the sailor says, and he hands me the yellow flag blazed with the red snake of Neith. Soon my flag flaps above, and I am symbolically on foreign footing.

"Welcome, maiden," says a female voice. I see only warriors before me, but some are women! Karkissan wives, having equal status with their men, seem strong and solemn. I wish I could show them my expertise with the bow, to earn their admiration. Their glances are kind and welcoming as they recognize Mother's torque.

"Thank you for your welcome," I respond in Tocharian. "I have never been on a ship before now, and I did not know there would be women...and warriors as well."

"We come with our men," one says, "for we are not just cooks!" That raises a laugh among the men as well, as all faces shine with exuberance from the festivities. "We Karkissan women have equal say in tribal matters, and we would not be left behind," says one. Another joins in and says, "I want to visit your merchants here, find cosmetics and jewels, and something to pass down to my children. My daughter will marry soon, a man of her choice, but her children will keep the maternal name, so something special is needed. We will go looking tomorrow."

Perhaps we women are the same, everywhere, looking for bargains and things to adorn our surroundings. All these women are dressed as warriors, but earrings, jeweled collars and torques are on display along with their leather armor. They move with ease among the men, sharing fruit and beer. I wonder if Mother is still watching.

Presently another vessel has eased itself closer to the Karkissan vessel, and I see by the flag that it is the Milesians. They are not so close that I could board, but Gamal raises his hand in friendship and waves. I do not see any women on his ship, only strong, muscular sailors. There is a roofed construction, like a little shuttered house, near the rear of the ship, with a raised deck for the tiller, and shuttered windows along the ship's side indicate another level below the deck. Oars protrude from this hull as it swiftly glides closer to Father's barge. Perhaps they want Gamal as interpreter. I wave to them as they pass, the sea breeze fills my hair. Uncle appears at my side, and says, "Scota, there are people here I would like you to meet."

Though the ship is full of warriors and warrior women, there are elderly people as well. Reverently people bow to them as they pass, though they do not bear special emblems or symbols of rank that I can see. Uncle would tell me if they were part of our family, but I am not introduced, and we move on. Soon I am brought to the feet of an elderly man, whose wrinkled skin seems to be part of the planks of the ship, pocked like wormwood. Yet, his teeth are shiny, strong and even--he is the *harper*!

"Welcome home, Scota," he says, taking his harp to his chest. The harp is larger than mine, but decorated with the same carvings, interlocking knots and swirls. He begins by strumming the harp sides, matching the rhythm of the lapping waves, then begins to sing while his fingers strum the strings. His song is about a long ago victorious battle, and the love between a warrior and his queen. The strings reverberate under his fingers as he sings, praising both love and battle. The song ends with the death of the loving couple, embracing as they draw their last breath, in praise for lives well lived. In his song, death is not a sad thing, but a victory. He sings of the funeral byre, flames reaching to a great goddess. No musty catacomb or mummy wrappings await a warrior from Karkissa.

"Thank you for your song, good sir. I will remember what you have played for me today." How different are these visitors to Kemet, each fervently praying to other gods, devoting their lives to favorable signs and oracles. For the Karkissans, the earth itself is The Mother, and all must be in balance, an unending cycle of birth, death and rebirth. They do not view Father as Osiris incarnate. His co-regents of Isis, Nephthys, Ptah and Horus are understood as aspects of creation, and other gods such as Maat, Nut, Neith, Selkis, Bastet, and the whole pantheon of gods are perhaps unnecessary in their mind. Here in Kemet we have so many temples, so many prayers to be memorized, so many incantations to master, glyphs and objects imbued with gods' essences. . . so much to believe. How foreign and confusing it must be to these tribal people, and so unnecessary.

Now the prow of the ship turns back to the harbor. Off in the distance I can see the boats of the Sea Peoples, but we do not approach. Those hulls are deep and tall, the sails are furled along two masts, and great rectangular shields line the sides of the ships. The sunlight blazes off this polished bronze, so that we are blinded by the intense light. But I can see men standing by their shields, firm footed as if on land. They seem unusually tall, even at this distance. They wear only belted cloths covering their manhood, and bronze helmets protect their faces and heads. The helmets are crowned with cock feathers, or even taller feathers from birds such as eagles. Some of the helmets have horns of bulls or other frightening beasts beyond imagining. The fearsome effect is not lost on me, for as they pass, loud horns and screams from pipes fill the air with frightful battle music. I wonder how the Persians, with their woven reed shields, could be any sort of foe to confront these warriors. Just seeing their might and confidence would bring cowardice to even the bravest of warrior. I am thankful for the gold of Kemet to have theses warriors in alliance!

As the sunlight begins to wane our ship glides back to the harbor, where the cheering crowds have diminished but little. Beauty comes with the setting sun, and all edges of things are tinged with golden light. We have eaten our fill, and the north breeze has filled our lungs with new vigor, and new awareness of the strength of Kemet. Father's announcement of the new Apis bull has brought even more optimism and faith in Father's rule. New dedications to the temples will bring even more peace and safety to the people of Kemet.

My mind is racing with the thoughts and spectacles of this day. The music, food, dancers, strange visitors, and the excitement will live with me always. Sleep will come mixed with vivid dreams tonight as I mount the litter to ride back to the palace. Tomorrow I must be a priestess of Neith, and not my Mother's fertile daughter. The new Apis bull will make a grand entrance of his own tomorrow, and the visitors to Kemet will moor their boats and fill the streets.

Back in my rooms Sher-Ri is sound asleep, curled into a ball, still in her dancing dress. No matter, dreams of dancing will be rewarded with wrinkled skirts. Other dancers have fallen asleep in their tracks, endurance finally finding its limits. Lamps are lit yet, and incense fills the air, wafting through the halls as the rowers continue their slow rhythm. Kenti-Sur raises her head to ask of my needs, but I wave "no" and easily remove my crown and hair netting. The tight corset comes off with the tug of the front laces, and the linen is damp from the harbor mist.

The corset feels so stiff while worn, but it adds comfort to my posture as if loving hands embrace my body. Still it is a relief to curve my body into a ball and blend into my bed. Sandals slip off easily, but I am too tired to bathe. The air is warm, incense sweet, and I find sleep as soon as my head meets the neck rest. As I drift away, the bed servant closes the curtains and finds her own place in the corner.

The dark sea swells under the deck of my ship as I stand on the prow. Salt spray lashes my flag but the red snake moves straight ahead with the wind, the sails full to bursting. North stars guide our path as row upon row of immensely strong men heave their oars, as if rooted to the deck. We are an army, fearless and proud, singing bravely heedless of the storm's violent wind. Deep baritone harmonies swell with each wave as the ship surges through the foamy sea. Like an infant rocking in a cradle, I feel the deep swells rhythmically soothing my entire body.

We sail towards a star in the night sky. The massive oars, silvered in the moonlight, drip with pearls and golden netting as we climb higher and higher into the starry sky. We ride the barque of Osiris, but it is not Father's. It is my ship, filled with kindred warriors. And I am their Queen, roaring with laughter, bathed in starlight. The indomitable captain at the till raises his arm to point at the brightest star. It is Selkis, warrior goddess of the hunt, and we are coming, coming, coming. Rowing, surging, coming closer until the brightness of the star explodes into a shower of sparks through the high palace window.

SIX

Spain, along the Vinalopo River, summer 1996

He'd been working at it for hours; dig a few inches, brush carefully through the sand, sift what was dug up, rinse, repeat. He was sweaty, his skin covered in a layer of ground-in sand he knew would take forever to wash off. But he didn't care. Donald Cameron was happy. This is what he wanted to be doing. If you asked him if he'd rather be on a beach, a cold beer and girls in bikinis all around, he'd say "nope." Donald sat back on his heels and mopped at his face with a cloth that didn't do much more than spread the dirt around. He reconsidered the beer and bikinis. Nope, he was happiest digging in the dirt.

As a kid he'd taken an aptitude test, and the teachers had had a hard time getting him out of the sandbox even then. Due to what they thought was a propensity to being dirty, they predicted he would grow up to be a janitor or trash collector. He fooled them all and became an archaeologist. Donald hadn't known what he'd wanted in life until one day in High School when he learned about "King Tut." At the time he hadn't been fascinated so much with the life of the boy king, or the history of Egypt, but the excavation itself snagged his interest. He'd never forget seeing those pictures for the first time, and he'd never forget reading the famous words of Howard Carter, the tomb's discoverer, "... everywhere the glint of gold..."

Finding stuff was what Donald was best at. His mother would say, "Where's my purse?" and Donald would fetch it. Or when something was truly lost, he would close his eyes and concentrate, thinking of likely spots to search. He could find strayed cats, misplaced keys, and even a dried out contact lens.

In Elementary school Donald could find capitalized names on pages by scanning, keeping the looked for name as an image. He was fast and teachers knew his hand would be raised first at any question they asked. Some kids resented his skills, and called him a "nerd." So, he was often the last picked for team sports, and certainly never picked as a prom date. He was at a loss where women were concerned.

As the heat of the Mediterranean sun bore down on his sweat drenched shirt, Donald paid no attention to the drops of perspiration rolling down his nose. At least not until one drop plinked into the dust below, revealing the glint of gold. He shook his head to clear his eyes, and wiped damp red hair from the back of his neck. He thought about a headband, maybe putting his straggly hair into a ponytail, or a haircut! Fleeting thoughts about Kemi's hair clashed with images of the hair of his boar hair brush. Donald's brush caught on something golden as it swept over the little patch of shimmering sand. A bristle was ever so slightly trapped on something he couldn't quite see. He grabbed a finer brush and swept it carefully across the area. A curved shape with ridges like a twist of rope started to emerge. Donald held his breath. He could hardly believe it!

"Hey Kemi!" he yelled, "you owe me a case of beer!" He heard her swearing in the shade of the tent, and then he heard another voice coming toward him across the sand. Donald bent to his task and the world fell away. All he heard was the soft scrape of his brush, and all he saw was the metallic twist of the torque emerging from the dirt. After a few short steps he placed the new find on the table in front of her. It glistened as it joined its brothers.

"Unbelievable," a female voice murmured. Donald looked down and met the dark almond shaped dark eyes of Kemi Houssein.

"Another one, Kemi." Donald grinned. She stared up at the big man as he smiled at her like an excited child. His auburn curls were soft even when coated with dirt and his blue eyes seemed darker when he was excited. His pale skin was toasted a cherry red. He looked like a child who'd spent too much time on the playground.

"Donnie," she said, her hands on her hips, "what the hell are these doing here?"

Kemi sat at a table under the canvas tent, staring alternately at her musclebound brother Masoud Houssein, and the collection of objects spread out between them. Then the brother and sister went outside the tent to talk. Their voices were hushed, but Donnie wouldn't hear anything above the swish of his brush on the dusty artifacts left on the table. For the most part, the table was littered with meaningless lumps of melted gold, what he would call "scrap metal," bartered for its weight rather than for the jewelry it once had been. Two Celtic torques and one plain bracelet bangle stood out, but the rest was unremarkable. Donald busied himself by organizing them with his brush, and soon he had little piles of like-seeming pieces that had been chopped apart.

Out of hearing range, Kemi said, " I don't know why Donnie wanted to come to this part of Spain, except that I told him the authorities away from the major cities would be easier to work with. He doesn't know we're illegal. But the stuff he's finding isn't Spanish, or recent enough to be Moorish. These things shouldn't be here. I think he actually steered us here on purpose."

"Kemi," her brother whispered in his gravelly voice, "*we* should not be here much longer. The locals are going to find out soon enough that we're not just fishing. All they have to do is contact some authorities and we're done for. And Donald isn't the clueless grad student you thought he was." Kemi looked up at her brother and narrowed her eyes.

"I don't give a rat's ass about the history of what we're finding out here," he went on. "We should have already left. Nothing here is worth a prison sentence in a Spanish jail."

"And leave this behind?" Kemi asked, spreading her hands to indicate the trove of broken artifacts, pottery shards, and twists of beaming gold.

"Masoud," she said levelly, "we came here to excavate this site because we believed the Spanish government is incompetent and hopelessly bogged down in corruption. The locals don't care what we do, and we can pack up stuff in an hour if we need to. This might be the greatest find since the Valley of the Kings!"

"We're here for the artifacts we can sell, like old coins and Roman swords," said Masoud. "Don't get all academic on me. You know we're here for the money. And whatever we find has to remain secret, because we're not legal. How can we even explain finding this stuff? We can't take credit for any 'great finds' as you call it. Are you going to say it was an accident we were digging here?"

"Of course we're here for the money," she sighed, "but now what do we do? We've found so much more than we expected! And the Celtic artifacts...I can't explain their presence. And Donnie isn't saying anything either!"

"Why not? Isn't that what Cameron is for?" said Masoud impatiently, "Hasn't he been able to tell you anything?"

"Oh yes," said Kemi, her dark eyes glittering, "and you won't believe what he thinks..."

જી જી જી

The day's work had revealed another Celtic torque, twisted gold like the other, but less weighty. Donald envisioned the Celtic warrior whose neck it once protected from a sword strike. Why was it left here amongst "scrap metal"? Such an item should have been part of an honored burial, or scene of a long ago battle with an intact skull. No, this was only trade cargo, purposefully placed for retrieval, as if the traders had run out of room on their boat. Or perhaps it was stolen booty, left for the thief's accomplices. There simply were not enough clues to explain the cache. What had alerted Donald to the site initially, was a palm sized clay oil lamp, sticking part way out of the sand. It's black clay, which stood out from the beige sand, was delicately decorated with curved feathers of *Maat* surrounding the central hole. It was clearly Egyptian. It had shown the way, perhaps left near the surface as a beacon.

What was even more curious was the discovery of several broken clay amphorae filled with rolls of papyrus. Most seemed to be bills of lading, written in Phoenician. The vessels had been carefully stacked long ago, then collapsed onto each other from the weight of sand and time. Amongst this jumble of distress was a white alabaster amphora, still intact. Donald extracted it carefully from the clay shards, brushed off the dust that clouded its shiny surface, and turned it over in his lap. It's workmanship was exquisite, and the stopper at the top was still intact. Donald hefted it under his arm and brought it to the table in the tent. Dried wax parted easily as he removed the stopper piece, and as he inverted the jar, rolls of papyrus slid out onto the table with a soft thud. Donald held his breath, and carefully set the vase on its side.

Before him were five rolls of Egyptian papyrus, each sealed with a dollop of wax. With a scalpel, Donald ever so carefully released the wax from the edge of one paper roll, and the curled pages opened slowly, as if by magic. The centuries of tension had formed loose curves, but the leaves opened like flower petals to the welcoming sunlight. Donald held a jeweler's loupe to his eye and studied a piece of papyrus laid out before him. His lips formed words as he slid the glass slowly over lines of closely written text. He bit his bottom lip in concentration. This particular roll was covered with Egyptian hieroglyphics, but closed at the end with a cartouche that read: "Scota Nefara-Selkis."

A noise made him look up. He smiled as Kemi brushed aside a canvas flap and stepped inside the makeshift laboratory. She returned his smile, and Donald felt something low in his stomach give a tug. Kemi had that effect on him, and even if he hadn't been obsessed with everything Egyptian he still would have fallen for her honey skin, dark eyes, and straight black hair that fell across her face like a raven's wing. Plus, her body was made for fine art. Past failures with romance were forgotten, and Donnie thought he had found the real thing.

"Donnie," she said in her low musical voice, "what else have you found out about our lost Egyptians?"

"Well, I don't think they were lost. If anything they lived here a long time. But there are no ruins, no stones configured like ancient dwellings. In Spain, these are called "oppida." Maybe they left in a hurry, but the site is too full of artifacts to make me think they were just passing through. A long time ago maybe this river was deeper and wider, and was an actual shipping route for Phoenicians. So maybe their homes are under layers of river mud. Except for this particular papyrus bundle, everything else could be trade booty or Carthaginian refuse." Donald was pensive for a moment, then continued. "We probably should pack up and go down to Alicante, and check out more local history. As much as I hate to leave this site, I need a better layout for organizing these finds. I still can't tell if our find is Celtic or Phoenician, but it could be Egyptian. There is another city nearby called Eiche that we should investigate, too. And if there's been any other archaeological investigations around here, the museums might have good information."

"So you're ready to leave?" Masoud asked as he entered the tent. He had been eavesdropping outside for some time. "We could find more gold here, don't you think?" And then, suddenly composed, he mumbled, "I mean more historical artifacts?"

"I sure as hell can't decipher this papyrus out in the sun! And it's so fragile that I need a safe desk, out of the breeze, just to open it any farther," replied Donald, shaking his head. Donald's frustration was mounting, having now heard unvarnished intentions from Masoud's mouth. Donald began to say something, then thought better of it.

With her hand out of Donald's sight, Kemi motioned to her brother to back off. Masoud had a habit of dropping conversations in mid sentence when Kemi was nearby. In this way she kept Donald happy, and Masoud under control. She had made sure that Donald had no idea that most of their ventures weren't 'sanctioned' so to speak. In fact, since Donald had joined the team, none of the digs had been approved by any official party. Kemi was determined to keep him in the dark. So, last month when some very official-looking men hiked over from some very official looking cars one afternoon, she made it a point to steer Donnie's interest back towards the artifacts. She preferred to leave the hard conversations to her brother. He was so much more...eloquent than she was. Kemi tended to get impatient, and she had been scorned for her messy techniques before. Masoud didn't even let her carry a gun anymore. She knew it was best to keep Donnie out of the loop. He had made them so much money after all.

"Who are those guys?" Donald had asked as she led him away that day.

"Don't worry about them, darling," Kemi purred, rubbing against his side, "it's just business. The men are probably trying to strong-arm Masoud out of more money. We told you about doing business in Spain."

"That's wrong," Donald said, frowning. He started to turn around but Kemi smoothly hooked his arm in hers and steered him towards the tents.

"Really Donnie, you don't have to worry. Masoud is an excellent negotiator." So, their travels in Spain went smoothly as Donald found more artifacts to ponder.

SEVEN

Masoud came back to the tent after about an hour, and found Donald pouring over a sheet of papyrus that to Masoud looked like all the other sheets of papyrus. Donald's red hair was stuffed out of the way into a dirty headband, but it was poking out everywhere making him look even more geeky. "Are you really ready to leave this site?" he asked Donald.

"There might be much more here, but as much as I'd like to sift more sand, I think that leaving would be best for the safety of what we've found so far. I really need strong light to decipher these papyrus sheets, and the camp lantern just doesn't do it," added Donald.

"Then we will come back," Kemi asserted smoothly, "but for now Donnie is right. The locals may think we have overstayed our welcome. And if they suspect we're doing more than just camping out like gypsies, they may guess we've found something valuable."

"Well," said Donald grudgingly, "promise me we can come back."

Kemi raised her right hand in a Girl Scout pledge sign, and said, "I promise."

They spent the evening cleaning up the dig site. Kemi and Masoud hardly ever asked Donald to do anything but dig, and tonight was no different. Eventually he gave up trying to help and went to his tent. Donald was a genius at finding things, but orderly packing was not in his skill set. He thought Kemi was excited that some scrolls were in Egyptian but he knew Masoud hadn't cared at all. It dawned on him that finding gold scrap was most important. Donald sat on the edge of his air mattress and rubbed his face. He hadn't told Kemi much about what he could read on the scroll, and he wasn't sure why. He'd always been trusting; something his family, especially his sister Alison, had always chided him about. Ali once told him he had crappy taste in women because he trusted unconditionally, and right out of the gate. True, he'd had quite a few women run all over him, but Donald was stubborn and convinced that all of them had really loved him, in their own way, of course. Essentially, Donald was still a geeky kid digging in dirt.

Ali had never met Kemi, but Donald was pretty sure she would disapprove. He knew that Kemi was controlling, but he didn't really mind. So why was he keeping secrets? He hadn't told Kemi or her brother that the scroll mentioned an Egyptian princess. If he was right about what it said, then it would be the find of the century. Still, Donald was pretty sure Masoud was less than honest about his dealings, but he thought Kemi must be manipulated by him. If Masoud turned out to be a crook, Donald didn't want this artifact to fall into Masoud's stupid hands.

Before long they had broken camp and gear was stowed in their battered camper. Donald made notations on his local map, marking the compass degrees to ease his mind about leaving the site. He knew he could find it again, just by the terrain, but the map was extra insurance. Then they carefully refilled any obvious dig holes and put the location back to its desolate self. They left some fish entrails on the shore, evidence of fishing, but that's all that anyone would really notice now. He felt uneasy about abandoning the site, but his more prudent emotions took over. Better to leave now and not suffer destruction of their finds, or be at the mercy of any outsiders. It wouldn't have been the first time his artifacts had been stolen by someone, nor his written publication usurped by some unscrupulous professor.

It took an hour of dodging scrub trees and rocks to get back to a real road, but after finding some pavement they were able to get to Alicante before nightfall. Spanish hillsides melted into broad vistas as they came closer to the Mediterranean.

Soon they found a hotel room that sported clean white sheets and a cool breeze from the seaward veranda. For once in his life, Donnie really enjoyed having a lukewarm shower and clean hair. Kemi was already sound asleep in their bed as he snuggled close. No sounds drifted up from the plaza below, the city slept and they felt safe. He lay down on the mattress and watched her sleeping face. A moment later Kemi turned toward him and slowly opened her eyes. There was an expectant silence and as he met Kemi's dark gaze, suddenly his mind wasn't on suspicions anymore.

That night Donald dreamed of ships. . . proud Egyptian ships covered in gold leaf and black lacquer, their brilliant sails of blue and purple raised against the sky. He dreamed of a woman standing at the prow. . . her red braids unbound blowing wild in the sea breeze. Her bright eyes were lined in kohl and her skin was brushed with golden powder. . .a beautiful princess. At her side a gleaming harp leaned against the rail. A man came to stand behind her, and they both looked toward the western horizon. It wasn't Kemi in the dream, but some beautiful warrior princess and her lover, going purposefully, somewhere.

EIGHT

Kemet, 363 B.C.E. A Palace Morning.

As my eyes open to meet the day I realize the other girls are quietly making ready for today's festivities. All are grooming hair and applying kohl. Platters piled with fresh fruits and smells of sweet bread prick my nose, and the girls are gleefully tossing onion cakes to each other. When they see that my eyes are open the noise level reaches its normal high pitch of a silly giggling harem. Sher-Ri is smiling at me.

"Who was in bed with you last night in your dreams? You were moaning and moving in ecstasy, as if someone was making love with you. We did not want to wake you, as it was enjoyable just to watch your rhythm. Now share!"

"I cannot say who was there. They were strangers to me, but I felt at home. Perhaps it was not an ordinary dream, but a vision of the future. . . I do not know, but it was *fine!*"

Sher-Ri nods, and does not ask for more. Perhaps today at the temple I will receive a missive from Neith. Three times have I heard from her, with a voice high above the chanting and chorus of words, that said *strength, honor, not yet. . . not yet.* .repeated.

There are rare times at the temple when all is still during meditation, when breathing falls into unity, and the air itself is still. I sense the Goddess Neith in our midst. I long for this to be truly happening, though Sha'Bet believes the Goddess comes only to the true of heart, those completely devoted to her service. She says therefore, that it is only my imagination, for I am just a novitiate. But Sha'Bet is careful not to dissuade my feelings completely, for she has her reasons for wanting me to become a full priestess. She envisions more tribute from Father, and perhaps other things. She enjoys her power, controlling the temple, and us naive girls. With her magical incantations and execrations we have all experienced the holiness of the chanting trance that comes upon us. If my dream last night was an oracle, perhaps today at the temple things will be made clear. Let Neith decide, for there is much I do not see or understand.

Sher-Ri is flitting around the room like a butterfly, as usual, for today she will be with the dancers parading down to the harbor in the midst of the musicians. It will be another magical feast day, for by mid-afternoon more ceremonies will honor the Apis Bull. He is Ra incarnate. The whole of the populace will converge on his litter to praise him. For all women wanting fertility, provisions will be made so that they can approach the young God. Women will raise their skirts to him as their husbands watch, as will even unmarried girls. People of Kemet concern themselves more with cleanliness than nudity, and it is usual to see a baby suckling at a mother's breast in public. I suspect Mother will have a private audience with the young god. Perhaps Father will conduct a magical ceremony for her. None of this is explained to me, for I will be at a distance with the priestesses and novitiates who intend to remain virgins.

Today I dress as a novitiate priestess, in layers of sheer linen, no jewelry, no kohl, and no special adornments that might set me apart. We will chant and sing our praises to the Goddess Neith, and weave in unison through the crowds, like a swarm of sheep. I hurry to the temple because it is past dawn, and I am late. It is well I do not have to attend to my hair or makeup today, as I would be even later. As it is, I may be scolded for this. But, I did enjoy my dream.

Our great Goddess Neith, Mother of Ra, is all knowing. She is the weaver of destinies, wise and powerful above all people and their primitive plans. She weaves all existence, and at death, she guards warrior bodies when they fall in battle. Her bow is strong, her arrows plan our future, so it is to her we pray for guidance. Only she knows our true path through life. We chant words, first in unison, then in a chorus of three voices, weaving the tones of the chant. Our linen dresses sweep the streets as we swirl to the chant and parade to the harbor.

I am the things that are, that will be, and that have always been. No one has ever laid open the garment by which I am concealed.

We repeat this chant hundreds of times as Shar'Bet leads our throng. People become silent as we pass, but are festive as soon as the chant fades from their ears. All people of Kemet believe their lives are planned in advance of birth, so it is prayers to Neith that offer guidance at life's crossroads. If only She would always answer! We chant our way all the distance to the harbor, finally reaching our assigned place where we will rest, for the second day of Shemu. Kenti-Sur and I find a low bench, sit together and watch children playing games.

"If we take final vows, such as those will never be ours." Kenti-Sur murmurs and gestures to a shady spot where families gather. We watch as two boys play a game of colored stones. Holes scooped out of the sand make a pattern for the bao stones as they are hopped from one depression to the next. The boys are concentrating on counting, predicting, and intensely ignoring the noise around them. A family nearby has a game of Sennet with carved game pieces, "hounds and jackals" are moved with abandon.

"The temple will be our family," I say, "with no worries and strife of daily life. These people have only occasional days when they can put away those concerns. I think the festival achieves Father's aims, for all cares are left behind and the people of Kemet feel safe. But it is an *illusion*, for enemies are at our borders."

A single tear streaks down her cheek, as Kenti-Sur watches a woman with a baby at her breast.

" Temple life will come upon us my friend, so enjoy this day as if you, too, were such a child. But do not make that choice because of your friendship to me. I could not bear that." Kenti-Sur nods, we hold hands, and wait for Father's address.

Father will address the crowds when Ra achieves his zenith, to tell all assembled of the alliances to protect our country of black earth. The Apis bull has arrived on his cart, fully decked with orange flowers that cover his back like a blanket. From our bench we can see Father and Mother on their litter throne. She is dressed in her finest linens, and under her black beaded wig her eyes shine with pride. She appears as the fierce warrior queen of past memory, and Father rises to his full height, like a mighty god to speak to the people.

"Great people of Kemet. Today we enter the second day of Shemu, in glory and strength, for I bring to you a new Apis Bull!" Father raises his hand in signal, and the cart drawn by four horses takes its reserved place before Phar'o. The young black calf, bedecked in lotus garlands, snorts, and stomps a polished hoof. His forehead is marked with the white star of Ra. His other holy markings are covered by flowers. A bin of grain rests at his feet but instead of munching the food he watches the crowd fearlessly. He exhibits the aura of a ferocious god. He is Ra Incarnate, and seems aware of his own importance. People form a queue at his head.

The fertility procession will take all day no doubt, as it has been many years since a new Apis bull has been discovered. Offerings of fresh green grass and grassy onions are offered to him, and he happily eats all that is offered. Steps in front of the cart are mounted by women one by one, each lifting their skirts for the Ra's blessing. The bull snorts occasionally, but watches each woman intently. Some women receive his grace as they feel the air from his nostrils thrill over their exposed nether regions.

I expected Father to make more speeches today, but instead he sits, looking pleased with the spectacle around him. Sometimes his interested eyes watch certain women approach the bull, but mostly he confers with various foreign dignitaries. More food is brought in, and another wonderful banquet begins. The musicians and dancers give their finest performances and the multitude is enchanted with the bounty of Kemet.

Shar'Bet claps her hands for attention. "Novitiates, you may have a day of relaxation. Remove your head veils and feel the light of Ra on your faces. You are dispersed, do as you like." Of course we will avoid the Apis calf, but we are free to mingle where we will. In my white plain linen I am easily absorbed into the crowds of people. Out of curiosity, Kenti-Sur and I move toward groups of foreign visitors. They do not perceive us as novitiates, but as commoners of Kemet.

"I heard news of late from Karkissa that King Masoleus has died?" I ask one foreigner.

"Yes, sadly, and our great queen is in terrible mourning. Our borders are not defensible by deserts as is Kemet, and the light has gone out of our land. Many people have decided to leave, for the Persians have levied heavy taxes and demand tribute. At least they do not concern themselves with everyday life in the cities, and Queen Artemisia has chosen to become a satrap to preserve peace for our people. We will not sacrifice our people with a futile war. We hope the tide will turn with our alliance with Kemet. Artemisia is building a magnificent monument to his memory, called the Mausoleum."

"Thank you for talking with us," I say, "feel safe here in Kemet." I bow, and take my leave. Kenti-Sur has wandered in another direction, toward the Spartans. We do not understand their language, but I see they are having contests of strength, and drinking more beer than anyone can imagine. This will surely brighten her previous thoughts. Instead, I make my way to the mooring where ships are docked. Sea birds are calling and diving for morsels of food left by revelers. They too will have full bellies this night.

To my left floats the ship of the Milesians, though I see no guards or persons in view. Is it the ship of my dream last night? The deck is smooth, the prow is curved, but there are no paintings or symbols as on those ships of Kemet. The deck rocks gently under foot and as I step onto the deck, I hear it creak from the touch of water on the hull. It is a lovely place to sit and partake of the north breeze. I turn my face to the sea.

"Who are you? You belong on the shore, not on my ship!" comes a voice. It is Gamal, and as I turn my face to him he is startled to recognize the princess he saw with the harp. "Oh, I beg your pardon, my lady. You are most welcome on my ship! I did not recognize you in this dress. Are you hiding your royalty for some reason?"

"No, my lord. I am both princess and novitiate in the temple of Neith. Today I am free to follow my own footsteps, wherever they might lead. Please tell me about your land and others beyond Kemet. There is so much I would like to know."

Gamal has the most open face and kind eyes. He smiles and begins wonderful descriptions of the places he has visited. Perhaps he understands now how cloistered I feel, and how ignorant I must be of the outside world. He explains things as if I were a school child.

"Miletus is a thickly walled city, open only at the seafront side, on the eastern shores of this Great Green Sea. To the north are other cities, Tyre and Ephesus, and even a place where the people live completely underground."

"Underground? For safety?"

"Yea, for protection from farther eastern tribes and marauders. They even keep their livestock in great caverns, and have huge cisterns of water for their crops."

"Their crops grow without the light of day?" I ask, incredulously.

"Yes, they have developed windows that bring the sunlight to open areas, for their crops. It is very unusual, but they prosper. Miletus instead has immensely thick walls to fend off attacks, for we are a very prosperous and wealthy city. We defend our harbor where most attacks come."

"Why do the Persians want a bigger empire? Is not their land fertile enough to feed their people? I do not understand this war."

"Perhaps it is their bloodthirsty god that sends them onward, rather than want of plunder or territory. Their leader, Artaxerxes II, thirsts for control of the whole world, including Kemet above all else. Through this common threat we must band together. Your Father has made strong alliances. I offer my help as translator often, and I have some skills as diplomat, soothing the feelings of certain envoys. Your father is often too brusque."

"Yes, he does not have your temperament, most certainly, good sir. His enemies are many, but he buys allegiance with Kemet's storehouse of gold. I understand our need of allies, but it seems to me that Miletus is able to defend itself."

"My city is constantly in need of allies, to preserve independence from the Achaeans, and the Persians, even Karkissa to the north. We have a most valued harbor, where money changes hands most freely. Our history is as long as that of Kemet, and while we have great mountainous areas and walls to the east, we are always in danger of conquest. In centuries past we have been ruled by Karkissa, Persia, Ionia, and even Samos. Our industries of purple dye and strong lumber for ships are unparalleled in the world. My father governs Miletus, as well as over sixty colonies around the Black Sea, but now with the death of Mausoleus, our independence from Persia is threatened. Our armies come to defeat the Persians in Kemet, but at the same time must defend at home. Your Father's offer of a colony here in Kemet may be our best move, for if Miletus is pushed into the sea I could not live under Persian rule."

Gamal's words show the concerns of a diplomat, but the love of his homeland shines on his face. He seems worried as we all are, but he knows better the difficulties of keeping alliances with nations that are often enemies. I begin to understand this balancing act of nations, all like vulnerable eggs in one basket.

"What of lands to the west? Are they threatened as well?"

"Perhaps you have heard of a nation to the west named 'Kart-Hadasht'? And the dark skinned people to the south?"

"I know of Nubia, and have heard of Punt, but not Karthage," I reply.

"There are settlements to the west, and north of the Great Green Sea, that welcome trade from Miletus. Beyond them are people supplied by camel caravans, but the sea is less precarious as the land routes are tedious and long. The people of Kart-hadasdt control the most territory west of Kemet, and lands where Milesians have not traded, but sailors tell of a great body of salt water too huge to cross. Perhaps Kart-hadast controls that as well, I do not know. We think of land as all of earth, but perhaps our land is really an island surrounded by unlimited water. The distances are so great that no ship sailing so far west has ever returned. Only the Sea Peoples sail beyond sight of land, and they do not share their maps."

As I listened, Gamal told me of distant markets, of strange animals, and wonderful fabrics in colors beyond imagination. He showed me green gemstones from far eastern mountains that have green ripples and swirls of deepest green. And he says there are metals so black and hard that nothing can withstand their cut.

"You have seen those called Spartans? Their culture reveres their women, because they are mothers of warriors. They rear their young with the intention of privation, a future of glorious death in war. War and battles are what they admire, and they train always for war."

"And the Ionians?"

"Those city states value knowledge far more than war. They have famous schools where learned teachers reside, so that those who quest for knowledge come to the academies at Athens. Would it surprise you to know that women also teach at this academy? Others are great orators, and the people value theater, discourse, and understanding above all things. One woman, Diotima of Mantinea, is one such teacher, and I have sat for many hours at her talks. "Please know, Gamal, that I am also schooled in many things, but not of the outside world. I attend the temple of Neith. The teachings I must master are memorization, no questions are allowed. I would love to go to such an academy that you speak of, where students are required to think rather than recite all day!"

"At least you feel safer here in Kemet, and you have the library that holds knowledge from all other lands. In Miletus, learned men cannot keep our city walls safe from gods who are fed by human babies. I have seen much of the world that you would not want to see. Keep here in safety, and do not wish to leave Kemet."

"Gamal, I am not safe here! You are deceived by appearances. If I were able, I would vanish this instant! I would stow away on your ship or join the Karkissan warrior women. I am no frail lotus blossom!"

Gamal gives out a little laugh with my outburst. He does not understand the ways of Kemet, though he believes he does.

"Did you see the Apis Bull in the procession today?"I ask.

Gamal smiles, nods, and says, "But I did not see you near that bull."

"Yes, I could be with those women as well. . . because I do not intend to complete my studies as a virgin in the temple." There, it is said. Gamal is pensive, does not look to me for more explanation, just waits calmly.

"Soon, my Father intends to take me. . . as his wife." Tears streak down my face before I can control them. Saying those words out loud unleashes a torrent of tears, and I weep uncontrollably.

Surprise and understanding seem to flood the face of Gamal. Recognition of my fate enters his eyes, and he now understands the reason for all my questions. Still, he does not speak, but holds my hands gently, giving comfort to me. Soon my tears dry, and I am again the proud princess of Kemet.

"Where is it written that my life must be planned by others? Only the Great Goddess knows my destiny, and I will weave my own fate through her direction. Could I not pay for passage to lands across the Great Green Sea? Think on this, good sir. . .would you take a princess of Kemet to Miletus?"

Gamal's brilliant blue eyes look me full in the face, and without flinching or hesitating he says, "No." Then in a barely audible whisper he says, "What you ask would threaten the alliance with Miletus if you left in secret. Surely you realize there is no safe port for such a runaway. Your father's arms would reach us beyond the known world. Then he pauses and says, "Unless it is well-known that you travel as an emissary, or on some other mission of your Father's. He controls the length and breadth of all Kemet, and all therein. All respect his power." There is no place to hide on my ship unless you were pickled in a barrel of wine. You would leave your birthright behind? You could not live long as a slave girl on a camel caravan, nor would I advise you to take such a foolish direction."

Gamal is prudent, and right. There is no hope for escape for me. Quiet hangs on the air like some tangible stone. My head is bowed, but then I look up at Gamal, into his eyes.

"Would you lie with your mother?" I ask. "Or your daughter? This is to be my future, to produce a son for the Phar'o. I would rather die."

Gamal's face shows his shock at my words, as he imagines such a thing. He nods his head as if there is now full awareness of my dilemma.

"You have some time, I think," he says. "Perhaps you could travel as an emissary or mission of your father's? These are strange days. Let us think more on what could be done, for your sake and that of the alliance."

Afternoon shadows are lengthening, and I must return to my sisterhood. Gamal's strong hands lift me by my hips onto the dock, and I take my leave with thanks. His eyes meet mine once more as I turn back to the crowded pier. I can blend into the crowds, and slowly reappear as if I hadn't been gone very long.

Kenti-Sur and other friends are there, eating fruits and everyone has had too much beer. The queue around the Apis bull has not diminished much, and groups of musicians and dancers weave through the crowds. Some people toss fruits to them and their purses are full with treats, even a few coins. Shar'Bet claps her hands for attention, and we must form ranks to proceed back to the temple. She has been busy giving audiences to people who want their fortune told, and she has amassed quit a tribute for Neith. She has been so constantly engaged that she did not realize I was absent. If she truly had the skills, she could read much on my face!

NINE

As evening begins to set, Father has the palace horn blowers announce that he is about to speak. The great bronze horns bellow their news, and all eyes turn to Father's litter. He rises again, like some indomitable statue, and with upheld arms, symbolically embraces his people.

"People of Kemet. Tomorrow I will begin the journey to Memphis, to present our new Apis Bull to his temple sanctuary. We will travel on my royal barge, and those of you who wish to go may follow, or travel with others on the shore. All will be made open along the distance to Memphis. The feasting will continue here in Rhakoti, but there will be an even greater celebration when we meet to honor this incarnation of Apis-Hapi." People cheer wildly and the crowds wave in admiration of this great Phar'o. Then he lowers his voice for special effect, starting quietly, but then raises to a crescendo when he names his his many titles:

"I have consulted the stars. The deluge is delayed, giving us more time to honor and pray for Hapi's return. Great is our Black Land! Let this day and my goodness be remembered for all eternity. I am the Life, Prosperity, and Health of Upper and Lower Kemet, Kheperkare, Son of Ra, Nekhtenebef, ever-living. May we be given all life, prosperity, dominion, all health and happiness with Ra forever!"

Such a mighty cheer swells out of the crowd, it deafens our ears. People are jubilant for more days without work, as well as the good portents for Kemet. Ships on the harbor will bring more soldiers, more provisions, and more commerce to our city. Taxes and tariffs on these imports will bring more prosperity. Our people will welcome all these faithful foreigners.

But, Father is not finished with his speech. He again raises his arms and as if by magic a hush falls over the crowd below him.

"I have directed my map makers to devise quadrants of Rhakoti for settlements for our foreign allies. The Milesian settlement shall be called Naukratis. Others have not been named as yet, but there will be dry land and space made for all who come. I decree that canals will be dug to divert parts of the river, as the deluge will soon bring its black fertility. Many plans have been put into operation to please our allies. With friendship all will prosper! Let it be so, Life, Strength, and Prosperity!"

Father's control of the people is masterful, and giving territory within our borders to our allies is powerful strategy, another perfect bribe for support. He must be smugly pleased with his control of these allies, else how could he leave Rhakoti for a trip to Memphis? It strikes me as odd, but I have never witnessed a new Apis Bull in all my sixteen years. No one else seems concerned, and just knowing that he will be out of the city and palace lightens my mood. Perhaps Mother need not accompany him? I for one, will find some serious excuse for avoiding the trip, for as novitiate of Neith I cannot be too close to that black calf!

As Sha'Bet assembles us into our ranks, each woman retrieves her clay oil lamp hung at the waist. Our heads are covered again, we begin our solemn procession back to the temple, now with lit oil lamps. Our little wick-lights flicker in the fading light of Ra. As we enter the temple our lamps are ensconced one by one in niches on the wall of the large meeting room. They look like bright stars flickering on the wall, like points of light in a vast sky. Shar'Bet directs us in chants, and prayers to Neith, for all the wonders of life. The sound of her solemn voice seems to fill the air, as if the Goddess herself has entered.

Tiny hairs on my arms lift in excitement, and we all bend to prostrate ourselves toward our high priestess. Oil lamps begin to sputter, and go out, one by one. We are left in darkness, but there is a rush of wind in the hall. Perhaps the expected north wind has begun. Sleep comes like a blanket over all who lie there. I will sleep in the temple this night; all seems well in the world as Khepher-Ra pushes his barque through the night sky.

Ten

Morning light filters down on last night's revelers. Our sisters rouse from sleep, and are quietly milling around. It is not the usual boisterous morning-time of a temple day. Some hold their heads from too much beer, and it seems no one is hungry. My duties of preparing bowls for washing is quickly accomplished, and I find Kenti-Sur as usual, arranging hair with her tortoise-shell combs. I bring moist linen for clean hands, and slowly our ranks come together and are ready for another day. But I must be present at the palace today, if only to attend a royal send-off of Father's barge. I find Shar'Bet arranging leaves of papyrus for today's calligraphy lesson. She looks up, irritated as always at my intrusion. I speak to Shar'Bet in a soft voice:

"Good morning, Mother. May I be dismissed?"

"Yes, you have importance elsewhere. But keep your distance from the Apis Bull."

With a short wave of her impatient hand, I am dismissed. How can she even say such a thing to me? The Apis-God is never kept in the palace, nor would I visit his paddock even under Father's orders. His eunuchs would have to bind me and serve me up like some nubile feast. Or is Sha'Bet's directive really a warning? I nearly fly back to the palace, hoping to find Mother and the palace still in a festive spirit. Terrible thoughts and images creep into my mind, fleeting scenes of hateful possibilities. Does Father have horrendous plans for me? Without delay I find Mother's rooms, but all is strangely quiet. Perhaps they have left for Memphis?

An eerie silence fills the chamber. No one is stirring. No lamps are lit. No fresh water in ewers for bathing. A dark, floating mist obscures my sight. It is *not* the smoke of myrrh. I smell the cloying taste of swamp air like rotting vegetation pulled up by a boat oar.

"Mother?'

No answer. I call for her again. No response. At least no human response. The swirling mist descends, blinding me. Breathing becomes difficult. I drop to my knees where the air is cleaner and cry out. "Has everyone left me behind?"

Dry, dead flower petals crackle beneath my knees as I crawl toward my mother's bed. My fingers touch the fine carving of the headboard and find an arm.

"Are you sleeping? Wake up."

I shake her shoulder until I realize her flesh has the cold, still feel of death. I start to scream, but the mist clogs my nostrils. I choke. My throat closes up. And I understand. *Do not breathe this air!*

A sudden whirlwind rocks me and lifts my hair as it sucks the dark, dense, poisonous fog toward the high windows. The putrid odor rushes outside like a cloud of ravens into the clear morning air. Able to see now, my gaze falls upon Mother's still, serene face. Eyes closed, mouth gripped in the grim determination of death, but there is no sign of pain. Just the empty shell of the woman who gave me life, but had never been a mother.

I draw a breath and collapse on the floor beside her deathbed. I do not know how long I have been there. A cry escapes me as I glance up to see my Father standing before me. Is it really him or a sorcerer's trick? I watch his formidable figure pulsate in the morning light. Flushed, he glares at me like a hunter eyeing prey and clutches his fists repeatedly in anger. Finally he has dispelled the last of the poison air from the chamber, and he speaks to me.

"Hariesis warned me of your treachery," he bellows. "You have conspired with Miletus. I cannot trust you to do your duty to Kemet. Do you not want to be Queen of our land? Others can fill this throne." A sneer of derision infects his ephemeral voice.

Despite my fear, I strive to speak firmly. "Hariesis lies, Father. He conspires with Articana to gain control over you. My mother and I have always been true to our vows. I am bound in truth to Maat and Neith. I could not do such things."

I feel his eyes burrowing into my very soul, seeking the truth of my words. He begins to soften, though he does not relent the clutching of his fists. I am astounded, as I watch his steely resolve begin to crumble. In a flash, I understand that with my mother's death his alliance with Karkissa is broken! It cannot be restored, even if he were to marry me. I recoiled to see such a powerful man, the God of Kemet, undone by this treachery.

Still flexing his fists he speaks in a distant, otherworldly voice, soft now. Then as if hearing voices from the palace stones, he cups his hands to his ears to listen. Quietly now he turns to me and says, "I go today to install the Apis calf in Memphis. I will take all the officials from the palace, leaving you behind. The senders of this poison will be damned, for I know who only could have done this deed. Nor was it my doing, for your mother has always been faithful to her promise to Kemet. I should have known there was terrible danger, for omens were all around me. But it is I who am cursed!"

I stare at him in wonder. His power could not avert such crimes? How could this happen?

"I have seen the future months as they will unfold. But I did not understand." With his fists repeatedly clenching he said, "These sixteen years Kemet has prospered under my rule. No one can deny I have been a great leader of our people. But Hapi is not delivering the deluge as expected this spring, and the Persians advance like sand in a haboob." Now, head lowered, "I have seen the Apis Bull slain. Persians will bathe in my nephrite sarcophagus."

Beads of sweat appear on his brow, as if great exertion was needed to remain standing. With a hand covering his red eyes he said, "It cannot be averted. The last three nights I stood at midnight to catch the moonbeams in a silver cup, but it was denied by clouds. Last night, whatever moonbeams were garnered, spilled out of the cup as it fell beneath the water. And I do not have any more potent spells to try."

He watches the corners of the room, as if expecting someone to be hiding there, eavesdropping. Finding none, he returns his gaze to me.

"My powerful visions reveal weeks and months, but only snatches of years to come. I will sail to Memphis, install the new bull, and go farther south to unite all of Kemet. But then I will travel overland to Abyssinia, and evade my entourage there. I am guaranteed refuge at the court of King Nastesen of Napata." His head is bowed, in obvious defeat.

"Kemet will fall, it cannot be helped. The gods have deserted me, for my sins are many. Maat's scales are tipped for I have transgressed my boundaries as Father to our land."

"What have you done, Father? I know people disappear, but I believed that to be Hariesis' doing. It is your right to have other wives, including me. What fault is yours?"

With more jerky movements, Father tries to control his words, which come haltingly. "I. . . sent my qarina to Macedon. It is there that I have sired a son, but without the rights of a husband. She is married to a king. I have opened my soul to more evil than it can hold."

"I have raped this woman, taken her during a storm while her husband was away. He has accused her of adultery, for he saw in a dream that she was embracing a serpent. She has borne a son, though it cannot be of her husband. Myrtale believes she was struck by a thunderbolt of her god, for her son has the marks of a great man."

"What marks? Is the child deformed by this evil? Father, you must explain this to me, for maybe you are mistaken and the Apis Bull will redeem Kemet. Our temples are faithful to our gods, as are our people. Your actions are not the whole of Kemet!"

Father's lips form a crooked smile, like a grimace.

"I am to blame and Kemet will suffer. The child has blond hair like his mother, but beneath the curls at his temples, horns have sprouted. The Apis bull has given his spirit to this child in Macedon. He will one day be Phar'o of Kemet, but only after much misery and privation has fallen upon our people."

Father's voice is even more measured, as if reading from the oracle itself.

"This son will ride triumphantly into Kemet one day, and the people will accept him fully as my son. He will defeat the Persians on their northern flank. His destiny as greatest of men will be fulfilled, as I conceived him with the most terrible magic. His mother will recognize me in him. I will go again to Macedon. My dance is not yet done! My end days show renown as a seer in the court of Macedon."

Were these words from anyone other than Father, I would bring them some elixir to calm them. He is talking like someone lost, fearful of shadows, seeing things that are not real. Or maybe he is seeing a distant scene. In a straining, distant voice he gives an order:

"Remove this princess to the Milesian ship."

And then to another corner of the room: "Receive my order. Take my daughter to safety."

His body shudders. Defeat is evident. He can barely stand. But then he looks at me, still and cowering on the floor.

"Know now that you are most precious to me, and I would not have you fall into Persian hands. Make haste today, take your ladies and ride with the ship of Miledh. Many cities are controlled by the Persians, but there are yet free places where the people speak your tribal tongue. Do not stay where the people speak Luwian. You will find sanctuary, this I can ensure. Orders have been sent to the Milesians. They will obey."

Father bends on one knee, and embraces me as I have never felt him do. Kissing my cheeks, he runs fingers along the tears there, then with hands circling my breasts, he pulls me upright and completely off my feet. His frothy lips cover my mouth in a kiss of such force that I am breathless and frail, like a lamb in the wolf's teeth. But then he gently set me down saying, "Scota, you are fruit of my loins. You will leave our great land. The prince of Miletus will take you to Tokai, to the west and to other lands, where your pennant will fly safely. I have seen temples to your honor in green lands and mountains. Take all that you have learned here and become the great queen of your destiny. Go now in safety. I release you."

Clenching and re-clenching his fists, Father then stands, and seems to be striking unseen things in the air. Like battling mosquitoes. Then his jerky motions abate and he becomes calm. Satisfaction and pride seem to flow over his face as he smiles at me, one last time. He then strides from the room, doesn't look back, and instantly I am alone with the lifeless corpse of my mother. I sit speechless, wiping his spittle from my lips, trying to open my mind to Father's revelations. Great Goddess Neith! What weavings are known to none but you! I turn and give my mother a parting kiss. "Ka of my mother, go now. Your work is done. Life, Strength and Honor is yours always."

ELEVEN

With wings on my feet I ran as fast as I could to my rooms. Sher-Ri was gaily dancing around the room. "We are going on big ships today! How did you arrange it?" But then she saw terror on my face.

"I cannot tell you now. . . make haste! We leave Kemet today. Pack everything. Men will be here to carry us to the ships." I looked around, and all my ladies were staring in disbelief.

"Everyone, give attention! I charge you with sealed lips from here on out, for today change is coming to our lives. My Father Phar'o has decreed that I am to go as emissary to the west, a city called Karthage. I will sail on the ship of the Milesians. It is Father's will that I go. As I will be gone many months, I will take all my belongings. I give you a choice this morning: Come with me on my travels or enjoy the festival in the city. You will be provided for if you stay behind, but if you choose to come with me, you must bid farewell to your relatives. Either choice requires your solemn promise that you will not divulge the reason why, or say where I go. Choose now. Come or stay?"

Sher-Ri comes to my side without question. "I will leave all my belongings behind if there is room for my mother."

"Of course! There is room for all who choose."

Kenti-Sur and Nabana choose to come, for their place in the palace has always been with me, having forsaken their relatives long ago. Another handful of maidens bow and come to my side. Others, who decide to stay, give me their sacred promise, signed in the air with the glyph of Maat, that they will divulge nothing about our absence. Then we set to packing all things, as Ra rose to his zenith over Kemet.

The streets of Rhakoti seem even more full of people today, if that were possible. More people from the fields have come to see Father leave on his great barge with the Apis calf. Carts are laden with food and drink, which is distributed freely today. Father's bounty seems endless and the people revel in his promise of a great victory. But the wind has not shifted, nor has the water begun to *rise*. Few people seem to notice. They are distracted by the merriment. My entourage of palace ladies moves determinedly through the crowds, which part easily, for we carry my royal flag.

Soon we are at the harbor, and many people are embarking on ships to go to Memphis. Father's barque is already loaded with the Apis calf. The whole of the railings are covered with flower garlands. Flags embroidered with gold threads shine in the sun. Many small feluccas await. These will trail behind the great barge, as it seems that most of the populace will travel to Memphis for the installation. At the quay I see Uncle directing people, as he will board the Karkissan ship. He stands and waves to me, not knowing it is good-bye, forever.

As we make our way to the Milesian ship, Father makes a grand entrance, with loud musicians' fanfare. Perhaps it is a well-timed diversion, for I and my entourage board the Milesian ship without undue notice. Ever in control, Father addresses the people. I hear the last words of this man I feared for so many years.

"People of Kemet, hear the words of Nekhtenebef Kheperkare, Ever-living, Mighty of Arm, Who benefits the Two Lands. I go guarding Kemet, enclosing all with my powerful arm as a sword master attacks the enemy. I do good to him who is loyal, they can slumber until daylight, hearts full of good nature. I bring He who makes green all lands when he rises, who sates every man with his bounty. All eyes are dazzled when they see him. Like Ra, when he rises in light, he gives light to all bodies. Let it be recorded on the stele that the Great Apis Bull will be installed in Memphis, for all believers to worship and adore. Have bold hearts, and fear not the future that is written by the Great Goddess Neith."

With mooring stakes withdrawn, the barge begins to surge with the current, and strong rowers take up their task. Crowds line the riverbanks as far as sight permits. The procession to Memphis fades from sight. The ship of the Milesians waits as men labor to stow the cargo. My reed covered stone rests beneath my heavy cedar chest of secrets. Other boxes of belongings are spread on either side to balance the hold. On top of this pile, my harp is perched, wrapped and thickly padded with yards of linen and string, like some mummified animal of unknown shape. But she is safe this way, and can wait for new harbors ahead, or calm waters aboveboard. Up on deck I see the banner of Miletus, purple-blue with a golden star. Our boat turns out of the harbor and we are away, with other Milesian ships in our wake. Three ships follow our lead, two warships with soldiers and another deep-hulled cargo ship. The sails unfurl, then fill and I feel the surge of the waves, pulling, pulling.

At the railing I catch my last vision of Kemet. Its towers glisten in the noon glare and the noise of the crowds slides away from my ears. Gamal is by my side, his face full of purpose.

"This is your wish, my lady?" *As if there is any doubt.*

"When I received these orders I guessed that your father's heart is changed. Are you disowned or banished? Whatever did you do to get his blessing for leaving?"

"My Father's will is his own, dear Gamal. Time will tell if he has read the stars correctly, but he sends me away for safety. . . he believes Kemet will fall."

I watch Gamal's face receive this prophecy, and his eyes widen with surprise. Perhaps it is beyond belief that the alliances so well formed will be of no avail. I answer the questions not coming from his lips.

"It is because the strength of Kemet is not from warriors, even as many as there are. Our strength is our Great River. Though the alliances may continue, the deluge of the Great River is delayed. Without the swamp filled marshes, we cannot stop the savages from the east."

"Nor can my homeland," sighed Gamal. "For there was much argument with my father before our ships left. We believed staying and defending Miletus should have been our best action, but Father ordered us to come to Kemet, thinking we alone would survive. Most of Karkissa has gone under Persian rule, though they have not pillaged or put cities to the fire. It is taxation and tribute they want, not desolation. So, if your father's visions are true, perhaps it will not be so terrible for the people of Kemet. Not for the temples, though. *Gamal is right about the overthrow of our Gods.* They would not allow your Father or Mother to live, nor his other wives and children, and most especially not you!"

With measured words I said, "Gamal, my mother is dead this day. I found her poisoned. It was not Father's doing, but he knew who was to blame. He has released me as the alliance with Karkissa is broken with her death."

I watched as Gamal's face received this news. He now understands fully why I am allowed to leave, and the subterfuge required. Gamal's face strains for composure. His diplomat's control breaks down and he bows his head.

"I am broken with this news, my Lady. I suspected something was terribly wrong when I received these orders, but I did not question them. In fact, I did not believe this was happening until I saw your entourage advance. I thought I had dreamed those orders."

Gamal's arm draws me close, and I feel the warmth of his skin. Sunlight surrounds us there on the deck. "You will be safe here with me. You need other clothing, my lady. This warm weather may not hold, and the salt spray will make your linens wet. Please go below and find thick tunics for you and your women. We will talk of plans when you are ready."

Gamal gives a soft embrace, parts from me, and goes to the stern. There are maps to consult and plans to organize, and much to think upon. But I am relieved that we have left Kemet behind. It is as if I were never there, erased from all memory. Surely the stone cutters will erase my name from the tablets in the Hall of Maat. As "deserters" our family will lose its name in history.

Below deck my friends are sorting through bins in the storage area. There are colorful tunics, even leggings, and sandals of coarse rope for sure footing on wet decks. I direct everyone to put away their dresses and change into these garments, and we arrange part of the hold for places to sleep. Sher-Ri has found a short girdle while others wrap linens around their waists so that the tunics fit more closely. I will wear my tribal dress and bodice, another short tunic will cover my shoulders. When all are changed we find places to sit, for I must address their questions. They have been so trusting, and accepted our leaving without hesitation, that I am amazed that they show no fear or consternation. Yet their faces are not happy, just blank.

"Good sisters," I begin. "We are voyaging with Father's orders, to lands in the west. I am to be an envoy of Kemet to cities along the Great Green Sea, to people who have never been allies of Kemet. Prince Gamal the Milesian will be trading with these people, and giving us safe conduct on our travels. But we are not to be seen as people from Kemet, but people from Miletus or other lands. For we do not know how the people of Karthage will receive us, even as traders from Miletus. When the sailors present the flasks of precious purple dye, and silks from the east, they will accept us as merchant traders. Beyond that, we travel in secrecy."

"For now, make yourself useful with ship tasks. The quartermaster will find duties and things we can do to help. Do not fear for your safety, for Gamal has promised to treat us well." Their fears abate somewhat, they nod with relief. Then I speak with a sterner voice:

"However, there are rules you must abide without question: No lamps lit below deck. No boxes left unstrapped. Cargo is stowed for balance, and you must not leave things lying about. If the seas become stormy, you must stay below, at least until your stomachs are used to the swells. If you feel sick, help each other, keep some bread to eat at hand, as this will quiet your belly. Try to imagine being rocked in a baby cradle, and the queasiness will pass. Those of you who are musicians should see to some music for each evening when we are at harbors, or when the sea is gentle. I would like you to feel peace here. It is our new home."

For days we sailed west, sometimes in sight of land, but keeping in deep waters. The cargo ship sails without oarsmen, to and fro with the wind, so it is much slower than the two warships. And Gamal's ship, being sleeker, is more maneuverable with its stern oars. But, we sail together, and speed is not our goal, but safety. Sometimes we saw shore lights of small settlements, but we sailed onward until many lights were seen which would be of a great city.

The lusty sailors were at home on the seas, casting nets from time to time, and hauling in all sorts of seafood. Some large fish with huge fins like sails were caught, and prized for their colorful skins which could be worked like leather. There were long eels, caught with caution to avoid their skins, which if touched caused painful itching. These were good to eat once skinned. And there were all manner of small fishes which the sailors hung to dry along the ship's rails.

While our sail was slackened and the nets were filled, we waited for the cargo ship to catch up. Many of the company took a swim in the warm water. They checked the hull for hull worms, and drag caused by the small shelled animals that attach to ships. Once the sailors dragged a rope along the hull to scrape off green growth and sharp shellfish, in order to clean the hull at sea. I marveled at their ability in the water as they floated and dove, playing like children in the bath. Gamal said he would teach me this skill in the water, but later, where he can be assured of my safety from the fierce fish we often see following our boats. Perhaps it is best now to just bathe with buckets of seawater, and rub the salt off our burnished skin.

As we did not need to stop for provisions, we passed what seemed to be small settlements and many coastal villages. None of them had harbors acceptable for mooring until at last we came to Tokai, a major city with a huge harbor. Now we were in Karthaginian waters, and we waited for small boats to come out to greet us.

"As we come nearer in," Gamal explained, "sailors will come out to us and arrange meetings for trade. We have hand signs, sort of a trade language, to let them know we are peaceful traders."

"Have Milesians been here before?" I asked.

"Yes, this is an established trade route. They will see our banners and know who we are. Our wares have much value to these people. They will be happy to receive us."

"How is it that they would not attack us to have our goods?"

"My Lady, there are rules of commerce! Ships are never molested in safe harbor. They need our goods and we can trade for food and water. Any city breaking such rules would endanger itself, for they would never be visited again. We will give them samples of linen, dyed with the purple dye from Miletus, and values will be established. See now, they bring amphorae of water and baskets of fresh fruit to show their good intentions."

"Then will we go on shore? I am curious to see these people and their town."

"No, not at these smaller settlements. We are safe here in the harbor, and will barter with their emissaries. They will go to the supply ship where I will meet with them, while our war ships stand watch. There is some distrust, but this is how things are done."

"Will they trade with gold coins? I have no idea of the value of the trade cargo. I could add to your trade goods with silk, and I do have coins from Kemet."

Gamal smiled. "These are Karthaginians. They control lands as far to the west that have ever been known, and far to the north as well. They do pay with gold coins. There are taxes and tariffs, and established trade duty on all items to be levied. I will meet with their officials and identify myself as a prince of Miletus. My skills with languages will help, and I hope to gain new maps and information about cities to the west. Our sails and flags are not unknown to these people, and our goods are highly sought after. You may bring some lengths of silk if you wish."

"Thank you, Gamal, for I wish to contribute to our voyage."

Then stone anchors were lowered and our ship is along-side the pendulous belly of our supply ship. The calm harbor and anchor stones provide a sense of land. I can breathe more easily now, as no one from Kemet has followed us. How long I wonder, before our people realize their royal family has deserted them? I quickly unlock my trunk and select two lengths of white silk, enough for several lovely dresses. I am very quick, for he is about to leave for the other ship.

"Perhaps these two lengths can help with the trade?"

Gamal nods, then tucks the folds of silk under one arm. He smiles at me as he swings on a rope with his other arm to the waiting deck. "Thank you," he calls, as his men receive him with open arms. In the distance I see the Carthaginian boats are arriving, laden with trade goods, food, and water vessels. But I do not show my face, my red hair is covered. Best to watch and learn.

At Tokai, Gamal learned of even larger cities to the west, another few days' sail. The people in this part of the world are all sailors, and are used to finding landings even within one day's sail. But we will continue to the large city of Karthage, which lies on a peninsula farther west. Gamal is pleased with the trade terms he has established, for his purple dye is highly prized. But we do not stay long at Tokai, for once our business is completed we make sail with fresh water, fruits, and bread studded with nuts.

Our sailors are easily distracted by having women on board, for this is unusual. There is much work to do, repairing nets, ropes, and attending to cargo, weapons and fishing. But my palace maidens stay below decks only at night. During the day they have found tasks, such as preparing food, which has delighted the men. Tonight as we leave the safe harbor of Tokai. We will have some music and song, and Sher-Ri will dance in the moonlight. Oil lamps swing gaily from the ropes, as the men form a circle. We have my harp, and a few flutes for music, and I find certain ship boards have timbre of drums. There is wine and beer, and everyone is alive and well in our home on the sea. Tomorrow we sail for Karthage, the city that controls these shores.

"The waters have befriended us so far," says Gamal. "Is there a prayer you have for a safe sea voyage?"

"No, my Lord, I have left all behind in Kemet. The great Goddess Neith perhaps directs my feet, but I no longer pray."

"The seas are not usually so calm, and warm. I think your harp strings have soothed the waves and winds. Does your harp carry a name?"

Gamal stands at my right side, with his left hand on the arch of the harp. He watches my fingers glide over the strings.

"Her name is Sirena, a nymph of the sea. She has had that name since before she was given to me, by those of Karkissa. Perhaps she is more at home now than ever before. But look, Gamal, some of the strings are becoming frayed. I will be gentle with them, for soon they may break. Can such strings be found where we go? I have coins to pay for them."

"I do not know if western lands have instruments such as your Sirena," Gamal replies, "but there is sinew on board for other purposes which may suffice. I will add harp strings to our list of needed supplies. Is there anything else I have missed? Are your ladies in comfort?"

"Perhaps a drum of some sort. But no, we are comfortable and have found our sea legs. My friend Kenti-Sur asked if we ladies are truly safe, for it seems you have directed your sailors to remain apart from us? It is not what some expected."

"I did not need to tell my men such a thing," replied Gamal. "My men have a code of honor and respect for women. They will not dishonor themselves. None have wives at home but have chosen this life on the sea. They will have leave to go on shore when we reach Carthage. And they are free if they choose to find their way back to Miletus, for I have told them I do not intend ever to return. If your Father is wrong, and Kemet is victorious, we will have news of it. For now you are safe, Scota, and your women are safe as well."

I start a new song on Sirena. The rhythm matches the lapping of the waves on our hull. The sound carries far, and perhaps people on the shore might wonder at the sound. Soon the sun dips below the horizon, and we watch the dancers in the twilight. If only this peaceful existence would last forever. My maidens have all adapted to the rocking of the waves as no one has been noticeably sick thus far. Who should we pray to out here on the sea? Gamal does not tell me his gods, though I have seen different amulets worn by some of the men. A few have body art that looks like some protective spell. I have much to learn.

As I wrap Sirena for her return to below deck, we douse our lights, and soon sleep will come. Gamal carries Sirena and takes me below, but only stays long enough to see that we are comfortable. Nor does he talk to my women, as if that is my responsibility only. "Sleep well, rock in our cradle," he says. As he turns, our eyes meet, and he smiles. The quiet lapping of waves brings peaceful dreams to all.

ഇ ഇ ഇ

Red clouds in the east bring the dawn, and we can see squalls off in the distance. The waves that were once so tranquil and soft have turned sharp, and we are jolted from our sleep. The great stone anchors are raised, and our boats begin to dip with stronger and stronger waves. Everyone rises quickly, but none stay below deck for long. Outside the winds are rising and sailors are working their oars to keep abreast of the storms to the east. Our ship takes the lead and points due west while the other boats follow closely behind. Thick ropes from the two warships are pulling the cargo ship, which has now raised its sail so it can be towed along and make the best speed. The men pull hard and fast to their fastest rhythm, one that they cannot do for long. Other men jump in alongside the oar, and taking turns, they jump like frogs, never missing the tempo. Soon we reach calmer waters, but the men are exhausted. The storm turns south, the sun rises into its third hour, and the men are laughing and relaxing as if it was just athletic fun. How strange these men are, that life to them is one big contest of wills!

We have outrun the squall at our back, everyone rests easy with food and drink. The sails are full with the promise of a light breeze, and our ships surge westward. Gamal comes to my side, pride for his men shines on his smiling face.

"I hold to your father's wishes, my Lady, to take you away to the west. But how far and to what lands I was not told, only to flee in haste! My people of Miletus know these coasts of Kart-hadasht, but it is not a country of safety for you." Gamal keeps his voice low, so others might not hear, and gives me some descriptions to calm my unease.

"Our trading at Tokai will reach other ears, and they will be expecting us in Kart-hadasht a few days from here. But it is not well for us to land there. The harbor is divided into the mercantile area and the warship area. I expect them to send out small boats to sample our wares, and then we may dock safely. But you and your women must not embark, and should stay completely hidden." Gamal has the serious look of caution, his tone is even and grounded, even though his words are full of anxiety.

"What are your fears? Are the people not civilized like those you dealt with at Tokai?"

Choosing his words carefully, Gamal says, "It is said they worship a god that demands human sacrifice, especially newborn babies. They are a great power because of this blood of babies and virgins. They have the power to capture us as a fly in honey, and their warships will wait at the inner harbor's mouth to measure our intentions." Gamal's lips are tense and straight, his teeth clenched.

"I will defend your freedom with my life, and the lives of my men, but I cannot give you free movement of the docks. The safe harbor laws might be easily broken by their thirst for virgin blood."

"Oh, Gamal, it is a small thing you ask of me and my maidens. We will remain out of sight, and will be as quiet as the temples at midnight. We will enjoy our time below deck with nothing to do but relax."

I am thinking that staying below deck, resting, and doing girlish things is really just another gift. Every girl would love the time to relax, attend to tangled hair or break into the many unguents to repair our skin. Just thinking of perfume causes my nose to twitch. "How long do you intend to trade in Carthage?"

"It is but a day or so at Carthage. If you understand the need for secrecy I will not feel I have mistreated you, my Lady. The maps I consulted at Tokai show other islands to the north of Kart-hadasht where we can go for sulphur, lead and copper, and then to Kurnos for wax and honey. Maybe then due north to Massalia. The people there are very likely to value our trade goods as fewer ships make their shores. But we were told, in no uncertain terms, that sailing further west will not be allowed. The Karthaginians control lands farther west that supply ivory and they would not have this special trade route entered. We will soon be depleted of our purple dye, but your father gave me special medicines and elixirs that those people will value most highly."

"So, as you tell me, we will not travel back to the east, or to Miletus or Rhodes, or other ports to the east. Nor can we go much farther along this southern shore. Is there another plan to consider?" I pause, and look out at the boundless sea. "Surely your men would make a life at sea forever if that is your will. . .There are not enough women on board for every man to have his own family," I say in jest, "and we cannot all be your harem."

Gamal gives a short laugh, enjoying the idea.

"No, nor can we take on more women. Though my men would like to have some time on shore to visit whatever Kart-hadasht has to offer. Perhaps our destiny lies on some uncharted island. There are smaller islands west of Sardu, where the people raise cattle. Do you want to raise cattle and make cheese?"

Gamal gives me a little poke in the ribs, so that I know we are joking about serious thoughts. Before, in Kemet, all I wanted was freedom. But not freedom to live in obscurity raising root vegetables or weaving flower garlands.

"My destiny is hidden from me, Gamal, and I am woven into a web too large to see. Goddess Neith has woven our fortunes together, let her direct our ships. I will pray for answers."

Gamal seems to leave anxiety behind, and smiles at me.

"We will wait for direction, there is no hurry for this voyage."

Two days pass, and at evening's last light we viewed a great many shore lights of the huge city of Karthage. Towers sparkled like gold in the last rays of the sun, and even at this distance we could see an immense double harbor ahead. This would be our last and only sight of land for us women, so I had all of them come to the railing to smell fresh air and see the extent of the lights. I spoke to them about Gamal's precautions.

"See ahead, my ladies? That is the city of Karthage. Here they worship a god called Baal, who devours children and bathes in their blood. The beauty of the city is a lie, and we are in serious danger if we so much as show our faces. Our time here must be spent in complete silence below deck, and we must remain hidden for the sake of all. Our sailors will trade with the merchants, and if visitors come on board, Gamal will dissuade them from coming below. Even if visitors are not aboard this ship, we must be quiet as mice in the grain bin. Give me your solemn oath that you will stay quiet and hidden these next few days."

All press hands to their hearts, and we all go below. We rearrange the sleeping area into a space for confinement. We stack boxes to make an enclosure that doesn't look odd, nor too tall, but gives enough space for sitting at least. Food, mostly bread and dried fruit was given easy access, along with water and toilet needs. It will be dark, even during the day, because no lamps can be lit below deck. Gamal gives a signal of repetitive knocks which he will use to warn us when he intends to check on us, but there will be no evidence of our presence. I think of this as a visit to the Osirion, and instruct the women in the mystery of Osiris and Anubis. We will all have close thoughts and vision of the dark night of our souls. But this is a blessing in disguise I think, to have some days of deep spiritual thought, of where we are going and who we are to become.

" We can talk until we feel the ship come to a stop, my ladies. After that, silence."

My smallest dancer, Benni-sha, seems more anxious than others. I calm her with what I know. "Prince Gamal will negotiate some trading, mostly for fresh fruit and provisions, but he does not intend to stay long at this port. He tells me that we will then sail north to Sardu, then to Kurnos, whose people will welcome our ships. So it will just be a short few days of restraint. Can you keep words inside?"

"Yes, my Lady," whispered Benni-sha. "It is my feet that want to move. I will not make any noise, I promise."

Keeping my voice low I say, "Maidens, consider the mysteries of death and the rebirth of good souls. We are going to the underworld today. You must keep still. Your heart will be measured for truth and goodness, and we are worthy, I believe, to come to some bright land ahead. Search your past behaviors, recite your prayers silently, and we shall receive guidance. Goddess Neith has plans for us, though her veil keeps all hidden. All will be revealed. This is not the end of our lives."

Presently we heard the thump of a boat coming alongside our ship. We could hear the strong, firm voice of Gamal, hailing the boatmen in various languages. Snatches of words drifted down to us as trade terms were established. By the sounds, some visitors did board our ship, and I imagine samples of silk and linen were passed to the harbormaster. Heavy thuds were heard of water amphorae or bags of fruit being loaded. *Why did I not offer coins to Gamal to help with the trade? The coins of Kemet might have been suspicious, though I do have some nondescript talents from Nubia. My thoughts were racing.*

Below in the dark I come to realize my responsibility on this voyage. I think my behavior has not been acceptable. Gamal has been loyal to Father's orders, and so far I have acted like a child. The playful flirting I've done with Gamal is easily ignored by his needs to attend to sailing, to maps, to necessary things to protect all of us. If we escape Karthage, I will make my wishes known, out loud. For I do *not* want to abandon my heritage and raise cattle on some nondescript island, like some lonesome hag into old age. I am a warrior princess! I have courage, and strength, and greatness to show the world. I want my soul blossom into its fullness, and reappear with tomorrow's sun!

Occasional bumps and noises are heard above deck, and once or twice the upper hatch was opened for sailors to bring down new amphorae of water and wine. With the sunlight behind their shapes, we could see foreign dress and hairstyles, and heard their language. I could hear Gamal and his helmsman barking orders, making those men withdraw in haste. My ladies were true to their oaths, and made not a sound, though the visitors might have taken special notice of our perfumed bodies and the smells within our hold. Soon enough though, all was laden aboard, and the the ship's anchors pulled. We felt the ship tip and turn, and slowly pick up speed, taking us safely out of the harbor.

Our hearts were light as seagulls, as a collective sigh of relief coursed through our hiding place. Gamal gave his signal for safety and one by one we came into the light, and saw Karthage far behind us. Gamal was at the stern of our beautiful ship, consulting maps and taking sun sights to steer us onward. Behind followed the cargo ship, now drafting even lower into the waves, while the two warships took up the rear. Beyond the harbor of Karthage, no ships followed us, and we were away free. We had made another successful docking, and Gamal was pleased with the trade. He was laughing and full of merriment at his helm, as if he had played a fine joke on a frightening place.

I blinked my eyes in the bright sunshine, for two days of darkness had weakened them to the sun's light. Soon Gamal was at my side, and he walked me to the prow where his golden star banner blazed on its blue background. We were headed north with the wind at our backs.

"Something happened to me," I began, and before I could get words out, Gamal threw his arms around me.

"What? I thought you were protected?" Questioning with his eyes and holding me close he struggled to understand. "Are you hurt? Frightened?" His embrace was even tighter.

I offered no resistance to this wonderful exuberance of care, but just said, "No, my Lord, I am much better than hurt or frightened. I am free!" Gamal released his arms, and took a long questioning look at my face, smiled, and patiently waited to hear my explanation.

"Below in the dark and stillness, we waited for our signal to rise up. For the first time I felt a communion, a unity of spirit. . .something I never experienced before, even in the sanctitude of the temple. It is a special kind of knowing, such that I am here in the fullness of being. I do not wish to be just your stowaway. I am a princess of Kemet, Scota Nefara-Selkis, and I am ready to have full part of this voyage, wherever it will take us."

"Think on this," I continued, "what would the islanders think of a flag from Kemet on your prow? Perhaps they would not recognize my banner, but putting them together in tandem would bring curiosity. I would like to join my assets of gold, linens, and silks with your stores and trade items. You have told me we will never again steer east. . . then let us steer west! Could we not barter our way through the passage to western or northern shores? In the darkness below, Great Goddess Neith spoke to me in dreams of green lands, where I will be Queen. And you are to be my King!"

Gamal took a sharp breath, as if my words had halted his breathing. His face was shining in the morning sunlight, and his eyes were as deep blue as the sea. He looked at me, sounding my depths like an anchor stone finding its rest. He looked away for a bit, then looked completely into my eyes, as if seeing me for the first time. Then he pulled me gently down to the deck and held my hand as if it were a flower. He embraced me tenderly, cradling this newly awakened soul of mine. We were curled together behind the prow, talking against the waves we plowed. There was a stillness there, no seabirds called, and we rocked together as one. Finally, he spoke.

"When your father appeared to me, it was like he was giving me your hand. He gave orders like a Pharaoh, and I was keen to obey him, for there was love behind his words. And he gave me hundreds of coins for your safe passage, not actually for payment, but for his love of a daughter, like a dowry. I would not have refused any of his orders, but this was much more like the wishes of his heart. Out of love for you, he gave you to me. His orders to me were the fulfillment of my heart's wish, for I have loved you since the first night I saw you.. There was something magical that evening with you and the harp. The palace felt suddenly still around us. I think you did not notice, but my heart leapt in your presence."

"My precious sweet Scota, I have done my utmost to wait for this moment, when you would come to me with your future. I hope I have proven myself worthy of your trust, and your honor, and that of your ladies. But I am not content to just sail the seas forever. We are bound together, you and I, whether by gods or circumstances, and I too am filled with your vision."

Gamal turned my face to him and with hands cupped below my chin, kissed me full on my waiting lips. The prow dipped in the waves, and love found its depths.

I'm fully sure there was a relieved sigh from stern to prow that filled the ship with absolute joy, or perhaps it was a thunderclap from the cloudless sky? Gamal and I sat together, talking of choices that might be open to us. When I was a child I played a game of cards. Scraps of papyrus glyphs, shuffled together, then laid in order to see what the future held. No matter how often I played this game, the same cards always appeared in sequence. "Far and away, green land of peace." I had always thought it might be somewhere south on the Great Green River, where I would become the priestess of a quiet temple. Somewhere green, but far away from the palace intrigue, and safely far from my fearful father. If I had my cards now, they would hold a different interpretation of "far and away," but *green*? Thus far we have only seen rocky shores, harbors buttressed against deserts, and blue water.

"Oh Gamal, I have much treasure below, in both coin and gold, as well as jewels for trading. I would like to offer my treasures for trading and provisions, and let us sail north to those islands, together. Would the harbor at Sardu or Kurnos be staffed with many warships, or could we expect peaceful trade? If we came only as traders and travelers, would they be suspicious of flags from Kemet?"

"We cannot know this beforehand, my dear Lady. But if the winds hold this direction, we shall make Sardu tomorrow, and I will question their alliances with Kart-hadasht. After that, perhaps we can fly your flag to Kurnos and Massalia. It may even be possible to offer enough gold for permission through the strait to the west, if they know our intentions are never to return. For now we must sail north, for I have no knowledge of the distance to the western strait. We will find lands to settle in peace, whether north or west. Do you hold to this plan?"

"Yes, wherever you will take me, I am yours, Gamal"

"Then, will you marry with me?"

Putting my right hand over Gamal's heart I said, "Yes, this is my wish. Let us find a quiet cove and be married under blue skies." Then I kissed him with all my heart.

We lay in an embrace there on the front deck in a timeless trance. Sher-Ri came upon us and said, "Are you going to couple in broad daylight? Are you going to tell us the good news?"

And when I turned my beaming face to her, she let out a tribal ululation that roused the whole ship. Perhaps the Great Goddess Neith could hear it, too! All the sailors and maidens were clapping their hands and Sher-Ri began to dance and spin. Soon there was music, drumming and dancing all over the deck, and the sounds reached the other vessels with our news. The sea birds were circling the masts and dolphins jumped alongside our prow.

"We were waiting, my lady, for news of your decision. All are jubilant, and will serve you even more heartedly now that we have a wedding to celebrate!" Sher-Ri's dance rose to its highest pitch, twirling with our joy. Gamal and I rose to our feet, and with the sun in my eyes, tears shown on both our faces.

"Yes, we are pledged. Surely the gods will welcome us to the next port. Back to your work, men, for we have good weather and good waves to take us to Sardu. I would like to make land by morning," called Gamal. And with that, all hands went back to their posts, while the maidens gathered me in their arms, and took me below to hear more.

"Gamal plans to find a safe haven, perhaps in a few days, but surely not by tomorrow. He tells me of other islands where we might find peace, lands where people would accept us as leaders. It is not our wish to roam the seas forever." I look at them all intently. "You have all made me proud with your faith in me, and that you have not demanded more assurances of future things. For this I thank you all." Sher-Ri and her mother just stood there, smiling.

"Now, what shall we give to the people of Sardu as welcome?"

The women look to arranging the boxes for some time, and then begin to prepare an evening meal. This meal will be a celebration they say, and I am not to know what is being prepared. As if I don't know what stores we have on board! But I leave them to their scurrying around and find Gamal back by the stern.

"Gamal, is this a dream? How can such good fortune keep with us still?"

He smiles and says, "It might not be always so. But we will have these memories to sustain us if fortune fails."

We stand together, while he guides the ship along. Soon we will drop anchor for the night, and the other ships will cluster nearby. Braziers have been lit, and a veritable feast is laid out. There is sweet wine and honey cakes, some sort of root vegetables from the brazier, and other delicacies from Karthage I have no name for. All will be content tonight, and the stars give their blessing for smooth nighttime sailing.

Around mid-morning we saw the coastline of Sardu, and made to the west side of the island. Seagulls greeted us with loud calls and dances in the air. There was a cove, and a breakwater constructed for sailing directly into the harbor. Sailors took soundings, found the harbor deep enough for our ships to safely drop anchors. Gamal and a small party of men set out toward the shore where they saw beautiful white sand beaches. This was the city of Thurros, and we on board could see round towers and many buildings. Soon enough Gamal happily returned with news.

"This harbor city of Thurros belongs to the Sea Peoples called Shardana. They trade with Kart-hadasht, but are independent, and prosperous. We went ashore to find that trade will be easy enough. You might laugh, Scota," he says, "but the people here value the color yellow above all others." Gamal is smiling as he holds up my yellow flag. "We will fly these colors here, and on to Kuros as well."

"Oh, Gamal! I have a box of yellow silks below, and also some yellow gemstones. . . a bag of them, I think. Let this be my first contribution. And I have gold, too, and I think a box of yellow feathers for arrow fletches." Gamal nods and is pleased.

"We shall both go ashore. I think you will like to see the beautiful white sand beach."

TWELVE

I dressed in my tribal girdle, with yellow linen beneath, and slung my unstrung bow and quiver over my shoulder. With no jewelry other than my gold torque, I coiled my reddish hair braids into rounds over each ear. Gamal lifted me into the small boat, and helped Sher-Ri and Kenti-Sur to sit beside us. Four sailors rowed us to the shore where we were met by city leaders, though presumably none was a king. Gamal spoke in a dialect they could understand.

"We come with trade goods and peaceful intentions. Please guide us to your merchants." We were led to the merchant stalls where there were many flags, many emblems that told of wares for sale. A commotion was raised in the marketplace when the merchants began to covet the wares we had brought to sell. Everywhere were people dressed in bright yellow. The men had breeches of yellow with embroidered short coats, and the women wore heavily embroidered yellow dresses that reached to the floor, as well as covered their wrists. Colorful skullcaps sported yellow embroideries and there were yellow ribbons and pennants flying everywhere. It was as if the sunlight had touched every inch of the land, and apart from the bright white sand, everything was dressed in yellow. Gamal opened a package of yellow silk which almost caused a riot, and people were grasping at the golden yellow fletching on my arrows. They were truly giddy over finding their favorite color on so many things to buy.

Gamal was laughing, "Let's set all this out, and have the merchants take turns before we cause hard feelings." And the main organizer of the market area clapped his hands for attention, and made it so. Gamal took charge of trading for sulphur. It was yellow, something I had never seen before, nor smelled. The odor of rotten eggs wafted through the boxes, but it would soon dissipate once well wrapped. I offered a small bag of yellow gemstones, some opaque that looked like the eyes of a snake, but others were translucent yellow like golden glass. The largest of these brought enough food provisions for many days' journey. Satisfaction was everywhere on both sides of the trades.

After several hours of wild trading, the chief magistrate led us to a great stone tower. Gamal spoke to him, pointed at me, and explained about our voyage, I think. Here there were many tables and cushions laid out on the open flagstone floor. Musicians grouped on one side played a fanfare, with tall curved horns. Dark skinned drummers played a march, as Gamal took my left hand and led me to the front of the crowd. As I looked around, I saw our sailors and warriors in the crowd, as well as Nabanna's dark skin. Everyone was here as the magistrate raised his arms for quiet. He spoke what sounded like solemn words, which Gamal repeated in translation to me:

"Here on this bright day, in the presence of friends and strangers, I ask you to be my wife. My partner in life, the mother of my children, until my soul departs. What say you?"

"I am Scota Nefaru-Selkis, Princess of Kemet. I am truly honored to receive such love. I give myself freely to you, and as your only wife, promise to love and support you in all things, for as long as we both may live. My vows to you are unbreakable and eternal."

Then we embraced, and sealed our union with a kiss. The crowd cheered, tall trumpets played a fanfare as other musicians joined in. Dancers invited us to a spectacle of dance, finger cymbals, and tribal ululations filled our ears as never before. Tables were laden with a great feast, piled high with wonderful fruits and basins of wine. Roasted meat and marinated fish was followed by toasted grains and nuts, and there were olives of every kind and color. Pomegranate juice flowed over a magnificent almond flavored cake topped with honeyed berries. Everywhere were jubilant faces wishing us good fortune and many sons.

As the sun was now dipping in the west, great oil lamps were lit on a wooden structure patterned with a huge star, and this was lowered from the top of the tower to light the scene below. We feasted and danced, and embraced in the moonlight of the full moon. Then Gamal and I were led to a bedchamber inside the tower. We felt fully safe with these wonderful people. Outside the revelers drifted homeward, while Kenti-Sur and Sher-Ri and our sailors were given safe lodging as well. Our bed was soft, but not as soft and tender as Gamal's body against mine.

We explored each other's bodies and knew them deeply and fully that night. We slept as a child's peace, wrapped in safe arms and heart-filled love such that neither of us wanted to rise from our wedding bed. But, realizing our duties to our sailors and shipmates, we rose, and were taken to baths of rose-scented warm water. Servants came and offered scented oils, which we massaged on each other, and we were given sweet breads and fruit to share. Soon we were joined by our friends, and led back down to the white sand beach. Some women gathered around me and gave me necklaces made of seashells and glistening pearls, a parting gift. As our sailors rowed us away, I vowed to return to this island again, many times, if destiny would permit.

Gamal said, "Our cargo ship is laden to the fullest, and though we parted with some boxes, it is clear that our trades were most beneficial to us, for the people valued your yellow goods most highly." Smiling, he told all, "Scota's gifts have brought us enough provisions to sail on for many weeks. My wife is a great partner!" He bowed formally to me, and raised my hand to show all the beautiful ring now on my finger. "This sapphire ring signifies not only our marriage, but a lasting alliance with the Shardana people, so pleased are they with our gifts. Long live our good fortune!"

Kissing me again, Gamal waved as the sailors cheered and steered us out of the harbor of Thurros. "I hope we will return here again, someday," I breathed.   "That's a promise, my Lady."

We sailed north now, to Kurros, happy with the knowledge that the harbor there at Aptoucha would be friendly as well. With the wind at our back, the sails were filled like wings to carry us north, to a port on the far side of Kurros. The people there are famous for their honey, and great stores of wax for candles and preservatives. Gamal will use the wax to reseal the boxes of sulphur, and any wooden staves that might have opened. He says we will spend only one night at the harbor there. However, if we want to sail northward it must be soon before the moon wanes and the tides shift. Before the north wind comes, we must be safely harbored, perhaps at Massalia.

There is much planning to do, for I would like to sail farther west along that northern shore, perhaps to lands where we might dwell. Surely there are people there who are free from the warring Persians, the bickering Ionians, and the demands of Kemet. Are there voices on the wind? I even think a bit about Father, and find a peaceful resolution around his image that I never thought would be possible. From now on, I will only think of Gamal and our future together.

Our ships plow the waves, and white furrows form as if we are planting our future with the surges of the sea. Surely there are bright green lands ahead where Maat will prosper with the blessings of the Great Goddess Neith.

" I hold my faience scarab high, to honor you, Great Goddess." Raising my arms, I offer my love and future to the sky as the scarab falls into the waves. "For all that I am and will be, grant us great love. Life, Strength, and Prosperity."

THIRTEEN

Scotland, 1795 — Dunsinnan, the site of MacBeth's Castle

"Och, aye! Terrible gandiegow for us to be out, lightnin' crashin' and all," said Keith as the lads looked for shelter. *"We stayed o'er lang at Lindsay's, I'm fair jeelit!"* The marshy field had turned to a quagmire in the warmer than usual weather. Every step squished and mud sloshed well above their woolen hose. They trudged on in this muck, sleet pelting their faces, when a shaft of lightning lit what looked like rocky cleft in the cliff face.

"Must 'a been a rockslide here, or happin' an earthquake," Neill yelled. *"But we can squeeze in here and bide a wee. Strike a flame and let's see the depth."*

Keith procured his flint and lit a bit of soft wad he kept in his pouch. Putting it to a stick, he lit it, and fashioned a small torch. They crept inside the cave to get out of the cold driving rain.

In the dim light, they saw a broken wall that had been part of a subterranean chamber. It seemed stable enough now, though they could see a stairway strewn with rubble from some long ago upheaval. At the bottom of these rock-hewn steps, many old broken items littered the scene, piled in heaps, as if hurriedly stashed long ago.

"Look o'er here! 'Tis a pile of dishes, an' boxes, an' even some metal cups!"

"Aye, but look what supports 'em!" said Neill, as he pointed at a large rectangular stone block, supported by four stone posts.

"Wha's the meaning o' it? Looks to be a buildin' stane, but look o'er the carvin' on it!"

"*Never saw the likes o' that writin'.*"said Neill. "*Looks like figures sittin' and talkin' wi' their arms. And ither carvin's be birds, walkin' aroond.*"

The stone had two large rings on either end for carrying purposes, yet it looked too heavy even for two men to carry.

"*Must hae been here a verra' lang spate,*" said Keith, "*for there's a lot o' broken stuff all aroond, too.*"

"*I dinna ken what it is, nither,*" said Neill, shaking his head. "*But sure a'pears to be hid here on purpose. Maybe some monks from the abbey that used to be on these lands used this room as a hidey hole.*"

"*Best leave it be,*" Keith replied, "*an not tell oor da's. Keep it secrit now that the rain's left off. Shake on it?*" With that, and the rain now coming straight down, the boys slogged home on the mire, thinking they'd return when weather permitted, perhaps bring a cart to take some of the things to the local parish.

Some time passed before they were able to take time off from their chores, so that when they returned to the area, they couldn't find the right place. Search they did, the whole day, but couldn't find the cleft in the rocks, nor any trace of the cave that had sheltered them.

"*Perhaps the rocks hae shifted again?*"

"*Not likely. I think we dreamt it,*" Neill mused. "*There's no bit of cave nor space in any o' these braes. We've lost our treasure!*"

"*Well, 'tis best, I think*" said Keith. "*These lands o' Scone are owned by the Earl o' Mansfield, and whatever micht be here b'longs tae his Lairdship.*"

"*True. But at school Thursday last our teacher told us a tale, of how King Edward I thought he'd found King Arthur's grave. Took the bones to London, he did. Thought he was some grand archaeologist,*" Neill said with a snicker.

"King Arthur? Like the knights o' the Round Table?" asked Keith.

" Aye, and he also said the monks of Scone were thinkin' he intended tae steal the "Stone of Scone"so they hid it from that bastard. The monks got a stane from Annety Burn that looked like it, and kept that in the church just in case. Some say it was the privy cover stane. Jus' as they expected, Edward stole that stane, thinking it was the Stone of Destiny!"

"An put it under the throne in Westminster!" said Keith with a laugh. *"Well, the joke's on them, their monarchs are no really graced!""Aye, but the monks were too afraid to retrieve the real stane from hiding, and by the time Edward Longshanks was deid, so were the monks that hid the treasure. The stane that is in Westminster Abbey is just like the rocks from aroond here."* Neill waved his arms at the nearby sandstone rocks and said, *"No way to prove they took the fake one!"*

"Well, we know better. I'm goin' lookin' aroond here, ever chance I get," replied Keith. *"An' I'm goin' to tell our story when I'm an old man if we don't find it oot!"*

FOURTEEN

Spain 1996

Like most southern cities in Spain, Alicante proudly shows its Moorish influence with patterned mosaics and geometric lattice work. Everywhere it was a bustling city, loud and awash with traffic, the typical opening of everyday mornings. It seemed easy to blend in with the locals; no one took notice of the trio, which was good. But there were plenty of jewelry shops that displayed fine Spanish filigree, and even "gold buyers" for many of the locals to sell broken pieces for cash. Masoud stopped in a few shops while Kemi and Donald went into a dress shop. In no time she had picked out a dress in white Spanish lace that fit her body perfectly. When they caught up with Masoud again, he seemed happy for the first time on the trip. Donald spent some time looking at mantillas, thinking about how Kemi would look with lace draped over her shoulders, and an organist playing the wedding march. While Donald was busy at the register, Kemi went over to talk to Masoud.

"Were you able to find discreet buyers?"

"Yes, I've unloaded all that broken stuff. The jewelers didn't ask questions, and I think they were happy to buy scrap. I even found an antiquarian shop that wanted some of the scrap papyrus, told him it had been in the family.

Kemi laughed quietly, "I guess that's believable with the amount of suntan we've been getting. I'm glad we don't have to carry that stuff around much longer."

"Did you sell the torques too?" asked Kemi. But she knew the answer before the words came out of her mouth. And her heart sank a bit inside her chest. Though the torques weren't particularly remarkable, they were obviously Celtic relics, something that should not have been chopped up and sold. Donald would have felt violated, but to Kemi and Masoud, it was just good business.

This city, in ancient times called Aka Leuke, was totally overgrown with buildings and paved streets. As they walked along the trio realized there would be no trace of the ancients here, except for what might lie below some building's foundation. The anonymity of the hotel provided some rest, and space for thought, but Alicante was not where Donald wanted to be.

"We should not stay here," said Donald. "Everything is too modern, paved over. I think we should just go to Eiche. The map shows that it's not far. It's older and smaller, more off the beaten track. I could do some digging there and possibly trace some trading routes."

"Masoud and I trust your instincts," Kemi said in a breathy voice, "don't we, brother dear?" as she nudged her brother's shoulder. Masoud looked quizzical, but Kemi gave a sly smile to cue him in. After a quick breakfast of coquettes they were back on the road, leaving no trace of them behind.

An hour later they were at the top of a rise where mountainous vistas reached down to the sea. Before them was the city of Eiche, with its Altamira Castle and Calahorra tower. Wide plazas festooned with date palms welcomed visitors to museums and the enormous footwear factories, for which the city is well known. Finding a welcoming restaurant was easy, and soon they had before them a feast of local fare. Masoud ordered paella, a huge dish of rabbit and seafood which was the first course. The waiter recommended their local delicacy, "pulpo a la galenga" which proved to be a Galician form of octopus. Another dish called pisto, was a mixture of broiled vegetables like a ratatouille.

"I almost forgot how good food is in Spain," beamed Kemi.

"It's time for a siesta," said Donald. "Let's get another hotel room away from noisy traffic where I can attack those hieroglyphs."

"You got it!" said Masoud, and after getting some suggestions from the waiter, they were off again, down a crooked little street festooned with olive trees. A quaint, white-washed hotel seemed a good choice, and after securing their camping gear they began to explore the ancient city. Masoud went off on an errand, looking for a bar no doubt, and information about those who deal in odd relics of some value or other. Donald and Kemi went to the city's museum of course, and Donald was gleefully viewing the exhibit of the city's history. Within moments they were treated to a hallway depicting the city's culture, dating from the ancient Ionians of

600BCE, through Carthaginian and Roman occupations, to the Moors in the 13th century, and finally to the Spanish Civil War. Evidently at one time there were salt mines, and the city was an important trading place for dates, pomegranates, and olives.

"What does "Eiche" mean?" asked Kemi.

"In English it would mean "oak" but that doesn't make much sense, as oak trees can't grow here," answered Donnie. "I think this place has much to reveal to us, maybe there is a Celtic influence everyone has forgotten about. Oaks were most important to the Celts, and I know all Spain was populated by Celtic tribes before the Greeks. People of Iberia spoke a Celtic dialect sorta related to Gaelic, but it wasn't written. You know that there was no such language as "Spanish" until the Romans invaded, I think around 200BC, so before that, the lands of Iberia were called Galicia. The language, mixed with Latin, became Spanish. But the people were Gauls. Gauls were the original Celts."

"So us finding some torques and other things with Celtic designs wasn't such a surprise to you?" Kemi asked.

"Well, not really," offered Donald. "The Carthaginians held the power over the whole Mediterranean coast for hundreds of years while the other tribal people lived inland. What we found could have been some Carthaginian booty, except for the Egyptian papyrus. That means our site might be pre-Carthaginian, or mainly Phoenician. The Phoenicians would have traded in Egypt and settled the Iberian peninsula, maybe even beyond. There are myths about sailors exploring the coast of Africa all the way south to the Cape, and up the west coast all the way to the British Isles."

"How do you know this stuff? Professor Donnie?" jested Kemi. "I wonder if you brought us to Spain rather than us bringing you!"

"You needed an archaeologist, and you picked Spain, remember? I did a lot of reading before actually meeting you, so I wouldn't seem like a total geek over here. But there's a lot I don't understand about our find. Just look at that statue ahead."

On a marble pedestal was the bust or partial statue of a heavily jeweled lady. It was all carved in smooth stone, and the placard read, "Lady of Eiche," provenance unknown. She was decked in many necklaces, long dangly earrings, and her hair was coifed in huge wheels over each ear. Her face was serene, staring ahead as if keeping her secrets and ignoring all eyes upon

her. At the back of the statue was an opening, a space for an urn for cremated remains. The description read, "This now greyish bust was once painted in a variety of vivid colors, two of which have been identified as natural vermillion pigment and Egyptian blue."

"It's hard to imagine this lady all colored up," said Kemi. "According to this description it must have been very garish."

"To our tastes, for sure," Donald replied. "But close inspections of residue on statues and pillars in Egypt revealed similar love of colored veneers. Ancient cities there must have been a riot of color. Because of that, I think this woman was an Egyptian."

"So, you are saying that some Egyptians were here, in Spain, maybe as traders?"asked Kemi, trying to categorize Donnie's previous statements with this idea. "Are you hiding something from me, now, sweetie?"

Donnie hesitated, then replied, "There are many sites in Spain, mostly near here, that show prolonged mining by Egyptian visitors. The salt mines, tin, and I think other minerals, were actually mined around here. But the Spanish bureaucracy tends to ignore the finds, and certainly doesn't fund much research. Some graves have been found that look Egyptian. I don't mean mummies in a sarcophagus but just with scarabs."

"Next you're going to tell me the Egyptians came to Nebraska!" joked Kemi. Or Cairo, Illinois!"

Donald grinned, and admitted, "Maybe as an archaeologist I'm on the lunatic fringe." Then he whispered, "You'd be surprised about what I believe. And really why we're here."

Kemi filed that thought for later, and was quiet for once. They wandered down museum corridors in silence, then got a cool drink in a secluded patio. Cold beer and a plate of cheeses and olives provided a quiet snack. Then, arm in arm, the pair walked back to the hotel to rest. Kemi busied herself with sorting clothing while Donald made preparations for unrolling the Egyptian papyrus. A narrow table faced the windows, and sunlight dazzled the smooth white tablecloth. With a scalpel he was able to open the thin wax, then he gently unrolled another scroll. It was about eight inches tall, and had five pages, or sections. He was intensely concentrating when Masoud entered noisily.

"How can you read that stuff?" Masoud asked, irritation in his tone.

"Practice," Donald said, frowning, "and that's what you pay me for!"

"Right! But I pay you for clues to treasure, not your history book." Masoud snarled. "Any chance that is a treasure map?"

"Give me time! This section describes a large stone being transported. But I don't know where. I'll do my best to decipher this stuff and tell you what I know. I get to keep this, though. It's not for sale."

"Agreed. You can have that moldy stuff," said Masoud. " I only want the metal things. The broken scraps are easy to sell here, and I've found some more goldsmiths who don't ask any questions. Most of that scrap stuff must be 22carat, nearly pure. I'll just tell them we used a metal detector on the beach to find this stuff. We've got enough out of last week's digging to cover another trip. Hopefully, you can get some good directions to a real treasure cache."

"I'm working on it," replied Donald. He felt hassled by Masoud, as usual, and wanted to retort that he was an archaeologist, not a treasure hunter, but knew that would only cause another unresolvable problem. He looked steadily at Masoud, trying to think of something carefully phrased to say, but all his thoughts were laced with emotions that Masoud wouldn't understand. The history, the struggles of past peoples, the continuum of civilization that Donald found so compelling were beyond Masoud's thinking. Masoud valued only gold, and the money it represented. So Donald quietly turned back to his transcription. Bowing his head, he painstakingly copied each glyph onto a separate paper, and left spacing to write translated words below the dancing forms. Egyptian writing can be read from right to left, left to right, top to bottom, or in a jumbled syntax to be poetic. Nothing is straightforward it seemed, but Donald could hear the words in his head, as if the writer were talking personally to him. Strength and pride echoed in the lines he translated, sadness was there too, along with a determination for success in the future. Kemi began reading over Donald's freckled shoulder. There were many gaps in the glyphs, and some strange ones he could not translate at all. But it seemed to be a record of an Egyptian princess named Scota.

"Here we have lived for thirty years, made a home (kingdom?) in this once fertile land. Spring and Summers brought good commerce (trade) to our island baths. Winters we lived inland, trading salt and dates. But now no rain comes, the olives are dead. So too are ...... my two sons, Breogan and Ith. Some tribes are barbaric, and value not our presence. Great is my sorrow to bury my sons without a maHat (cenotaph?) I have not the workmen to build their resting place.

Great Goddess Neith! Bring back the rains! Where are the traders from Kemet? What has befallen our great land to the east? Kemet has fallen? Do the filthy Persians butcher the Apis Bull? Where is your strength? I am in sorrow deep. Hear me, oh traveler. I am Scota Nefara-Selkis! Great is my father, Nehktanebus! May he rule forever. I am Princess of Kemet, great is my name. Six sons have I bore here, faithful to Osiris! Reach to us your support, O Mighty One! We suffer privation. Warring tribes beat at our doors!"

"This part is even more interesting," said Donald. He realized Masoud was still standing there, waiting for news. "This lady is talking about leaving this place, and these records were left behind for her people to find. She is taking her people away in ships."

"How many ships?" Masoud asked, his dark eyes wide.

"The scribe was unclear on an exact number," said Donald, "but it was probably around twenty or so."

"Twenty?" Masoud's excitement spilled out, his eyebrows raised expectantly. " Twenty ships is no small entourage! Who was this woman?"

"She's described as an Egyptian princess, and she was fleeing the country. Something about leaving due to a bad drought and being attacked by tribal people."

"But she didn't leave empty handed?"said Kemi joining the conversation. Her eyes glinting with excitement that paralleled Masoud's.

"Definitely not," Donald said with a smile. "She took off with a ton of stuff, including treasures, and a retinue of staff. It wasn't your ordinary trading trip. She was planning to stay gone. She talks about taking all her people, and treasure, and some sort of engraved stone."

"A stone?" Kemi asked.

"Yes, she describes a "stone of her lineage" to be set into a future temple or palace. She wants this stone as evidence of her royalty, for her immortality."

"How old is this stuff you are reading?" asked Masoud. "I know about King Tut and his gold stuff. Who was Pharoah at this time?"

"If this papyrus is truthful, this dates to 340BCE or so, and the pharaoh was Nectanebus," said Donald. "Not much is known about him though. I think he was the last native born Egyptian leader, because after him it was the Persians or Greeks. You know, Cleopatra and Anthony, that time period."

"Oh, right! Like I should know this history," snapped Masoud.

"That's what we pay you for," soothed Kemi, her attention drawn to their conversation. "I am very intrigued with this fairy tale, Masoud, and if this lady had twenty ships, let's find out where she went! She mentioned an island of baths....where might that be?"

"Might not be too far from Eiche," said Donald.

"Let's do some more exploring!" Kemi clapped her hands. "Can we afford a boat trip?"

"Probably," said Masoud. "I got good coin for all that broken stuff. I saw some small boats at the harbor, and seems like there are islands not far off the coast. We need to follow the clues to that treasure!"

Donald went back to his documents. Food was sent up by room service, and he worked long into the night. The last piece of papyrus was very fragile and faded. It seemed to be a copy of what was on some sort of monument, or stone, called a *talaTat* that the princess was transporting with her, always. She evidently made speeches while sitting on it or standing before it, like some sort of tangible proof of her heritage. The papyrus didn't describe the size of the stone itself, but it must have been a large building block, carried along wherever she was going. What he was able to transcribe was odd, and didn't make a lot of sense:

Hear me, oh Traveler! It is my "shay"(fate? destiny?) to be Queen. My lands lie far north, we go to claim them. Our ships are laden fully, our sailors have courage. Strength of Gamal Miledh (resides?) in me always. May he live forever! Great Goddess Neith guide our way in safety and victory! Thy bow is great! I say this, Scota Nefara-Selkis, this day _____!

It was clear that whoever wrote these lines of glyphs wrote them as if the words themselves contained some magical assurance of success. This princess seemed to believe that her destiny was to become queen of some far away nation, and that she was strengthened somehow by the spirits of her sons, and the other named person, and that the goddess would add benevolence to the voyage. Donald hoped they might find clues on some islands, if they found the right one. The adventure of a lifetime was upon him, and Donald didn't want to reveal his cards too soon. He felt distrust around Kemi and Masoud even more than usual, and tried to decide what if anything to tell them about "Scota". She was the myth of his childhood, in fairy-tale bedtime stories from his parents about Scottish history. He did know that Nectanebus really was an historical person. So, just telling them about the Egyptian pharaoh should be enough.

"Are you finished with the translation?" asked Kemi. "It's way past time for bed, but I'd rather know what you've got before I go to dreamland."

"Yes, though lots of it just brings more questions," Donald answered. "I think this lady really was a princess, probably a daughter of Pharaoh Nectanebus."

"Nectanebus? Fill me in."

"Well, from what I remember, Nectanebus was the last Egyptian born pharaoh of Egypt, the Thirtieth Dynasty. The first of that line was Nectanebus I, the "falcon", who revived monument construction all over Egypt, and united Upper and Lower Egypt. He constructed one hundred human-headed sphinx statues in Karnak, and was victorious against Persian invasions. He was succeeded by Tejos, who must have been completely incompetent, since he defected to the Persian leader Artaxerxes, who was attacking Egypt at the time. Then came the last one, Nectanebus II who ruled for less than 20 years, but who lost Egypt to the Persians. What followed was the second Persian Period, around 343BCE. Not much is written about this period in history, though I think it is really important."

"Why is that?" Kemi asked, oblivious to revealing her lack of education.

"Because if we hadn't had these wars and victories against the Persians, and the birth of Alexander the Great who was finally victorious against them, we wouldn't have had the Golden Age of Greece! We wouldn't have Egypt's culture, we wouldn't even have Christianity!" Donald was getting irked with the obvious lack of understanding shown by Kemi. He expected this from her burly brother Masoud, but he was uncomfortably reminded of the distance between his own motives, and theirs. Having her as a girlfriend was one thing, but as a life's companion? No way!

"So tell me about Nectanebus," prodded Kemi.

"Nectanebus," Donald said quietly, "was a *magician* king."

The magician king! There were so many stories about Nectanebus that some professionals had at first doubted his existence. They must be only stories, they reasoned, no real person could have existed that people truly believed had magical powers. Donald remembered

some of the accounts he had read, and how he thought they had sounded like pure fiction. Nectanebus could fly, read your mind, invade your dreams, speak to the dead and destroy you

utterly if you crossed him. He had secret chambers and performed rituals to defeat his Persian enemies. He was a sorcerer and a very powerful man. Whether or not the tales of magic were true, Nectanebus had a lot of power. He was the last native Egyptian king, the last of the 30th dynasty. Eventually the Persian army did defeat him and he fled the country, probably ending up in Nubia where he still had some power. Anyone fleeing from Nectanebus was quite brave, Donald thought, even if only a quarter of the accounts were true, the man had certainly been a force to be reckoned with.

"Just know that the history books say he got control of the throne of Egypt by some sort of magic, but probably killed off all the other family members or something like that," said Donald. "There's no record or written stuff about him that explains his rule, or where he went. The Persians used his sarcophagus as a bathtub. Had to drill a hole it in to let out the water. That's all I remember. We should give it a rest, and get some sleep. I'm to the point that my eyes want to fall out of my head."

Their bed was waiting, but Donald was still deep in thought. Deciphering the scroll was a painstaking task, and Donald liked to take his time. He knew this made Kemi anxious, but he didn't want to get it wrong. This could turn out to be a major discovery, and the simple fact that the scrolls mentioned Nectanebus' involvement was huge. If this woman was *really* Scota, then Donald was *really* interested. Who is going to believe what I've found? Donald sat back in his chair and rubbed his eyes. The dreams he was having recently had both amazed him and shaken him. Before coming here he had never had dreams like this, and figured it must be this place. This small site with it's big implications, talk of sorcerous Pharaohs, a mysterious woman fleeing the country, it was like a movie script. Donald's dream had reminded him of a movie; in all it's technicolor glory. It had also spooked him a little.

He shook his head slowly and stared at the scrolls in front of him, his eyes unfocused. He knew who this woman was. It could be a defining moment in his life as well as his career. Problem was, he finally realized their dig was illegal. How could he publish his findings, or follow this trail without involving the authorities. The major problem was Masoud, and his back alley dealings. Donald couldn't just forget his dream, nor could he trust Kemi much further. This papyrus was significant in so many ways, he'd wished he'd left this place yesterday. It might be time to vanish completely, just like Scota. He climbed into bed with Kemi but lay on top of the covers. A cool breeze wafted from the windows, but Donald wasn't chilled. He simply slept like a baby.

FIFTEEN

In the morning, the three of them found a ferry boat charter to take them to various islands. The captain identified one as "Illeta dels Banyetas" which was also called "The Queen's Baths." It took two hours to sail there, the motor chugged rhythmically as the waves kept time. The beautiful crystal green Mediterranean waters seemed shallow and calm on the trip. The island was a narrow strip of rocky limestone, and had hugely scalloped harbors on its eastern side. These coves were tourist destinations for scuba diving, and the waters were warm with colorful coral estuaries just below the surface.

"Este Illeta tiene muchos banyas y torreones," said the charter captain. "Enchoy yourselfs todas dias!" he said in broken English. They soon found a hotel, rather more like a hostel, to stow their packs, then set out to explore the island.

Children gathered around everywhere they went, begging for coins or candies. These ragamuffins were like a gaggle of geese surging down the streets until they figured out that these "touristas" had no intention of supporting their begging. A few glaring warnings from Masoud and the children melted away into doorways, and the trio was left to their exploring.

The island had once been a major retreat for wealthy Greeks, Phoenicians and Carthaginians. Everywhere were mosaic floors and ruins of great temples. The temples seemed to be dedicated to a goddess named Tanit who was a Phoenician fertility goddess during Carthaginian rule. There were huge limestone baths, now open-air pools fed by fresh spring water. A central avenue ran the length of the island, with temples and palaces lining the route from north to south. There was some supposed Greek influence here, but to Donald the scene seemed even more ancient, with carvings of the goddess Tanit over what looked like altars. Donald knew that the Carthaginians were devoted to this goddess of fertility, and to infant sacrifices. Her symbol was a triangle topped with a head and arms. And often it looked more like an Ankh with a triangular skirt. This, he knew, was also the symbol of Neith, the Goddess of War. This was clearly Scota's island for commerce that he had deciphered from the papyrus!

Along the main avenue were shops advertising massage and baths. The trio entered one, and soon found shelves filled with a variety of bath salts, in various colors and scents.

"Let's take a bath and a massage?" suggested Kemi.

"Not for me," said Masoud. "I'd rather do some exploring, maybe go for a scuba dive."

"That's ok," replied Donald, "we can catch you up later at our rooms."

Kemi and Donald made reservations for a private, two person bath and massage. The lady in charge showed them a change room where they hung up their clothes. Plush Turkish towels were draped over them for modesty. Soon they were enjoying the heavily salted and perfumed water, which was almost too hot for Donald to enjoy.

"Oooo!" purred Kemi. "I could live here forever."

"Good to see you so blissful, lady," replied Donald. "But I don't think I've ever been this clean in my whole life."

"Just wait for what's next!" added Kemi.

They were led, towel wrapped, to white towel covered tables where they lay in cushioned comfort. Soon mixtures of salt and perfumed oils were rubbed all over their skin. Two pairs of masseuses began to smooth their muscles with deep massage until their skin glowed like polished granite.

"If this is anything like the business our Egyptian queen had going, she must have made a ton of profit!" said Kemi. "This must have been the 'Best Spa of the West' in her time!"

Donald roused himself from his dream state, and began conversing with the attendants in Spanish at first, then found that they also spoke English.

"How old are these baths?" asked Donald.

"Our island baths are two thousand five hundred years old," said the woman, with pride in her eyes. She was middle-aged, with strong hands accustomed to giving long massages. "Our baths were constructed by a great queen, "La Reina," long ago. We have many stories about her work here. She also had a school where she taught the people how to worship the great Goddess Tanit. This was most important, for she outlawed the sacrifice of babies, which had been the custom."

"Thank goodness!" said Kemi. "Who could give a baby for sacrifice?"

"In those ancient days the people were pagans," replied the woman. "When the gods don't cooperate with crops people starve, and they don't even need more mouths to feed."

"They must have believed in their gods," said Donald, "for we have seen many inscriptions adoring Tanit, everywhere you look."

"Yes, but now we are Christians to be sure," said the woman assuredly. "You are safe here. Please visit our shop and buy our goods." With that, she gave a little slap on Donald's butt and they dressed to explore more of the shop.

In the shop, were shelves of bath salts, some in glass jars, which glistened in the sunlight. Donald selected two bags of perfumed salts, one in lavender, the other scented with roses. The colorful cloth bags were stuffed, even hard to the touch.

"I'm going to send these to my sister Alison," said Donald. "Her birthday is coming soon and this stuff would be a hit with her. We can mail them when we get back to the mainland. That way we can avoid any custom's charges."

"I want some too," said Kemi, "for us to share next time you can be talked into taking a bath!"

Donald smiled. Kemi somehow understood his love of being dirty, if not smelly. She at least would enjoy herself in a bath or two with these lovely perfumed salts. But Donald had other plans for the two additional bags of bath salts he was purchasing. Soon their bundles were bagged, and they set off to explore the island.

A small building came into view that was a makeshift excuse for a museum. Donald was happy to find that the locals had made some effort at preserving the artifacts they had found. There were a lot of cracked amphorae, and Phoenician pottery, even some Greek blackware, but little else. There were no traces of Egypt here as far as Donald could see, until he saw a bowl full of what looked like inscribed rocks. Many had the triangular carving of Tanit, just a simple circular head above a wide slanted base, with a horizontal line for arms. These looked like votive offerings, carved in soft limestone, for dropping into the offshore waters. But Donald thought he could see a scarab form among these stones. There was no attendant, and no way to reach through the glass case to turn it into the light to examine it.

Another alcove displayed statues, mostly broken busts of long dead officials. None of them were painted, or reminiscent of the "Lady of Eiche." But one "goddess" had a distinctive bow with arrows clasped across her chest. It could have been "Neith" Donald thought. The years had not been kind with weathering though, and it bore no inscriptions.

"Look at that one," he said to Kemi, "she has the bow and arrows of an Egyptian goddess, one called "Neith." She was a goddess of the hunt, but also a metaphor for the future, or fate, I think."

"So people prayed to her for good fortune at hunting?" asked Kemi.

"Well, not exactly. It was more of a prayer for guidance in life, like how the arrow could fly to its mark. Like a river of time flows and our place on the river."

"Makes me wonder why we are here, too," said Kemi, "and maybe there is some purpose to our travels." They both were quiet for a time, then Kemi said, "We should be getting back to our rooms, and see what Masoud has found out about the harbor here."

With that, Donald and Kemi returned to their room. Kemi decided to take a short nap. Soon she was lightly snoring, relaxed from the day's experiences. Donald busied himself by emptying the bath salts onto a tablecloth. He carefully inserted the tubes of waxed papyrus inside each sack, then refilled the sacks with the bath salts. It was easy to retie the ribbon into a pretty bow. Excess bath salts went down the bathtub drain. He then wrapped both presents in the local newspaper, tucked in his translations and a note to his sister Ali. Then he set out to find the post office, assuming there were postal facilities on the island. Sure enough, they were used to mailing bath salts for the tourists, and he found the "Correos" sign hanging a few doors down from the hostel.

The lady at the post office was happy to find a sturdy box, and shortly had the bath salts wrapped securely with brown paper and string. Donald addressed the package to his sister Allison in California. He paid for insurance, and got his receipt. The lady behind the counter promised they would be delivered on time for Ali's birthday, "via aereo."

As he turned to go back to the hostel, Donald had a second thought. He slipped into the next shop he saw and bought two more identical bags of bath salts. He needed to do some serious thinking about how to extricate himself from his predicament. Selling artifacts of gold had never been in his original bargain, no matter how much he liked Kemi. And now, he was getting scared. He did not trust Masoud's temper if he couldn't produce a treasure map.

When he returned to their rooms, Kemi was still napping. He snuggled in beside her, confident that he had done the safest thing for his scrolls. Besides, he had made excellent copies of all the hieroglyphs, and he felt sure that neither Kemi nor Masoud could discriminate between the various papyrus pieces that were left. They would not realize some were missing.

Masoud barged through the door, didn't even knock. He seemed a little irked to find his sister and Donald curled up together like children. He was slamming around the room, shifting chairs when they sleepily opened their eyes.

"How was the water?" Kemi asked. "What was the harbor like?"

"Water was warm, not at all cold, but there was no equipment for rent for scuba diving. I just did some snorkeling," shrugged Masoud. "And I walked the shoreline, saw a bunch of fishing boats, and old harbors. The locals said the island was the refuge of some "Reina" or Queen, but they didn't have her name. They just call it ""Ilyeta de la Reina" but don't know why. Stupid fishermen."

"We looked at some museum stuff, didn't find any clues, either," said Donald, "but we had a very indulgent afternoon with the bathhouse masseuse." Donald gave Kemi a little nudge, and she gave a little giggle. "It was an unforgettable afternoon."

"Well, Donald, what do you suggest for the next stop on our treasure hunt?" Masoud asked.

"Maybe try a trip to Gibraltar? Our princess must have gone through the strait if she was truly making an ocean voyage to the north. One of the local boats might take us there cheaply, and besides, that might be quicker than driving on the narrow roads on the coastline. I know there are a lot of caves on the ocean side of Gibraltar that we could explore. The whole mountain of Gibraltar is riddled with limestone caverns and tunnels."

"So much for "as *solid* as the Rock of Gibraltar!" quipped Kemi.

"Okay, sounds like a plan," said Masoud. "The local fishermen I met are looking for charters, and no doubt are easily bought. Some of them could smuggle us on shore, no questions asked. I can sell the camper and rent something else in Gibraltar."

After a dinner with several bottles of Spanish wine they found the hard beds at the hostel inviting. All too soon morning broke with the screech of seagulls at the windows, and the intrepid travelers set off to find a worthy boat. Soon they were floating west, toward the "Pillars of Hercules," following the trail of possible unknown treasure. Masoud was intent on finding riches within the caves at Gibraltar, while Kemi was intent at getting a commitment from Donald, perhaps a ring. Donald was intent on getting out of Spain, back to his sister, and safety.

The large fishing boat Masoud chose wasn't luxurious by any means, but the languid hours on calm waters gave them hours to contemplate their next moves. Masoud was closed mouthed about how much money he had garnered by selling the gold scrap. But at over a thousand bucks an ounce, he must have close to 50K. Donald wondered if he'd sold the torques as well. Everything about his situation was making Donald madder than hell as he lay on the sunny deck. They watched the horizon ahead as the sailor tacked into deeper waters along the coast.

"Tell us about this Egyptian princess we are following," suggested Kemi.

"Her name on the scroll was "Scota" and there are a lot of myths surrounding that name," replied Donald. "Her name appears in oral stories about Ireland."

"Are you kidding? Ireland?" Kemi began to giggle.

"We aren't sailing to Ireland!" snorted Masoud. He was not amused.

"It's just a myth," said Donald. "No one believes those "invasion stories" are historically true about Ireland. I guess because it wasn't written down anywhere they're just bedtime stories for children."

"So, tell us the story," suggested Kemi.   "Scota was a princess from Egypt, maybe one of two princesses with the same name, who left Egypt because of wars. The first one was supposedly during the time of Moses and the heretic pharaoh, Ahkenaton. The other one was later, during the time of Persian wars against Egypt. The Irish folklore just says they came across the sea and invaded Ireland, and named the counties there after Scota's sons. She got killed in a battle, or fell off her horse. Who knows!"

"Scota? Isn't that the name on the scroll you found?" asked Kemi.

"Yeah, I think so, but lots of Egyptian names can be read however you want. We don't know how the vowels sounded, or any of the words for that matter. We just fill in the blanks like some word game, and hope we got it right." Donald was being evasive, but even he couldn't be sure it actually was the same princess. He had no idea how old his scrolls were.

"Now you tell us!" said Masoud. "Is there a treasure to find?"

"Look. They left in a lot of ships. Took their stuff. Went west, and sounds like they went north after that. That's all I really know," said Donald. "The stories are just myths, and nothing can be verified. It's a tale told to children at bedtime. Believe what you want!"

"Anything else?" asked Kemi.

"Just that the stories are also connected with Alexander the Great, that he was the son of Scota's father. No one believes that bit of fantasy either."

"What?" Masoud asked, then looked at his sister, "What is he talking about? Who's Alexander?"

"Alexander the Great, o' brother of mine," Kemi said, rolling her eyes, "Donnie is telling us a romantic myth that Nectanebus was Alexander the Great's father."

"Alexander the Great," Masoud said flatly, "*the* Alexander the Great. The son of a Pharoah?"

"That's the legend," said Donald sitting back. "When Nectanebus was finally defeated by the Persians he did not go to Nubia, but to the court of Phillip II of Macedon."

"Ok," Masoud said, looking to his sister again.

"Phillip was Alexander the Great's real father," Donald said, leaning forward a little, "but the myth goes that while Phillip was away on a campaign, Nectanebus tricked Phillip's wife, Olympia, into sleeping with him. The baby from their uh...union is said to be Alexander."

"If that's true, then this woman," said Masoud, finally catching on, "would not only be a princess, but also Alexander's older sister." Kemi grinned and looked over at Donald. Masoud's eyes had gone dark again, and she knew he was excited.

"What else, Donnie?" she asked him, "what else do you think?"

"That name, connected with these stories, could change all the history books!" exclaimed Donald. "But no one can prove it. It's just a myth."

"I'm not interested in changing history!" snorted Masoud. "We're not here for a pleasure trip on the Mediterranean! I'm here for one thing, one thing only, and it better be bigtime!"

"Be patient brother dear," soothed Kemi. "We might as well enjoy the trip! Besides, we found a lot of things to line our pockets already. You didn't say how much we got!"

Masoud's eyes became slits. He gave an evil stare towards his sister and Donald, then stomped off towards the prow. He was not about to reveal the amount of money the gold scraps had brought. He acted as though there would soon be a parting of ways. He'd take what he had and part ways with the lovebirds. He separated himself from them like some obstinate child having a temper tantrum. Masoud angrily squeezed the boat rail, and was sullen, looking at the sea as Donald approached.

"I'd like to know what's left from the dig, and what's left in our packs," said Donald, rather tentatively. "We might meet some kind of customs officials at the port, and it would be hard to explain the artifacts I found for you. Is that too much to ask?" Kemi looked at her brother, but she could tell his anger was mounting. And now even the sky began to turn dark. The sea was getting choppy. Kemi could tell her brother didn't want to say anything, so she had to intervene carefully to smooth the waves between the two men.

"Masoud, Donnie is right. We need to know what we're heading into, and what kind of money we got. Why are you so stubborn!"

"There's no gold left," sneered Masoud. "I sold it all. Broke up the torques into small sections so they wouldn't be recognizable. I know we can't be caught with that stuff! Do you think I'm stupid?!"

"Calm down, bro! We just don't like being in the dark!" said Kemi, trying to soothe his feathers. "What about the papyrus, and the potsherds?"

"One of the antiquities buyers bought that junk, even gave me a receipt," said Masoud.

"So, all we have left is Donnie's stuff? I guess he can hide that," Kemi admitted softly. "How much richer are we?"

"We've got expenses, don't forget!" Masoud said forcefully. "This fisherman alone is costing a bundle, and I'm waiting to see what I can talk him into taking, with extra for "no questions." First he said $500, but I'd guess he will demand more. Plus the hotels and camper, a vehicle to rent....we've spent more than half of the take."

"So what is it?" Donald demanded.

"We sold around twenty four ounces, give or take," offered Masoud evasively.

"I still can't do the math on that Masoud!" Kemi's voice showed the exasperation and impatience that Donald felt. "Is this twenty questions?"

"Keep your voice down!" grumbled Masoud. "That scrap was worth around $1500 an ounce. I don't want our captain to hear this stuff!"

Wind was howling, which made it hard to hear words between them. The captain was at his wheelhouse, waving to them to take cover for the night. Masoud went to talk to him, then came back shortly.

"Mr. Otero says the storm will actually help us get there faster," said Masoud. "But he says soon it will be raining on us, and we should take cover. He knows we were arguing, but I told him you lovers were having a spat."

Kemi nodded, and left the men to find cover for herself under the stern shelter. She snuggled into her sleeping bag, and to her, the swells were like being cradled in safety. Soon swells larger than their boat began to toss them around like fish at the fish market. Masoud stood at the rail, peering into the darkness ahead and rather enjoying the ride like a roller coaster. He even laughed out loud once or twice, as if enjoying the thrill of adrenaline. He was like some gnarly pirate, beckoning the waves to challenge his will. Soon they were in complete darkness, clouds obscured the moon and stars. The captain was busy checking his headings in his lighted cabin.

Masoud seemed to count the crashing waves, matching their cadence, waiting for the next one. At his right, Donald was getting nauseous. He looked at the wine dark sea and felt like some long ago ocean wanderer. As he leaned over the side to vomit, Masoud helped him the rest of the way. There was no sound of a struggle, and Donald flew into the foam between the swells. No moonlight pierced the thick clouds, thunder clashed, and rain pelted the deck like sharp tears. The dark swells belied no trace of Donald Cameron. Masoud went forward to his bunk, and slept soundly without a care in the world.

Calm seas brought morning light. Masoud bent over his sister's face, and gently wakened her with a face full of determination. Looking her straight in the eyes he said, "Donnie was so upset that you wouldn't marry him, that he left last night. That's all you need to know."

"What?" Kemi wailed.

"That's our story! You two argued, and he left. Period!" Masoud repeated tersely.

"Donnie left? You mean into the water?" whimpered Kemi.

"I don't need to repeat it again, do I?" Masoud sneered. "That's our story. I'm betting the captain of this boat won't want to doubt me. If he wants to report someone lost at sea, his payment will be cut in half." Masoud then rifled through Donald's backpack. He found the passport, wallet with some money, clothes, and two bags of bath salts. No papyrus. Must have had it under his shirt, he thought. Masoud replaced everything but the money, and zipped the bag shut as finally as closing a casket.

Up on deck Masoud found their captain bringing out some pastries for breakfast. "Señor," Masoud began, "my sister and Donald had a terrible falling out last night." And with some hesitation Masoud asked, "Did you hear them arguing?"

"No, storm loud," the old seaman replied.

"Well, my sister told him she wouldn't marry him, and he got extremely upset. He left the boat!" said Masoud in a terse voice. "I think he is gone! I don't know when it happened, but when we woke up this morning, he was gone."

"El era un suicidio?" exclaimed the captain. Fear and suspicion flashed in his eyes, but soon he calmed, and said, "Señor, it is no use to look for such a person now. It is too far late. Perhaps he was a good swimmer, and will float to shore," offered the man. "Perhaps not."

"This is a choice of tourists, sometimes," he said with a lowered voice. Then he turned and offered a pastry, watching Masoud's face as he did so.

"No, I am too upset," said Masoud. "And my sister is in distress. When we reach shore she will visit the church for confession."

Nodding in agreement, the captain said, "Es un consuelo."

Ahead the massive butte of Gibraltar came into view.

The sea was getting choppy again, as winds were swirling around the massive cliffs. The motor chugged as they steered toward a jetty. Donning their backpacks the solemn pair stepped off the moored boat. Masoud handed the sailor Donald's backpack.

"This is our friend's belongings...passport and clothes. If you want to report the man lost at sea, this is payment for the trip." Masoud showed the captain his left hand, holding a stack of bills. "But if you wish to forget us, this is better payment," and Masoud's right hand held a wad of money, enough to secure his secrecy, and probably a month's wages from fishing. The man accepted the money from Masoud's right hand, bowed his head and said, "no reporta."

Then Kemi grabbed Masoud's hand and started whistling the "Happy Wanderer." She could have won an Oscar for her performance of a carefree adventurer on holiday, though her eyes were swollen from crying. They walked from the dock, intent on disappearing into the expansive city. Many villas and opulent hotels graced the shore of the Mediterranean coast. The city itself was dotted with skyscrapers, and it felt like being in a major city, like London.

"This doesn't look much like Spain," said Masoud. "Everything is in English!"

"Gibraltar is part of Great Britain," said Kemi, quietly. "We will probably have to pass customs or immigration to even get off the boardwalk."

Sure enough, at the end of the quay was a processing center for visitors. They got in the queue and got ready for inspection. "Anything to declare?" asked the female official, "Passports please." She smiled at the pair, assuming they were on a honeymoon. "What is the purpose of your visit, my dears?"

"My *sister* and I are touring the Mediterranean," said Masoud. "We have a few days left on our holiday in Spain, so we thought we'd visit Gibraltar for a few days. See the sights."

"Everything is in order," said the woman with an embarrassed look on her face. "There is no duty on bath salts," she said to Kemi, as she proffered them to the woman. "You have clearance for three days, anything longer will require immigration paperwork. Enjoy your visit."

"Thank you," said Kemi, "we'd like to see the caves and caverns here. Please point us to the visitor's information place?" Nodding, the woman pointed to the sign. "Follow the arrow."

At the Visitor's Bureau Masoud made reservations at a hostel and found brochures about scuba diving and cave exploring. A pamphlet displayed some history, with glossy pictures of Phoenician ships, Moorish armies, and Galician musicians. One photo showed dotted areas on a map of the strait, marking shipwrecks and submerged masonry. "I guess this is our treasure map," said Masoud. Another underwater photo showed a jumble of Egyptian scarab amulets by the thousands, offerings thrown into the sea. "So much for treasure! Donald would be pleased to find Egyptians here." Kemi shrugged and looked at her brother in silence. She simply didn't know what to say.

SIXTEEN

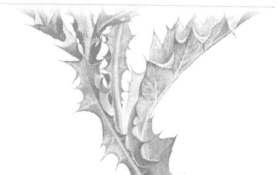

Scota at UCLA, September, 1996

United States, Los Angeles California

The student ghetto around UCLA was more artistic than slum-like. Tibetan prayer flags hung off front porches, music wafted from different apartment floors, all coming together to make a constant drone that never really shut off. Ali Cameron climbed the stairs to her apartment through layers of sound. The first floor boasted some kind of Reggae funk, followed by the metal head on floor two, classical from the professor's place who thought it was cool to live where the students did, and finally to the open door of her own apartment which was blasting Benny Goodman. Ali's roommate Pam was gyrating in their living room. Ali stood for a minute, pushed back her red hair, and watched until Pam's enthusiastic hip swaying turned her body toward the front door.

"You got a package from Spain." She swiveled her hips to indicate the brown paper wrapped box.

"Oh, my gosh! Must be from Donnie!" Ali knew Donnie was in Spain since she had received postcards from various cities. But it wasn't like him to send things, especially since it wasn't her birthday or anything. She opened the box to reveal two bags of bath salts from a place called "Illeta dels Banyetas." A letter scribbled on yellow paper lay on top.

"Dear Sis, Happy Birthday! I'm sure this will be a safe gift, hope you like it! I might not be home for awhile. If I don't get back on time, just know that I love you, Donnie."

Bath salts? How weird, thought Ali. Safe gift? Like her brother, she loved playing in the dirt, hiking in the mountains and recording strata. She could discern Pleistocene alluvial from Jurassic at a distance, and knew which strata would give up brachiopods or trilobites. She had a great collection of fossilized fish, whose bones were caught in the sand where they once swam. As children, she and Donnie were the "dirty duo" much to their mother's chagrin. She was always slathering sunscreen lotion on their freckles, as her red-headed children spent so much time playing in the sunny dirt. Studying geology had always been Ali's goal, while Donnie wallowed in the history of long dead civilizations. So, *Bath Salts!*

A flash of insight said this was code for mystery, or danger. She knew Donnie was in trouble! It wasn't her birthday, and since he never told her when he expected to be back, he wasn't late. The message was between the lines.

"What'dya get?" Pam faltered when she saw the concern on Ali's face.

"Donnie sent me bath salts from some island off the coast of Spain," she whispered.

"Yeah, well, that's weird. Even I know that's not something you'd use, even on your wedding day." Not waiting for the downbeat, Pam stopped dancing. "Anything else?" she asked.

Ali unrolled the Spanish newspaper to find Donald's scribbled translation, lots of crossed out words and glyphs, and enough of the theme to realize that Donald had found something very ancient. She handed the pages to Pam, and showed her Donnie's note.

"Is he in trouble? What are you going to do?"

"Who can we call?" Ali slumped in a chair. "Do you think the "Spanish Immigration Office" or American Embassy, or what?"

" Maybe Student Affairs or the State Department? There is a cute professor in Archaeology who might help too. I mean, he's old and cute. Maybe Donnie wrote something coded in those hieroglyphics."

"Let's see what he *really* sent."

Like an emergency C-section, Ali split the pink bag open along the seam, delivering a waxy tube with a thump. The strong scent of sweet roses filled the kitchen as the plastic tablecloth received the tiny pink crystal salts. The purplish bag delivered another waxy tube. Identical twins of what looked like rolls of fibrous paper, ragged on each end. The aroma of lavender blossoms masked the odor of patchouli that had commanded the apartment since the girls had moved in. Amazement flooded their faces. Two tubes of ancient wax-sealed papyrus lay like silent messengers unable to speak. Several pages of Donnie's translations gave no information about her intrepid brother. The Spanish newspaper had the date, which she could read, but little else. It wasn't the Spanish people spoke in southern California. Nothing else about the package gave a clue to the meaning. It just spelled foul play.

Ali settled down at the desk, pushed her hair behind her ears, and began making phone calls. She dialed the last phone numbers she'd had for Donnie, but that proved a dead end. She called the police department, and talked to a lady at "missing persons," which was fruitless as well. Finally, she called the State Department, and told them she thought her brother had met foul play in Spain.

After hours of repetitive conversations, and being put on hold with seemingly countless official-sounding people, Ali came to the conclusion that besides waiting, there was nothing she could do. She had no real evidence to support her fears, nothing to start the wheels of investigation by any authorities. They listened politely, but that was all.

The next day she took Donald's notes and scribbled translations down to the basement offices in the Archaeology department in search of a professor who specialized in Egyptology. She thought maybe the offices were arranged chronologically, since his was in the oldest part of the building, while the upper floors were flush with Native American artifacts, stuff she often found lying around on the mesa. *How did those people remain so primitive for so long? No metals, maybe.* Another flight of stairs down and she found ARCH103.

Professor Angus Morrisson's office had enough free floor space for his desk, chair, and a folding chair for visitors. Walls were lined with bulging metal bookshelves, which couldn't hold another inch of a book. More books and folders were stacked precariously on the floor, with slips of paper sticking out at odd intervals. Ali's geologist eyes immediately understood the chaotic filing system, stratified by time and subject. The door was open so she rapped on the door jam, then waited patiently for the professor to accept a visitor. He looked up over glasses perched at the end of his nose.

"What can I do for ye, Lassie?" came the brogue-infested speech.

"Hi, I'm Alison Cameron. My brother, Donald, sent me some papers that are translations of something he found. And he is missing... may have met foul play." Ali fought the tears that threatened to swell over her eyelids, but soon lost that battle as they made wet tracks down her cheeks. She handed the papers to the professor.

"Can you tell me what you think of this?"

Dr. Morrisson opened the folding chair and invited her to sit. He was not a tall man for a Scotsman, but stood straight and composed in his charcoal grey Harris tweed. He had a blue origami folded handkerchief poking out of the pocket, that blended with the blue and green tartan necktie. Resisting retirement, his grey hair and closely trimmed grey beard spoke of meticulous attention to detail in all his actions. The soft beard framed sparkling blue eyes surrounded by laugh lines, evidence of fifty odd years of study, exploration, and scholarship. With deft hands he repositioned his reading glasses, as they were using his nose as a slide. He stood there skimming the lines, pausing occasionally to look over his glasses at Ali. He could see that she was near to breaking down, wiping her tears on her sleeve, but trying to look composed. He tried to console her saying, "There, there, Lass, we'll sort this oot."

Ali watched his face transform as he read the paper. His eyes widened as his forefinger came to the name that closed the translation: "Scota Nefara-Selkis." Dr. Morrisson crashed into his chair, shocked. His legs went numb, his mouth agape, he then burst out with "I'm curgellit! Och Aye! At last! At long last!"

"What is it?" Ali asked. Her tears stopped mid-slide at the professor's reaction.

"Where did this come from? Where did you say your brother is working?" Dr. Morrisson's voice, at first insistent and demanding, softened as he looked at Ali and saw the distressed look on her face. "Start from the beginning. Dinnae fear, we will set this right."

"My brother met a girl at the Boston restaurant where he was working. She and her brother had a company called "Finders/Keepers." Here's the business card."

Dr. Morrisson read the silvery paper card that said, "Finders/Keepers—We find it, You keep it." There was no website listed, just a phone number, and the names of Kemi and Masoud Houssein.

"According to Donnie they worked the Boston area for Revolutionary War artifacts on private land. They have some sort of sonar machine and metal detectors, and get hired by people to search their property for stuff. Evidently they found a bunch of Celtic sites near Groton, Connecticut, and helped people sell artifacts to museums. Donnie thought they were reputable, but I don't know much more." Ali regained some composure and continued.

"Donnie wanted to work in Egypt, but they said the bureaucracy was impossible, especially for small time companies like theirs, but they were planning to go to other countries, more like a vacation, I guess. Anyhow, they hired Donnie and took him to Spain, and I got several postcards. I think he was pretty serious about this woman, Kemi Houssein, but I don't have any real information about her, or a photo. He does seem to hook up with girls I don't like, so lately he hasn't told me anything about this one. He says that since he's no great catch I shouldn't be so suspicious about his dating scene."

"But your brother has studied Archaeology? And can read hieroglyphics?"

"Yes, he finished his Master's degree two years ago, but couldn't find any position, either teaching or excavating. He's been working at a Boston area restaurant since he finished his last Teaching Assistant thing. Then he met these people, and got hired for this trip to Spain. This last postcard is from some island off the coast of Spain in the Mediterranean."

Dr. Morrisson listened intently while turning the postcard over carefully. A pretty picture showed a sliver of an island with ruined stone temples and towers. He looked at Ali with soft but intense eyes and said, "Go on."

"Donnie mailed two scrolls, hidden in two bags of bath salts. They are sealed in wax. I knew not to open them, just kept them safe. I put them in my safe-deposit box."

"And you've heard nothing else? Have you called the State Department? How long has it been since the package came?" Dr. Morrisson's questions tumbled out in rapid succession , and soon the professor knew everything Ali knew about her brother's cryptic note.

"If I don't hear more soon, I mean it's been nearly a week now, I think I have to go to Spain to look for him," Ali said. "What do you think about the transcription he sent?"

Dr. Morrisson looked at Ali closely, and said, "If ye are a true Cameron, then ye'll neither "give nor yield!" But you need help. It appears that Donald has found written evidence of a princess believed to be only a myth. Her name was Scota. From her we get the name 'Scotland'!"

"What in the world are you saying, sir?"

"You've never heard the tales, then? The 'invasion' stories or the oral history of the Scots called the "Scotichronicon?" Dr. Morrisson sighed. "These are the masterful stories of old, of seafarers and warriors who settled the Isles long before the Roman invasion. An Egyptian princess, named Scota, is in our oral history as the first Queen of the Scots. The story says that she and her sons traveled from Egypt, lived in Iberia, and then conquered the island of Ireland, which is named after her son "Ir." Supposedly the land was parceled out to each of her sons. They buried her in Glen Scohene after a violent battle. It's never been excavated as far as I know, so there's never been a shred of evidence that any of those stories were true. I've waited all my life for some written account with her name. This is a great find!"

"Those are the sort of tales that Donnie would love," Ali admitted. "But I've never heard that fairy tale. You are telling me that Scotland was named after an Egyptian princess? That's incredible! Maybe I'm too far removed from my genealogy... our father did his best to fill us in, at least I've heard the "March of the Cameron Men" you were quoting. But that sounds like the height of make-believe. If Disney made a movie about it though, we'd believe it. My mother was of Irish descent, but never told me this myth either. She gave me her Irish harp, and lots of songs, but none of that history stuff. 'Course I'm more interested in Geology than stories."

Ali was trying to put on a brave face, but she was melting under the kind gaze from the professor. With a more confident voice, she continued. "I have not touched the wrapped papyrus that Donnie sent. I know enough about finding fossils and artifacts to not harm them. Donnie must have been under extreme danger to have removed that stuff, and to trust the mail. I can't imagine anything except danger that would cause him to mail...I mean *smuggle*...artifacts out of Spain. He obviously feared for their safety. And his own!" Ali was nearing her breaking point again. Her eyes began darting around the room as if looking for an exit to her fears. After taking a few deep breaths she said, "The pages I showed you are only his translations. Are we in trouble just for having them?"

Dr. Morrisson left his chair and came over to console Ali with a hug. "Calm yourself, my dear. You did the right thing by putting them in a safe place, and that's where they should stay until we unravel Donnie's disappearance." Ali nodded, and seemed calmer. She felt she had come to the right person for help.

Dr. Morrisson sat on the edge of his desk, but held Ali's hands as if she were his daughter.

"Well, your brother's package came from Spain, from an island," the professor said, calmly enumerating the facts they knew. "That's enough clues to trace his last location. I doubt that the authorities know anything about it. But if Donnie is a well-trained archaeologist he would know he was breaking all the rules of his profession. The 'provenance' is almost as important as the artifacts themselves. The scrolls are safe for now. We'll see what to do after you find Donald."

"How can I find my brother? I'm not a world traveller, able to go to other countries by myself. I wouldn't even leave L.A. by myself. I know it's a lot to ask, but would you be able to go to Spain with me... and help me find my brother?" Ali asked.

"Aye, you do need help. Lucky that you came by today, as I'm not supposed to be here. I just came by to get a particular article, which took some time to find." Dr. Morrisson threw up his hands in exasperation. "I usually know where everything is. I'm on sabbatical this Fall, and I don't need to keep office hours. I'm not offering any Summer Session classes either, just doing some research for a publication."

Dr. Morrisson fussed with a stack of notes, and rearranged some books as if to be rearranging his schedule. He closed his eyes for a few seconds, blinked, and then said, "Sometimes the greatest finds in Archaeology come because of a fluke like this. And if Donnie has found Scota, this would answer a lot of questions about Scotland's history. Even our DNA." Dr. Morrisson had a faraway look in his eyes, thinking of broken lineages that could be connected. As he leaned on the edge of the desk he began to tap his fingers as if playing a Scottish bodhram. His fingers marched a quick-step as he drummed suddenly to a halt. Then he looked up excitedly.

"I hope you have saved the postcards so we can follow his trail? Perhaps go to the last major city first, and of course the island. Though I've never heard of it, if it's small, the locals may remember him. It hasn't been too long ago. Do you have a current photo of Donald? Start with that and we'll make an itinerary." The professor was doing his best to sound practical, acting business-like to hide his excitement. Then he said jokingly, "I've needed an excuse to go over the Pond for some time! After we find Donald, I'll make my way home to Lewis! An unplanned and unexpected homecoming tae the Lew's!"

"Were you born on Lewis?" Ali asked. "I think it's an island?"

"Yes, I'm from near a wee village called Tolsta Chaolais. It's a cluster of homes, a signpost, and a wide view of the cold ocean. Once the island had hardy fishermen, though not many people lived there year long. If you can believe it, the fishing lanes were depleted. So now only fish farms are there. You can see multitudes of fish pens offshore. It's strange to think they have to raise fish in a pen, out in the ocean."

"What else is there besides sheep? Maybe I'd like to go there, too?" asked Ali.

"Not many sheep, there's little forage for animals. Being so far north, no trees grow on Lewis. It does grow thick peat moss that the locals use for fuel in their "black houses.""

"Why are the houses black? Do they use black rocks?"

"No, but the geology is curious. They're black because there's no windows. The old way of having a home on Lewis was to cut the turf out of the hillside and build a wee house, with a thatch roof. Keeping it low and partially below ground provided protection from the fierce winds, and the merciless cold. Usually the house had no windows, just a chimney hole. The climate is just too harsh. But they do have electricity now, which has helped tourism."

"Doesn't sound much like a tourist attraction, if you don't mind me saying."

Angus nodded. "People come to see the famous standing stone circle called Calanais. Great dolmens were erected there thousands o' years past, but the rocks come from somewhere far away. Can't see how they came to the island, either. My sister runs a wee "bed and breakfast" there, for tourists that occasionally stay for more than the single day. Some come to get Harris tweed from the local weavers and sweaters from the knitters. I've not been back for many years, but a visit would surely make her happy. We will definitely have a trip to Lewis."

"I have my inheritance money," said Ali, "so I won't be a burden. Donnie is my only family, and I'm willing to spend any money and time to find him."

SEVENTEEN

No further word came from Donald Cameron. No reports from any official source came, and after three weeks of waiting, it was clear that he was not coming home. Ali had enough money to cover her fare, and the professor used his frequent flier points, and soon they had airfare to Alicante, Spain. Ali promised Pam she would keep in touch, packed up some clothes and went to the airport with Dr. Morrisson. He'd told her to dress for cool, if not cold weather, as the warm summer days would soon be past. And if she went with him to Lewis, she would need many layers to keep warm. The professor brought several copies of what he called "Invasion Myths" for Ali to read on the flight. Just as he said, the oral history of the Celtic peoples was very involved, and spoke of many generations of travelers.

"You told me that this is an oral history," said Ali, as she settled into her window seat, "so who wrote this stuff? It must have been written down somewhere?"

"I'm not a linguistic archaeologist," began Dr. Morrisson, "but the ancient Celtic people did not allow writing, except for simple tallies for bartering goods. Of course they had a common language, but they believed that writing things down could be subject to false statements and lies. So they relied on trained "bards" to remember their histories. All the births, deaths, famous battles, and every event worth remembering, was set to verse and song. These bards and harpers were highly respected parts of the culture. Youths were trained at an early age and were able to develop phenomenal memory ability. And probably being blind would have been an asset, I mean, not being distracted by everyday things. Everything the clan wanted to remember was set to verse, as in a song, like the Iliad and Odyssey."

"But I thought Homer wrote that," said Ali.

Professor Morrisson smiled, "Aye, but we know the battle of Troy happened in 1186BCE or thereabouts. The story of those heroes, if they were real people, could not be written until the Greeks had developed Linear A, then Linear B...I mean that it wasn't *able* to be written down until the Greek alphabet itself was codified around 440BCE. That's why there is so much repetition in the Odyssey...how many stanzas start with "the rosy fingers of dawn" or other repetitive phrases? That's so the bard could remember the number of times he'd said that, to know where he was in the story. Those tales must have been told orally for hundreds of years before they were written down."

"So Homer just wrote down what he was told?" Ali asked.

"Even the name "Homer" means 'hostage', or the blind one who is lead around on a tether. It's a name that might not have been a real person," said Angus. "Researchers think he might have lived around 800BCE, but that is based on what various Greek historians said. Nothing could be written by his contemporaries, again, because there was no writing until the alphabet got organized."

"But the Egyptians had writing all this time?" Ali said.

"Yes, they were the masterful keepers of knowledge of the ancient world. At least until the great library at Alexandria was burned. There are some papyrus scraps in Phoenician that talk about the Trojan war, another "eyewitness" account. But those pages, some on bark, could still be someone's fiction. Anyway, Celtic people didn't have writing until the modern age."

Ali realized that the best way to date something that old would be radio carbon dating. But as a geologist, she could rely on the strata, for the history of rock was reliable. Ancient people probably didn't even have paper to write on, thought Ali, which was why using papyrus filled that need. Rocks like the Rosetta

Stone, were much better. Just had to find them! Dr. Morrisson, like Donnie, trusted evidence from people, not stone.

Dr. Morrisson interrupted her thoughts. "Even if there was a written language, it is debatable as to whether or not it was used by anyone other than the priestly class, which the Romans called "the Druids." That language is called Ogham, and it is a simple alphabet cypher of hash marks and lines. My people on Lewis speak a language called Gaidhlig, that only began to be written in the 20th century. I think they had an "orthographic convention in the '80's to figure out how to spell their words!" Professor Morrisson threw up his hands to show his frustration. "So much is lost, just lost!"

Ali began to read what Angus gave her. First, a passage from the "Declaration of Arbroath" written in 1320, demanding freedom from the English, which had this curious passage:

They journeyed from Greater Scythia by way of the Tyrrhenian Sea and the Pillars of Hercules, and dwelt for a long course of time in Spain among the most savage tribes, but nowhere could they be subdued by any race, however barbarous.[1]

Angus told her that Thomas Jefferson knew about this document when he was composing our Declaration of Independence. It seemed that long ago this migration myth had credence with Scottish nobility. The Tyrrhenian Sea was off the west coast of Italy, which was on the way to Gibraltar, which used to be called the Pillars of Hercules. At least the landmarks were real. The other documents given to Ali were various 'chronicles' and mythological stories about Finn McCool. These were more like fairy tales, with shape shifters and various battle sagas. Soon

---

1 Declaration of Arbroath, Scotland 1320

Ali couldn't concentrate on all the names and "genealogy." It was like reading the "begats" in the Bible. In no time she drifted into a fitful sleep. Angus had the stewardess bring a light blanket for her, and he carefully retrieved the paperwork without disturbing her. Better she should sleep, he thought, as all this stress of her lost brother was wearing her down. Then the cabin lights dimmed, the engines droned on, and Angus found sleep as well. The plane carried them to their landing in Spain.

EIGHTEEN

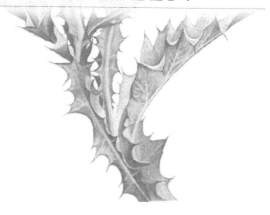

Alicante, huge city as it is, had no clues to offer as none of the many hotel concierges remembered Donald Cameron. Angus and Ali rented a car and drove to the next spot on the map: Eiche. A smaller town, but with lovely Spanish Mediterranean architecture, shaded verandas and date palms growing everywhere. On a whim, they checked at the youth hostel first, and were rewarded with news. "Si, I remember theese peoples," said the innkeeper "y la postcard. Illeta dels Banyetas. Si, they did go there." he told them.

So, soon enough they managed a boat to the quaint island, with it's many towers and crumbled ruins of open air baths. The main street had more than a few bath houses, but one in particular stood out because it was built within a ruin. Columns and marble statues decorated the place, making it look more Italian than Spanish, so it seemed distinct from the others. They checked them all however, and found that this last one was the bathhouse where Donald had purchased the bath salts. Of all the many tourists who came through there, the lady in charge was able to remember both Donald and Kemi, for they had been there late in the tourist season, when most crowds had gone for home.

"They made such a lovely pair," mused the woman. "I think they were planning to marry soon?" She alluded to the sensual nature of the massage, and how beautiful the young girl named Kemi had been. "Such a perfect couple!"

"Do you have any idea where they went from here?"asked Ali, hoping there were more clues to follow.

"Sí, I think they were charting a fishing boat. Many touristas come to me *after* going scuba diving, so maybe they did that too, *no se*. There are boats to be found along the eastern harbor side, and they would have needed a boat to go back to the mainland. I'm sorry for no other thing to tell you." The woman sincerely tried to help, her kind eyes showed concern, but she had nothing further to say. They had found the bathhouse but the breadcrumb trail ended there. Dr. Morrisson and Ali walked the length of the main street in silence, not knowing which way to go from there. Ali stubbornly kicked pebbles out of the street, angry that Donald had gone so far away without her. She felt guilty too, about not knowing more about the Houssein pair, as if being immersed in microscopic crystals had distracted her from her only living relative. *He wouldn't have gotten married without telling me, would he?*

"Let's return to the hotel," suggested Angus, "perhaps they will remember something else, or have some other ideas. The police here are certainly no help!"

"But I think Donnie would have left from here. There are boats for hire, and since the bath salts were mailed from here, maybe they left by boat? Let's go down to the waterfront and see who remembers them. It's worth a try, and I don't want to leave without every stone unturned."

The waterfront had only a few boats at anchor during the day, as most of the trawlers were already at sea with their nets. So it was an easy task to show Donald's photo to the various captains that were still in the harbor.

"Do you take tourists around the island?" Angus asked. "Do you remember a man with red hair that might have been here a few weeks back?" And as they showed the photo, one particular captain's face showed recognition. The man was agitated at first, then bowed his head and said, "Si. I took them to Gibraltar." But his face took on an even more suspicious cast, as he held his hands to his head and started to leave. Dr. Morrisson grabbed the man's arm before he could leave, and said, "This man is now missing! Please help us with information! I can pay you!!"

"No, No, señor! No mas dinero! No mas!" sobbed the man, clearly upset. "I will tell you of him. They had an argument at night, there was a storm, and the young man could not be found in the morning. I have saved his belongings because I could not report him missing."

"You did not report him missing?" screamed Ali. "What is wrong with you!"

"The other man paid me for keeping the secret," said the captain, shaking his head. "And really there was nothing anyone could do....the sea is deep. I would have big trouble with an investigation, especially taking touristas all the way to Gibraltar. Lo siento mucho." The seaman began to cry. He slumped down on the dock, curled into a ball, hoping the foreigners would simply leave. Then he looked up from under his arms to see if they'd left.

"Señor, we do not wish to cause you trouble. But you must tell us all you know. This lady looks for her brother, and you say he jumped overboard? Please give her some answers as to why he would do such a thing!" Angus was now crouched over the Spaniard, not to threaten him, but to plead with him. His tone was firm, like a brother to a brother.

"I think they were lovers, the man and the lady. But her brother, who hired me, said they no longer were in love, and the wedding was off! And he was upset that she didn't want to marry him anymore. In the morning the brother told me that the man jumped off, en suicido. There was a big storm, thunder and lightning, and I heard nothing else." Finally some word of Donald Cameron! But was this the truth?

The captain motioned for them to follow him into his boat, where he retrieved Donnie's backpack. He then sat back, resigned for the expected trip to the police station. Ali searched the pack, found no money, just Donnie's documents, and another map indicating a trip to Gibraltar. Fighting back tears, Ali said, "How far did you take them until you knew he was gone?"

"Oh, that was the morning we docked at Gibraltar that he came up missing! If he was a good swimmer, he could have made it to shore. It is what I hoped, or I would not have taken the money!" The captain tried giving his best assurance, that Donnie could have swum to shore. "Yes, I am sure he could have made it!" said the captain, repeatedly. "Es verdad!"

Angus and Ali looked at each other, knowing that it would do no good to report this man to the authorities. As a smuggler, he could spend many years in prison for something that might not have been his fault. The thought of foreign legal systems and proving anything now seemed beyond their abilities, would only slow the hunt for Donnie. Angus looked again at Ali, shrugged his shoulders, and they silently agreed to leave the captain there on the dock.

"Señor, we have your name and information. If we find that you are not telling the truth the authorities will be arresting you. If there is evidence of foul play on your boat, you will not get away with it. Do you swear you are telling us the truth?"

"Si, es verdad, con Jesu Cristo y la Madre. Es verdad." No more words were spoken, Angus nodded, then put his arm around Ali and they walked back to the hostel. He waited patiently for her to say something. When the shock had subsided, Ali said,

"Please take me to Gibraltar!"

NINETEEN

Stirling Castle, Scotland 900AD

"Until the Romans came and brought Latin to the Isles, there were no written records of our people" said the monk.

"But I've no need o' this writin,' I want to play ball wi' the other lads! Why must I learn this history? I can read. 'Tis enou' to have it written by scribers...they can tell me whatever I need to ken."

Father Mortimer was exasperated. "We're no English! We do not use 'primogeniture' to choose oor kings! You shud ken that at least! You are the Tanist. Oor kings are chosen by strength o' mind as well as arm. If you want the kingship, you'd best learn this history well! Mayhap I'll tak yer play stick tae yer backside?"

The monk was charged with educating this young Prince, stubborn spoiled fop that he was, but there was little hope for enticing the boy into the scholarly information he would need were he ever to be crowned king. The boy knew the empty threat of a beating with his ball stick was as useless as expecting maturity from the twelve year old. Silently, the old monk prayed for guidance, if not deliverance. He too wanted to be outside in the sunny courtyard, instead of sitting at the desk in the lengthening shadows.

"Alright, I'll niffer wi' you. Transcribe these next sentences correctly, an' I'll release you early. But they must be perfect, no wrong letters."

With that, the boy dipped his quill and wrote diligently, knowing that if he could control the ink he would be out playing very soon. He knew his whiny refusals would only carry him so far, and copying the few sentences was a better trade than having his mother called down to the scriptorium. So he set to work copying what the monk set before him.

As it is written in the Annals of the Four Masters" the Milesians had extended their territory to encompass the extreme northeast of Eire. Ui Niel and his people had argued over territory to the south and west, and there had been famine in the south, such that more land would soon be required. Across the water along the Oban shores, better holdings awaited if the Cruitne could be subdued. The first migration of the Dalriada began three hundred years before the birth of Our Lord. Our bloodline descends from Angus, King of Dalriada, who reigned from 384 to 325.

"Well done, my son. Clean your quill, and tell me something else about them."

The boy smiled, easily remembering this bit of history: The Dalriada are descendants of Lugh, "Long of Arm." "Riada" means "long arm." King Conaire Mor of the Erainn Kingdom, broucht his people frae Antrim in 498 Anno Domine."

"Good enough, go now and play. We will continue tomorrow. You have done well."

Father Mortimer watched as the young prince bounded out into the sunlight to play stickball with his friends. Their curved oak staffs knocked the stone ball against the castle courtyard walls, hitting shins and table legs alike. How could he interest this boy in the history of the people? Perhaps a visit to the Dunadd mountaintop where kings were enthroned, to see the carved footprints of those that came long before. There Erc, Fergus, and Loarn, sons of King Erc had invaded the shores of Jura and Islay. Soon they had driven the barbaric Cruitne all the way back from the Mull to the river Add. All of southern Argyll now belonged to the Scotti. King Erc was king until 474, and was the father of Fergus Mor. It was recorded that Angus held 430 septs, his grandson Gabrahn held 560, and Loarn held 420, so that the Dalriadic kingdom comprised at least thirty thousand souls. The "kining" was protector of the kin, both by strength in battle and provider of safety for the people. Father Mortimer did not see any such attributes in his young charge.

But those carved footprints were no longer used to sanctify their kings, as the capital had been moved from Dunadd.. Nor did he know the location of the Tanist stone throne said to be covered with runes and knotwork spells. Father Mortimer had read something curious in the Annals of the Four Masters, that his young pupil did not notice. The writer claimed that Muirceartach of Antrim had given the Stone of Destiny to Fergus, King of Dalriada, and that it was described as 'black marble.' He would love to view the stone that Kenneth MacAlpin took to his capital in Scone, in 840. But the journey to Perth would have to wait until he was free from tutoring his young charge. The image of such travels intrigued Father Mortimer for a few minutes, then left his thoughts when bells sounded for vespers. Tomorrow would be another trying day with his disinterested pupil. For now, he hastened to the peace and calm of the cloister.

TWENTY

Gibraltar: St Bernard Hospital, October, 1996

He knew he was dreaming because that same, repetitive science question plowed through his brain, as black towering waves, frozen like something out of Cecil B. Demille's Exodus, thundered all around him. The wave roared into a terrible crescendo, but didn't fall. It was suspended, anticipating some crazed conductor's baton. It was like some thundering ovation, crenelated by Valkyries mounted on watery dragons, who were crossing the crest of the wave. Little shimmering fishes were pinioned on the face of the icy wave, positioned in patterns that he knew he would see on the Jaquard bedspread when he was able to waken.

His shoes had long ago been lost, but he struggled valiantly to remove his trousers, thrashing and scissor-kicking his way to freedom. He had to hold his breath. He needed to swim to the crest of the giant wave before it could crash down and smother him. He wanted to move his arms and stroke, but his arms were held down by women, sirens of the deep, who were calling to him. "Stay with us, we will love you."

And then he was ten years old, sitting before a a bowl of lumpy oatmeal, swimming in cold milk with ice cubes. His spoon made ripples in the milk instead of moving spoonfuls to his mouth. And he hated cold oatmeal. Then Mommy, urging him to eat.

"But Mommy, when lightning hits the ocean do the fishes get electrocuted?"

"No, Dear. God tells them to swim away."

"But which way do they swim? Do they just go deeper, or do they swim left or right?"

And then, Alex Trebek waits for the $2000 question on "Double Jeopardy" as he struggles to find breath to speak. He is in a cold sweat, more lightning flashes as the buzzer sounds. Too late!

He shivers, and the stupid science question is framed again. When lightning strikes the water, how deep does it go? Does it zap only the large fish? Will it hit me? I want to live! I must find the shore, but this isn't the Charles. This is the ocean. I can barely thrust my body to the top of each swell and hope to see land. Lightning flashes in cadence to the waves, which suddenly become mobile again, cascading into thunderous roars of surf. My feet touch rocks, but all is dead still as I lay there to wait for answers. Water conducts electricity. The charge wants to be grounded. My feet touch the ground, but no answers come.

Daylight stabs his eyes as the woman in the light blue scrubs pulls the window curtains aside. Sunlight streams into the room. Something like indiscriminate elevator music wafts through the warm air. The blue and white bedspread is hopelessly tangled into knots around his feet.

"Good morning, Sir." The elderly matron of a nurse beams a soft smile toward the wreck in the hospital bed. "Tsk, Tsk. I see that you are soaked through again, and have wet your bed.   Can you be calm? You are safe here. You are all right." Her nurse's voice is soothing and kind. She touches his shoulder and smooths his damp hair from watery, red eyes.

"If I remove these restraints we can get you into dry clothes. Are you ready to get out of that wet bed?" Her eyes question his readiness, but the weary man smiles, nods, and breathes a sigh of relief.

"Today is Tuesday, and we have porridge for breakfast." She shows him a dry gown, saying, "I'll tie it for you when you are ready. First let's get you to the shower." She smiles as she helps him stand. He is still lost, but the sun shines brightly, and he can hear traffic down on the street. He makes his way to the shower, and with warm water trickling over his bruised body, he begins another day without memory. Except for the dream.

While he showered, the nurse made her notes on the bedside clipboard. She mutters, "Another nightmare, wet sheets, needed restraints. Suggest more p.m. sedatives."

In the hospital dayroom, patients sat at breakfast. Four to a table, distant stares filled each face, as medications kept the peace and quiet. He had learned to control his fears whenever he was in the dayroom. He could eat quietly, speaking little, as there was no one to really speak with anyway. Recently however, he was allowed to wear regular clothes, as he had been promoted to the freedom of eating with others. Still, if they made him sit at the window that looked over the bay, he would become agitated.

Little by little, he could manage calmness while sitting at that picture window. But it was not where he wanted to sit. He preferred his room, staring at the pink walls. The doctor though, told him he must face the world in order to reclaim his memory.

The hospital staff gave him magazines, and newspapers. He learned he was in Gibraltar, at the Inpatient Recovery wing. He knew the date, the names of his nurses, his doctor, and even knew two fellow patients by name. But little else was certain. He thought he might be a Spaniard, but he couldn't speak Spanish. Some days he thought he was British, but his accent, he was told, was American. Funny that he could talk but not remember his name.

So he sat in the dayroom, either watching the traffic or gazing at the ocean. He tried to trap stray thoughts or analyze his dream. That repetitive dream had themes he could dissect. He remembered the TV show and losing the money on Jeopardy. He remembered the Wagnerian opera as it crescendoed into Valhalla. And he remembered a kind woman called "Mommy" though he was unable to see her face. Wasn't there a fishing boat? There were nameless women. But he was nameless, too. Disjointed thoughts came and just sat.

Every morning, bright and early, his very British doctor made rounds. Dr. Alan Harrington, "stiff upper lip don't you know," was dapper and business-like, but wasn't hurried as you might expect. He called his patient Jerry Flotsam rather than "John Doe" because of the curious mystery of his arrival in Gibraltar. His advice to "Jerry" was to coax memories into consciousness, but to not try to force things. Tranquilizers or sedatives would be administered to offset violent tendencies. This was much less a threat, rather more like a safety net. But straightjackets had been employed not too long ago.

Harrington's diagnosis was "indeterminate." Either his patient had a closed head injury with 'brain damage oxygen privation insult', or an "emotional trauma" survival loop that blocked memories too harmful to remember. His prescription was "social interaction" with "behavior monitoring" in the hospital day room, as well as psychiatric counseling. He told his patient to try organizing bits of memory, either good or bad, to share with the psychiatrist once a week.

It took concerted effort, but he tried valiantly to follow those orders. His earliest, clearest memory was lying amidst rocks in the surf. He remembered crustacean covered rocks, mossy and green, in front of his swollen eyes. He remembered tiny crabs crawling over his bruised face, little white spider-like crabs looking for tasty human flesh. He remembered drinking brackish sea water and vomiting into the lapping waves around his shoulders. And he remembered being bone cold in the blackest of nights. And seagulls screaming and swooping in the brightening sky.

In the hospital library he found a book of ancient Greek myths. The mother of the muses was Mnemosyne, goddess of memory. Another myth told of five rivers where the recently dead souls were taken to drink. The river Lethe provided "oblivion, concealment, and forgetfulness" to those who tasted its waters, for the reborn soul should not be expected to remember past lives. He thought about this. Did he want to remember, or should he just begin anew? Still, he thought his name wasn't Jerry, and certainly not "Flotsam."

Other books of interest were various non-fiction titles such as "The Rise and Fall of the Roman Empire" or "History of War" in two volumes. He spent hours in the book room, looking at travelogues, political maps, and magazines such as "National Geographic." He liked that publication the most, because of the variety and beautiful photography. He felt drawn to an article about a new tomb found in Egypt, and he found comfort even just holding the open pages in his lap. Day by day his nightmares subsided. More of his personality rose to the surface, as if he was finally swimming toward the sunshine. But progress was excruciatingly slow. He still could not remember his very name.

Most days, he seemed happy, calm. He smiled at others, he learned to play some games. At first it was a simple memory game played by children. Animal pair cards were shuffled and spread face down, and whoever managed to match the most pairs was the winner. He was unbeatable at that game, because he could remember the location of the pictures even if he couldn't remember the name of the animal. The therapists had many versions of this game, some with farmyard animals, others with historical landmarks like the Eiffel Tower. He was making progress as the deck of fifty pairs was not much challenge even to his battered brain.

And there were other games. He learned to play Cribbage. Pairs and combinations of cards adding to fifteen, or runs in sequence, variations of face cards and little pegs. He liked the numbers as they were understandable and constant. The cribbage game could fill hours of distraction. When he was occupied and engaged, he was less likely to dip back into the anxiety and depression of his situation. Dr. Harrington hoped his patient would regain enough memory to function in a sheltered work place. He thought that with the British disability assistance support, his patient could eventually leave the hospital and live a relatively normal life.

Hospital routine was safe and predictable to the minute. There was little turnover with patients, so friendships began to form. Apart from oatmeal cereal and British treatment of vegetables, the food wasn't all that bad. The library in the day room filled other needs. If this was to be his life, he could accept it. On most days that is.

TWENTY ONE

Scota in Spain 303BCE

Three unhewn dolmen formed the back and arms for Scota's throne. These reddish sandstone boulders encircled the bluish-black stone seat. Engraved with the names of her birth-right and Egyptian charms of the Goddesses Maat, Neith, and Mother Isis, the stone had received additional symbols known now to her people. Spirals and triskelions adorned the topmost surface, while intricate knotwork patterns circled the stone's perimeter.

Queen Scota was dressed in her mossy green robe, embroidered with golden threads. The last rays of the sun glistened over these patterned threads so that as she entered her robe shimmered in the receding light. Tall and strong, with her red hair wild and free, Scota took her place at the head of her people. Countless gold bracelets and tooled arm guards covered her raised arms, while her tribal bodice framed her uncovered breasts. Her mother's ancient torque guarded her royal neck as if it were part of her skeleton. Rays of sun danced off the points of her golden crown. She marched the perimeter of the open air palace to tunes on harps and bagpipes, for it was to be a great celebration and feast, the advent of a new migration.

Scota lowered her arms as she seated herself. The music died away. A hush fell over the excited people, as happy faces turned to hear their beneficent queen.

"My fellow Milesians! Tomorrow we leave these lands, not in retreat, but in our nature of seafarers and adventurers. We go to conquer! Our mighty ships are ready, our plans are well formed, and tomorrow we sail for new lands. Our best breeding pairs of livestock will come with us, yet our stores are filled to bursting. Tonight we feast on the rest. We can enjoy the fruits of our labors these thirty years. We will leave behind nothing of value, and those barbaric tribes that have buffeted our settlements will find our city abandoned. Amergin and I will charm these hills against entry, so that those who enter will sicken and die. The souls of our departed will guard these lonely hearths, but their graves will never be found nor plundered. "

"My dreams have directed me to take you to our final destination, a green island of pure water and massive oak trees. These past years of drought will become distant memories. Future crops will not wither in harsh sun, for our new lands will be blessed with gentle rain and misty green valleys. This I have seen, and Amergin knows this to be true. Fear not, for the future is ours to win. We will be victorious in battle, for our arms are strong. Our people are battle ready. Open the wine casks! Let all celebrate our great migration!"

Tables laden with roasted meat were then thronged by the cheering people. Music and dance filled the open plaza. Soon multitudes of oil lamps graced the walls and niches, so that though the sun had set, all was lit and warm. A great bonfire received the bones of slaughtered cattle, sheep, and goats, bone marrow was piled in heaps for feasting. Much fruit had been dried for the journey, but other fruits had been turned into nectar for drink. Sweet candies and fruit pies were relished, for they could not be taken aboard. People ate until they could eat no more.

As many as ninety ships were boarded in the morning. Scota's three sons captained the largest ships, while Scota herself sailed on her husband's sleek warship. It saddened her to leave his grave behind, but she believed his spirit was with her always. Whatever pestilence had befallen them would stay behind in their abandoned city. As she stood on the prow, she looked out onto the receding shoreline. She could see the drystone circular houses, many now roofless, as they lay quiet and still, devoid of the bustling life that once labored there. Soon enough land was out of sight. Her brave voyage north began.

Scota remembered her many days and nights at sea of her first voyage from Egypt. She remembered the feel of the swells beneath her feet. She remembered Gamal's arm around her in safety. Tears welled in her eyes as the wind and spray buffeted her face. She wore thick woolens against the cold that was to come, for although she believed her visions of warm sunny green hills, she also knew winter would approach soon. Much work would need to be accomplished in this new land, shelter and sturdy homes built, for she had not seen visions of her new country in winter, only spring. Still, there was the promise of freedom and adventure was in her heart. She had the "Sight" as did her son Amergin.

Many times she had asked him "What do you See?"

"Tallest of trees, thick trunks. None were saplings or pale. Everywhere dark green, hills and more hills, and all green beneath the mist. Much grey rock protruding everywhere. Strong rock for battlements. And the smell of pine boughs and flowering heather filled the air."

"And what do you *See?*" Scota asked again. Her coppery hair shone like a helmet, now overlaid with silver threads. A white forelock curved across her forehead like a scythe. Amergin's mother stood straight and strong, belying her years. Her blue eyes, clear blue as cornflowers, looked on her middle son with pride.

"I see Victory." Pain flitted across Amergin's eyes, but his mother heard only his words. Amergin Gluingel was called "the poet" for his Sight gave knowledge beyond words.

So onward they sailed, north and farther north, until seagulls greeted them near the new lands. Then came a bright sunny day, with seabirds swooping their masts. Gray fins of dolphins followed alongside ships, as if to pilot them to the harbor ahead. The fleet of ships calmly lowered huge stone anchors, and men waited for the word to advance. It was decided that Amergin would make landfall first. To the new shore ahead, he recited his song of defiance. The wind and waves brought his words to those who waited on the shore. Amergin's voice sailed above the waves. His words were received, and never forgotten:

I am the wind in the deep sea,
I am the wave of the ocean,
I am Roaring sea
I am the stag of the seven combats,
I am the vulture upon the rocks,
I am the shining tear of the sun,
I am the fairest of flowering herbs,
I am the wild boar in valour,
I am a salmon in the water,
I am the tumulus of poetry
I am a lake on the plain,
I am a word of skill,
I am the point of lance of battle,
I am the God who created thought in the head of fire.
Who knows the secret of the unhewn dolmen?
Who invokes the ages of the moon?
Who teaches in the place where couches the sun?
It is I!

I am the Song on a spear,
I enchant the Wind.

Then Amergin, his brothers, and a small party of warriors rowed to a sandy spit of beach, separated a short distance from those strangers on the shore. With his mastery of languages learned from his father, Amergin Gluingel of the "white knees," delivered his ultimatum of conquest to those assembled on the beach. They seemed to be small in stature, dressed like farmers rather than warriors, and they seemed cowed by the tall Milesians dressed in battle gear. As Amergin waited, more small people came furtively out of the trees to see the ships, as they had none like the great warships of the Milesian invaders. They wanted parlay on the shore, so Amergin and his brothers Eber Finn and Eremon approached. With certainty of words with hand gestures, they told their leader they would claim this land. Unexpectedly, the people replied with courage. They asked for terms.

Amergin returned to the fleet, and came to Scota's ship to tell her of the people's request.

"What terms?"

"They asked for nine waves, time to gather their forces. Three waves for each of three queens of their land. It was an honor I felt they could have, so I agreed. We also can use the time."

TWENTY TWO

Having given his report, Amergin bowed and went to find his wife. She had finally finished the new flag, larger than the others. Her tiny stitches appliqued the edges of the red snake firmly onto its yellow background. This flag was not silk, but sturdy linen, and would withstand the slings of war. Sceine looked up, saw deep concern on Amergin's face. He was never able to hide his feelings from her, nor did he need to.

"What troubles you, my love? I know you saw victory ahead."

Amergin dropped to his knees and fingered the edge of the new flag. "I see much that I would not see. Yes, victory is ours, but not all will survive the battle. The cost is foretold."

"We could sail farther away! What good is your Sight if we cannot avoid or change it? Perhaps this flag can fly on other shores."

But Amergin was already in mourning, for the loss that he had seen was too great. Words came haltingly, as if their hearing would harden them into stone, and reality.

"No, all that I have seen will not allow change. Our Queen Mother will find her death here in this green land. It is what she has waited for with her whole life. Amergin held his head in his hands. Grief overwhelmed him. For he had foreseen the death of those closest to him.

"The lands will be ours to have forever, in peace and plenty. Even if she knew what was to come, she would give her blood willingly for our people. I did not tell her."

Sceine stroked tears from her husband's cheeks. "She is a warrior, Amergin. We have fought many times, invaders have cost us many of our people. We are not afraid of death, for it is the price of life."

"You are wise, wife. It has always been so. Yet, my heart is near breaking. It is my burden to know, and to act within this truth. Mother says my inheritance from her father is not to be questioned or dissuaded. So we will keep strong. I did not see the fullness of battle, only the outcome." Amergin struggled with thoughts, then formed more words.

"With this green misty land, of water and rivers so clean and clear, we will not suffer privation of the drought that parched our fields, nor the misery of failed crops. This new land is full of good fortune. We will build a new homeland here."

"Come, let us find sleep. Let me hold you in my arms. Your bed is prepared." Sceine snuggled close and Amergin released his cares into her breast. She was wise and spread her care over him like a blanket. He would be strong and clear-headed by the morning. The ship gently rocked as it headed north for safe anchorage. But his heart ached with his secrets, and were he not the son of a great warrior, he would have accepted defeat then and there.

In previous years, when the rains stopped and the fields gave no promise, water was more precious than gold. Bathing basins stored dry grain instead. Dust-caked skin formed wrinkled, careworn faces. There was no respite from the dry skies, and though their defensive towers kept them safe, the land had not given them enough reason to stay. They moved their enclaves farther north each year, searching for mountains that held rain clouds or rivers that could be tapped for fields. But everywhere the land had dried, forcing them finally to the ocean.

Still, freedom was not denied them, and strong ships were built for the voyage to new lands. Many ships formed their armada, filled with strong, skilled warriors. Years of defending against warring tribes of barbarians had served them well. Scota's people were prepared for whatever challenges lay ahead.

In her cabin, Scota went to her prized cedar chest. She opened the lock by turning her ancient key. In the stillness of her cabin she could hear the wooden levers click as the lock fell open. She lifted the heavy lid. Within were treasures, healing medicines and herbs, magical talismans and amulets, all packed securely within folds of silk. The chest was lighter these days, for much had been used in those years to procure health and safety of her people. She longed for a haven where there could be baths again, that luxury of soaking cares away. She had saved many linen bags of perfumed bath salts for these future baths, as she had not used them for a very long time. Water had been too scarce.

Under these top layers of bottles and bags of herbs, rested the gold relics of her childhood. Gemstones from far away Kemet slept in little silk bags, each marked with glyphs identifying their color. The Horus glyph guarded the bluest sapphires, the Maat glyph signified yellow topaz. Scota sorted through the bags until she found Kheper-Ra, for this bag held the green stones from her mother's homeland. Green bands swam over their surface like ribbons. She searched through the stones until she found the largest one, whose swirls were circular. The fine green circle in the center looked like a dark green eye, banded with varying shades of green. She held it in her palm as if it could look back at her. Scota thought of her husband Gamal, who had always been the keenest merchant, able to garner the highest values in trades, such that this original cache was but little diminished. This stone she removed, for its purpose would find it centered on her war shield.

The cedar chest was still replete with golden armlets and bracelets embossed with the glyphs of now far away gods and goddesses. They held no sway over these foreign lands. Prayers to Neith, or Tanit, or Great Mother Earth became interchanged, taking turns. Now it was an internal courage that governed her spirit. Scota felt complete. She closed the lid, secured the lock, and was satisfied. Her feet led her to the other end of the ship, to the armory, which was now a hub of activity. Koiriko and his apprentices were preparing weapons in sequence, first arrows, then spears, then short swords. Shields were vertically stacked and carefully stowed for their razor sharp edges falling free could slice an arm, or worse. Strong ropes tied through the handles kept the shields from shifting free.

Koiriko produced Scota's shield when he saw her enter for he expected new designs to charm it for the battle ahead. The old Milesian's bright eyes had not dimmed with age though his skin was as tough and brown as the leather he worked.

"I have a green gemstone for my shield's heart," said Scota. She extended her palm to show him the stone from Karkissa, the green bands seemed to writhe around their central eye. "And I would like the red snake to flow around it, arching upwards, much like the glyph of Isis. For I am the Mother."

Koiriko positioned the stone under the bend of the snake. "Yes, it will fit perfectly here. The soft leather bezel will harden soon, making it irremovable. It shall be done today, my Lady." He smiled with reverence, for their friendship had stood strongly for these thirty years. Then Scota looked to her recurve bow, examined the string, and found it was healthy and strong. Arrows fletched with bright yellow feathers filled the quiver, no room for even one more, though there were bundled groups of matching arrows nearby. No mere bird points here, only sharp, deadly death. She thought of the island people so long ago who had valued her yellow fletched arrows. And of Uncle, who had taught her to aim them.

Interrupting her from this reverie, Koiriko wanted to show off the war shields. Milesian shields were round, nearly impenetrable layers of leather, reeds, and more leather.

"My Lady, here I have the top leather surface, tanned stiffer than wood. It might permit an arrow point partway, but then the spongy reed center can spring up to collect the missile's force. This makes it lightweight, but nearly impenetrable."

Scota fingered the unfinished edge of the shield, and she could plainly see the layers Koiriko showed her. As she pinched the edge of the shield, she could feel the sponginess, and understood his cleverness.

"Your invention of these layers will protect many warriors. How fortunate that we have your skills! Our shields are much superior to those we saw of the hated Persians. I am thankful for your creation."

Koiriko bowed and smiled. "It is not my invention, my Lady, but from our city of Miletus far away. We learned much in our marketplaces. But, my invention is on the reverse."

Koiriko turned the shield to show the back of the shield, where he had positioned two handles which allowed the warrior to support the shield with the entire forearm. At close combat the shield arm could slice and deflect sword and spear thrusts.

"I am proudest though with the outer edge..." Sharp-toothed bronze formed the perimeter, able to slash spear shafts or break sword blades. Shields were both offense and defense, covered with magical glyphs and family crests. This was the pride of the clan, much more than a sword. Scota fingered the sharp edge carefully, imagining its destructive force.

Koiriko's work would assure superior weaponry over the more primitive island people, putting the odds in the favor of skill rather than sheer numbers. Amergin had given no estimate of the defenders' strength of number, but they seemed vulnerable in weaponry.

"Have you made new helmets as well?" Scota asked, as she looked at a bin filled with headgear. Thick tanned leather was often used for helmets, though some warriors preferred polished bronze. Some were plumed with cock feathers, but many sprouted horns like some charging bull. All had chin guards, curved like wings over cheekbones. They were longer in the back, to protect against a neck strike. Each one was light in weight but protective, and covered with magical glyphs, and the wearer's name. Some Milesians wore the gold torque of Scota's heritage instead.

"I think there are enough, my lady. Also, I have made a new leather cuirass, shin guards, breastplates, and leather aprons. My apprentices have not been idle."

"With these garments and arms, our warriors will be invincible," said Scota smiling. When you feel the ship turn south, you will have but a few more days' preparation. But I see you and your workers have already prepared much. Be sure to find rest soon, for the battle is not only about our weapons, but about my heart's promise. Victory has been foreseen."

Koiriko was pleased. "I do not doubt your magic, My Lady. The weapons are our finest we have ever had. I will give the men rest. Perhaps you could bring your harp here to play for them, let the sound fill every sword and sling stone." He smiled, knowing that was Scota's plan to complete preparations.

"You have my thoughts exactly, Koiriko," said Scota. "I know just the song to play, for both our weapons and our warriors. We will wait for the ship's turn to the south.

TWENTY THREE

Spain, October, 1996

Dr. Morrisson made preparations immediately upon returning to Eiche, and with bus fares in hand, they would make Gibraltar by the next morning. Ali still wasn't saying much, as if speaking about the story would make Donnie's death actual, rather than just a disappearance. She was hoping against hope that he would be found. But where?

Finally, Angus began to list the possibilities for searching. "We should visit the police station, the hospitals, and go from there. Was...Is Donnie a good swimmer?" he asked.

Ali nodded, "Yes, he had a lot of experience swimming while he lived in Boston. He was on a rowing team for years, and laughed about swimming in the polluted Charles...It's very cold, you know, but cleaner these days."

"That's good information, my dear," said Angus. "Dinna fash yerself. I mean, keep your hopes up. We will find him for sure!"

Gibraltar, with its British dependency, has an efficient bureaucracy unparalleled by anything in Spain. Ali and Angus went first thing in the morning to the British authorities in charge of immigration, and opened a missing person file. But Immigration had no record of either Donald or the Hussein pair. They had disappeared as well, though the trawler captain had assured Angus that he had delivered them safely. Then Angus and Ali took photos of Donald to the morgue, where Ali was relieved to be told that they had no body resembling her brother. Having the photo of Donnie was a saving grace, as at least, Ali did not have to view any corpses.

"Where to go now?" asked Ali. "If he had washed up on shore he would have been in the morgue." Her voice was quavering, and she began to lose hope.

"We haven't checked the police," said Angus. "Perhaps that is our next stop."

The police station proudly displayed the colors of the Union Jack. Uniformed officers sat at various desks, quietly arranging papers, and computer printers were spewing reports. It looked rather like the office of a large business, rather different than an American police station with guns, lapel cameras, and booking stations.

"It would have been three or four weeks ago," Ali told the sergeant in charge. "He might have had some injuries or nearly drowned. We think he may have floated to shore. Please check any records of that week."

"Your brother is one lucky Yank!" said the sergeant, his face beaming over the happy coincidence. As the excellent detective he was, tying up loose clues gave him the greatest pleasure, though happy endings were few in his line of work. With a dramatic pause, he smiled at Ali, as if he was Santa bringing the best gift of her life.

"A fisherman pulled a young man from the water only half alive. None of the fishermen recognized the lad, nor had there been any boats in distress. It was a complete mystery to find him, not only alive, but obviously he was not from around here. He was sent to hospital immediately. By my records, he is still there. Seems to have amnesia by this last report."

The detective was leafing through his reports, but found no updates on the man's condition or identity. He then procured the appropriate paperwork to give to Ali.

"We had no way to contact relatives since the man had no identification, and couldn't even remember his name. Please fill out this paperwork with your contact information and we will have you taken forthwith to St Bernard's!"

Ali nearly collapsed with this news. Her knees began to buckle. Angus reached for her waist, then had her sit in a nearby chair. "Great news, Lassie! We have found him!"

Ali seemed to be in a daze, speechless at first. Her emotions had been kept in such tight control that the sudden release was overwhelming. Then she exploded with , "Thank you! Thank you! Thank you!" It was like thanking the Universe for all things good in the world. She hugged Angus. Tears of joy streaked her cheeks. "Thank you! Thank you!" was all she could blurt out.

Angus took the clipboard the detective offered, and began filling in the required blanks. The detective made copies of their passports, then called for transportation to take Angus and Ali to Gibraltar's hospital.

"The hospital will be expecting you. Don't hesitate to let us help you in any way. We wish you the best! It's been my pleasure to assist you."

TWENTY FOUR

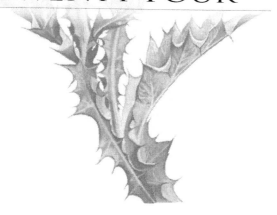

Harbor View Road curves to the north of St. Bernard Hospital. Its massive building blocks any view of the harbor unless you are on the top floor "day room," which is where Donald Cameron sat, viewing the harbor. Angus and Ali had a meeting with the head nurse before going into the bright room.

"We do have a patient that fits your description," said Nurse Jenkins, "but he has been non-verbal and very agitated. It's only been this week that the doctor has removed his restraints and decreased the tranquilizers. He had been difficult to manage, you see."

"What is the diagnosis, please?" asked Ali.

"He presents a "closed-head injury," which is internal brain damage. Swelling inside the skull or oxygen starvation may be the cause, as he might have hit his head severely. Or, it could be mainly severe emotional trauma. He was pulled from the sea."

"What is the prognosis?" asked Angus.

Nurse Jenkins shrugged her shoulders as if to imply that nothing could be done, but then replied, "He may suddenly snap out of it, or maybe never. He has been non-verbal to all the languages we tried, but a few words in English make him sound American. Perhaps seeing a familiar face will jog his memory. You should not give up. At least he seems happier these last few days."

Ali nodded, anxious to see her brother, she started to enter the room.

"You might try music," said Nurse Jenkins as an after-thought. "Sometimes hearing a certain tune or song will click. We only play mild background music on the ward, indiscriminate sound that is soothing. Perhaps you have some ideas?"

Ali thought a bit, then began to whistle something from their childhood. A music box, shaped like a little wooden chalet, had played this tune when they were children, and it was Donnie's favorite, because the song didn't resolve. It was like the "song that never ends" since the music box kept repeating the same twenty odd notes until the spring wound down. Then he would give the crank more twists, and the notes would tinkle for more minutes. Her whistle was clear and strong as she formed the notes to the theme of "Rigoletto."

Donnie was sitting by the window, just staring at the harbor below. As he heard Ali's whistle a smile emerged on his lips, and he closed his eyes. Ali kept whistling, and eventually stood before Donnie. She smiled as she recognized her long lost brother, but there was no recognition in his eyes.

"Donnie? Are you there? It's Ali...."

Slowly, like walking up the last of the long flight of stairs near the top of the Empire State building, a dawn of recognition moved into the eyes of Donald Cameron. His eyes became focused on the red-haired freckled girl he remembered as his sister, and he said, "Ali?"

"Yes! Thank God we've found you!" Ali threw her arms around her brother like never before. Tears exploded and soon they were both crying. As were all the onlookers on the ward. Many had tried to converse with him these recent days, to no avail. Everyone was cheering for this welcome sight. The floor nurse called the doctor assigned to Donnie, who arrived hurriedly, his white coat flapping as he ran to meet them.

"What luck! I've been sedating this handsome young man because of his agitation. He was violent toward the nurses until just lately. You are relatives?"

"Donnie is my brother. I'm Alison Cameron, and this is Dr. Angus Morrisson, who is helping me find my brother. We came all the way from California, tracing postcards that Donnie had sent. Is he able to be released?"

"Yes, with supervision and proper identification. He appears to know you, thank goodness. The MRI showed no physical brain damage, and all our tests were unremarkable. It may be an emotional blockage hindering his memory. We can release him to you with a bit of paperwork."

Ali showed Donnie's passport to the doctor, who was genuinely ecstatic over the good luck of his favorite patient. The records clerk began typing up release papers. In short shrift he was free to go.

"No charge my dears," said the receptionist. "It warms our hearts to see Jerry find his life again. We are relieved to see a happy conclusion to his stay here. Best wishes to you all."

Soon they were walking out the front doors of the huge hospital, traffic hustled down the Harbor View Road. Ali could not contain her excitement.

"Oh Donnie, I've been so worried. Meet Dr. Morrison, who helped me. We have searched and searched for you. What do you remember? Do you know where you are?"

"Am I in Boston?" asked Donnie, seeing all the traffic on the busy road.

"You were in hospital, this is Gibraltar! And you swam here!" said Ali.

Donnie looked perplexed, and Ali could see that he was still lost. It would take time, but she was going to make it her life's mission to restore her brother. "Let's get something good to eat!" said Donnie, and they knew he was on the road to recovery!

Physically, Donald Cameron appeared strong and hardy. Even the deepest bruises and contusions had healed. But mentally, he seemed broken, as if he'd lost part of himself in the cold waters off Gibraltar. The trio checked into a large hotel near the waterfront, the butte of Gibraltar was off in the distance covered in mist. The weather had been stormy, with low clouds and rain, and seagulls perched on the balcony outside their room. They squawked for tidbits, knowing that tourists often fed them if they were persistent. As soon as Ali closed the draperies, the birds took off to find other prospects.

"Donnie, we need to get you some clothes. The good news is that we have your passport, but you can't go around Gibraltar in what the hospital gave you."

"You have my passport?" Donnie did not understand how that could be, but nodded about his need for clothes. The khaki tan one-piece jumpsuit wasn't even long enough to cover his ankles.

"We found the fisherman who brought you to Gibraltar. He told us you had committed suicide, and that he didn't know what to do with your backpack. Luckily he saved it, I guess guilty for not reporting you missing. But that's past. No worries, now. Do you remember why you're here?"

Donnie's face was blank as if the answer to that question was caught in some quicksand bog far away. He was struggling to remember, as he had been these many weeks, but nothing would dredge up. He shook his head, sadly.

Ali's eyes filled with unwept tears, her eyes shone as she tried to keep the tears from spilling out. "Do you remember sending me a package from a bathhouse? I got bath salts from you, from Spain."

Still no sign of faint recollection was on Donnie's empty face. Thankfully, he remembered his sister's name, and how to talk, but little else. Dr. Morrison was watching from the next room, then came to offer some ideas.

"Let's get our chap some clothes, some good food, and get some professional help. A full belly can do wonders to ease all this upset, Dinnae push him. He's no yet ready."

Ali nodded, gave Donnie a quick hug, and they walked out to the street into the hubbub of the crowded British city. A large department store loomed ahead, and in no time they had Donnie dressed like a tourist, with several changes of clothes in the shopping bag. Donnie picked out several shirts in blue, a light jacket, and a pair of sunglasses finished the effect. They explored a few streets, but they were all hungry after the morning's excitement.

Restaurants had menus in their front windows, and Donnie chose one place called "Gatsby's." It was quite late to call it lunch, but now the restaurant was nearly empty, and would be taking dinner reservations soon. They feasted on thick, hot soup, fish and prawn kebabs, and let Donnie order several desserts to fill his sugar barometer. Hot English tea calmed them all as the afternoon sun began to set on the horizon. Still no memories bubbled to the surface without a framework to fit them in. Ali began to form a scaffold of memories, thinking Donnie could just fill in the blanks bit by bit as he recovered. Gently, she began to talk about herself, and their childhood, to see if he remembered anything beyond her name.

"We grew up in California, where Dad was a machinist, and Mom was a librarian. Do you remember our house there in Los Gatos with lots of tall trees?"

"Yes, and I remember the music box tune. We used to play it in our treehouse. And we pretended pirates were coming all the time. But Mom and Dad are dead."

Ali nodded, sure he could remember more in time. "You went to school in Boston to study Egyptology, but I stayed near home to study Geology. I have a roommate named Pam back in California, where I'm going to school at UCLA. I'm studying geology 'cause I like rocks." Donnie nodded but only listened distractedly. "Dr. Morrisson is a professor of Archaeology there, and teaches about Egypt stuff." Still, no glimmer of interest crossed Donnie's eyes. "Do you remember living in Boston and rowing on the Charles?"

"Maybe, the water was cold there, and I don't like the cold water. I swam and swam, and it was dark. I hated watching the water in the bay at the hospital. But they put me there to watch it every damn day. I tried to get away!"

"No wonder they had you in restraints! Donnie, you did swim there in Boston, but it was here that you were swimming in the dark. You swam to shore here in Gibraltar," explained Ali.

"That's silly, Sis. Nobody could swim from Boston to Gibraltar."

Repressing a giggle, Ali said, "No, you were already in Spain." She spread out the postcards on the tablecloth for Donnie to see, in sequence. He looked at the first one, then several others, but stopped when he saw the card from "Illeta dels Banyetas." Like sunlight coming slowly through an ever so slightly cracked boat hatch, memories filtered in like wounded soldiers. Donnie nodded his head, and remembered the massage he had there. He remembered dark almond eyes of a girl but not her name.

"It feels like closed little doors in my head," said Donnie. "Doors I want to open but they are locked. That's frustrating because I don't have keys. I feel like letting them stay locked and closed up. I'd rather know what we should do now. Are we going back to the States?"

"We could, Donnie, but since you're well enough, let's pretend we're on vacation here. We could look around Gibraltar first. Dr. Morrisson wants to go to Scotland."

"Why? Are you from there? I guess you do sound Scottish. We had a very Scottish father who taught us to like haggis and oatmeal. I do remember that thick porridge scooped like an ugly blob into my dish. But shortbread and scones were nice."

"Leave it to a boy's stomach to know what he likes," jested Dr. Morrisson. "But please call me Angus. There's a lot to like about home cookin' for sure. But 'tis the history of my homeland that brings us here to Gibraltar and Spain. You sent your sister a translation, and some papyrus artifacts that talked about a princess. That's the mystery at hand now. I don't think we need to stay here for a vacation. A trip to Ireland and Scotland will make a more sense now, as we're following a princess named Scota."

Donnie blinked his eyes as the echo of the name was repeated on his lips. "Scota, Scota. I found her name, didn't I?" Donnie smiled, because he knew something more. "She was an Egyptian, and I did some excavating. I remember finding something important, and being happy about that."

Ali hugged her brother. "That's right, and that's enough for now. Let's get some flight plans and start a new chapter on this mystery! I'm for heading north!"

Knowing it would take a few days to plan a trip to the Isles the trio visited the points of interest in Gibraltar. The Butte had walking trails, views of the ocean, and history that seemed to refill Donnie's reservoir. Caves and tunnels riddled the massive promontory, but sunshine and sea air revived their spirits. Little by little facts and dates, history and anecdotes began to fill the empty crevices in Donnie's memory. The "long-term" knowledge was just under the surface, waiting to be snagged by little hooks of recognition. But the short-term traumas seemed gone forever, taken like some computer virus.. The hard-drive would open, but the screen saver and all the new data was lost. A blessing really, thought Ali, best to never open those chapters again.

There were fierce Barbary macaques in cages at the zoo. They no longer ran wild, too dangerous to tourists. Modern cages kept them safe from the predatory raptors that used Gibraltar as a flyway. Still wild, they pretended to charge with teeth barred, howling their distinctive shrieks, as the tourist guide pointed at them. Their shaggy brown fur blended in with the scrub juniper in their caged enclosure. They moved as a troupe to share fruits at feeding stations. Donnie had a wistful look at seeing the baboons. Ali took a photo.

"I remember reading that when they were excavating Stonehenge they found the skull of a Barbary ape," Donnie said suddenly. "I always thought that was weird, since they wouldn't make good pets. And surely not used for a sacrifice. It couldn't have been indigenous to the British Isles, so someone long ago brought it. Maybe they had a zoo, too."

"Yeah, couldn't have been their mascot," laughed Ali. "I can't see why anyone would bring that screaming thing for a pet. Do you remember if there was anything special about the burial site, I mean were there other relics found?"

"No, just the odd skull of an ape. No reason for it being there. I don't think any human burials were ever found at Stonehenge either. But near one standing stone they did find some faience beads, like from a broken necklace. You know, Egyptian paste beads."

Ali nodded, happy inside that he remembered the name for the beads. "Trade stuff no doubt. Or some ancient tourist lost her necklace there. Plus the odd Roman coin or two. Would you like to go to Stonehenge?"

Angus chimed in, "Sure, but there is another site like Stonehenge not very far from here. Actually it's in Portugal. It's called Almendres Cromach and has 96 standing stones in a circular formation. It's not as impressive as Stonehenge, but we could walk among the stones. At Stonehenge they don't let you walk through it, too many kooks, I guess. I propose we go to Portugal first, then Ireland, because according to the invasion stories, that's where Scota's people made landfall."

"I'm in favor of leaving this bay for sure," said Donnie. Why Portugal?"

"There are Celtic sites all over Spain and Portugal from Neolithic times up to the Iron Age. The "oppida" look just like Bronze Age sites in the British Isles. The dwellings are circular drystone walls, which at one time supported timber walls and thatched roofs. The ancient Celtic style in Scotland looks just like those oppida in Spain and Portugal. But since we are here in Gibraltar I think we could go north to those Celtic sites I've heard of. They would be on our way. Let's go to Evora first to see the standing stones, then on to Mozinho, in a city called Penafiel. We can take the bus north to Evora.

Angus was as delighted as a schoolboy on a field trip. He danced a little jig at the bus station window, turned, and with a flourish, presented three tickets to Evora.

"My treat," he said. "We'll be there tonight."

At the ticket line at the bus station, Donnie's tall frame and red hair stood out among the shorter travelers. His face was bright with adventure, excited to leave Gibraltar behind. The station was crowded, for it was the weekend, and many tourists would be on their way home. In a far corner, a dark-haired girl with almond eyes watched the trio board the bus. Her heart skipped a beat and for a second, a tear threatened to wet her lashes. "*Out of all the gin joints,*" she murmured to herself. She was alone, going somewhere, with guilty memories of what could have been. She watched silently as the man she once truly loved, strolled arm in arm with a red-haired chick out of the bus station, out of sight.

TWENTY FIVE

On the bus Ali watched the tree-filled scenery go by. Mountainous vistas and curvy roads made her feel carsick for awhile, and the bus air-conditioning wasn't really up to standard. Angus tried to distract her stomach with information, but Ali was intent on fixing Donnie's memory.

"I thought those Stonehenge circle-type things were only in Britain," said Ali. "Now we're finding them here, too?

Angus said, "Megalithic people were all over the world at one time. Their stone structures are all that remain of their civilization. It is next to impossible to date the stones as they weren't burial places, though sometimes cairns or other rock tombs were found nearby. There are stone megalith structures in Egypt, some in the near east, but mainly they are in Brittany and the Isles. There's a place in Turkey called Gobekli Tepe that is really similar. There are strange ruins in Peru called Puma Punku that once were near sea level. It's now high in the mountains, like 10,000 feet up. You know how tectonics and geology can cover whole civilizations. You'll see the one in my hometown called Callanish when we go there. But there's no way of telling if the standing stone circles belong to one culture, or which millenia. But they are similar."

Donnie was listening, then said, "I like that the one in Portugal is called 'Cromlech' cause that reminds me of those stories about Conan the Barbarian. Wasn't his head god called "Crom?"

Ali laughed, "Yes, I remember those stories. Crom wasn't very touchy feely, he liked death in battles. You would think of that!"

But Donnie was secretly happy to remember those childhood days, of reading Conan stories. He could almost feel the thoughts coming up from the depths near the base of his neck, moving through his head to his forehead. He was happy and content just thinking about Conan, Stonehenge, and being with Ali and Angus. They settled into watching the villages go past their windows. It was all like a dream to Donnie.

A small city called "Guadalupe," outside of Evora, offered hotels and rest for the trio. But in the morning they hired a driver to take them down the dusty unpaved road to the stone circle known as Almendres Cromlach. There were no guides, and the only people there were a few young explorers having a picnic in the shade of the stones. Trees surrounded the site, and Donnie could tell by the orientation that the ancient megalithic people were concerned with astronomy. One stone had many circular pits, as if they had been doing 'trial and error' to find an orientation for the equinox. But there were no carvings other than a few circles carved into one standing stone.

"I thought the stones would be fat on top, so they could support a crosspiece," said Donnie. "This is really different than I expected, with their rounded tops."

"Seems like a ceremonial place rather than a temple with a roof. We will probably never know who built these sites, or why," said Angus. But, it was a lovely site to visit as they walked quietly among the stones for several hours. Like Stonehenge in Britain, the civilization that raised these standing stones was older than the pyramids. With no written language, few symbolic carvings, and no ceremonial burials, the stones just stood silently in their circle, like a gigantic clock face with no hands. And always the local people claimed the circles were erected by giants.

Ali began to hum an old song as they continued weaving through the stones. She wished she had her little lap harp, to play that mournful song playing in her head. It was a song about leaving the misty mountains of home, a song for people leaving their homeland. As the trio came full circle, back to their first stone, it was time to head back to the village. Everyone was quiet and pensive, as if the dolmen had imparted the forlorn feelings of a lost people. Hardly a breeze stirred, and a quiet hush came over the tall pine trees as the piney smell followed them like a shadow. Time to go, and the sightless stones watched as the trio of visitors rode with their driver back to Guadalupe. They would be back to Evora at nightfall, and another day's travel would take them to the airport at Porta.

"Our next stop out of Porta will be Penafiel," said Angus. "There are many Celtic or Galician sites nearby that I've always wanted to see. Near Mozinho there is a huge statue of a Celtic or Galician warrior, and he is wearing a kilt!"

Donnie smiled as another lost memory began to surface in his thoughts. He smirked with the recognition that some old memories could be snatched. "Our dad always wanted me to wear the kilt, but I felt very self-conscious. We had to dress up for Burn's Supper and parade the haggis into the banquet room, with the piper blaring, leading the way. As a little boy I hated dressing up like that, but now I'd wear it anytime."

"The kilts were worn by many nations in the Bronze Age," said Angus. "But people forget that the Celts were in Iberia before coming to the British Isles. The tartan dyes and their formulas originated in Spain, too. I just would like to see those ruins, since we have the opportunity."

"I think walking among some ruins would help Donnie's memories," said Ali. "It's a good idea to go see Mozinho." And to Donnie, "Do you remember being an archaeologist?"

"That seems right, Sis. But didn't you say there was an Egypt connection? My head seems fuzzy about things, but I mainly remember the name "Scota.""

"We will fill you in little by little, my boy," said Angus. "We'll get you back in the saddle, and Penafiel is a good place to get the feel in your fingers. We can take a plane though, no more stuffy buses."

TWENTY SIX

Angus, Ali, and Donnie settled into their seats, and soon the plane lifted off for the short flight to Penafiel. After stowing away their carry-on bag in the overhead, Ali retrieved some of the papers Angus had given her. She had the aisle seat, with Donnie in the middle. She wanted to share some things with Donnie, and let him read the highlighted passages for himself.

"Angus gave these things to me. I haven't read them all, but this part about the Milesian's Invasion of Ireland is cool." She passed the clipped paper to Donnie as she sat down, and pulled the tray table down to her lap, to hold the rest of the documents.

"Here it says they sailed across the Tyrrhenian Sea, through the Pillars of Hercules, and spent years in Spain." She pointed to the highlighted portion of the Declaration of Arbroath.

Donnie looked at the passage, and remembered something, something about a translation that told of privation, drought, and attacks from warring tribes.

"Did I translate something Egyptian about this?" Donnie asked.

"You sent it to me from some island off Spain. I have your letter, and the translation here." Ali leafed through the papers in the folder and found the notes Donnie had sent so many weeks ago. She handed it to Donnie, as if they were gold leaf, fragile and tentative, worried that it might cause harm to his rehabilitation.

Donnie began to read his notes, his translations, and looked at Ali. Quietly, as if dawn was breaking, he said, "Don't worry, Sis, I can handle it."

But moments later tears formed and he began to weep uncontrollably. Donnie buried his head in his jacket and quietly cried. The realization that he could still read hieroglyphics was little solace to the fact that he couldn't remember where the inscriptions came from. He knew he'd mailed the pages to Ali, but he couldn't remember where he was when he mailed them. When the cloudburst of despair finally lifted, he dried his eyes and returned to the pages, reading down to the last words on the last page.

Angus, at the window seat, also watched Donnie's face as his eyes moved over the translations. Donnie smiled when he came to the name "Scota Nefara-Selkis." Angus was relieved as he saw that Donnie had regained his calm pensive attitude. But to Donnie, his note to his sister was a mystery. He could not remember why he wrote it or why he sent bath salts. It was like reading words written by another person, a person he didn't know. But the copies of ancient papyrus and their Egyptian translations brought a sense of proud expertise to Donnie. He was proud of what he had written, proud to know he had had a valuable skill. He vowed he would regain this ability.

"I have a pamphlet about the museum at Penafiel," said Angus, as he put the shiny trifold into Donnie's hand. You can see the layout of this Celtic fortress, clearly Bronze Age, and the artifacts they excavated there. And here's a photo of the "warrior statue" on the grounds. Quite a pair of huge strong calf muscles on that guy!"

Donnie looked at the glossy photos that showed the half pillar of a Galician warrior. Incised lines portrayed the woven threads of a kilt, tightly wrapped around a strong pair of legs. The torso and head were missing, but the warrior clearly wore a kilt.

The other photos showed remains of a mountain fortress with fifty or more ruined rock dwellings surrounding a central hub. A thick drystone wall encircled the hill fort, evidence of needed protection from invaders. There was a long gated roadway with well worn ground, and what looked like wells and storage areas, but no standing stones like those at Cromlech. It was called " Castro Monte Mozinho."

"These people also built round towers," said Donnie. "I think they were called 'Torreon.'"

Angus smiled, knowing that little pieces of Donnie's memory were returning, like being in a curiosity shop where more things were returned to their dusty places on the shelves.

"I'm from Lewis," said Angus, "where we have something called a 'Tor', a tower just like those found in Spain and Portugal. When we get to my home, I'll take you to the Lewis Tor. It's also called a Broch, but it is the same construction, round and conical, but no outside windows. They don't seem to be used like watch towers to our modern eyes. It would be great to know what they were really for."

Donnie nodded, contented that he was on this trip with a professional archaeologist. Ali was listening to them too, realizing that Donnie's memory was returning layer upon layer, like artifacts unearthed in chronological order. The engines of the plane droned on as Donnie looked at more papers and read more passages of invasion stories. His face was bright and shiny by the time they landed and his feet tripped with exuberance as he bounded down the stairs.

"Hey! We're in Portugal! I'm not in Boston anymore! Oh, yeah, we were in Gibraltar, I know," said Donnie when he saw Ali's stiff grin.

Ali tried to hide her concern with a big smile whenever she saw that Donnie's understanding was still very flaky. He was more like a little boy than her older brother. He would need a lot of careful tending in the days and weeks to come.

The bus trip from the airport to Penafiel turned into a day-long trip, as there were many stops along the way, giving the feeling of the mountainous area of northern Portugal, its friendly people, and the Galician character of the many town names they passed. Angus filled in much of the Castro culture history, and talked about Late Bronze Age metallurgy, details of the worshipped gods and goddesses, and the typical Celtic motifs carved everywhere, like the triskelion symbol. Donnie soaked it up like a sponge, filing similarities between Scottish and European Celts, though he could see no connection with Egyptian culture other than the princess' name.

Finding lodging in Penafiel was easy and the tour of Mozinho fortress was a gift to legs tired of sitting. They walked the ancient city, which had been an expansive fortress for thousands of people. Though wooden buildings had long since disappeared there was evidence of long ago battles. Ali pointed out this evidence, especially along the outer walls and main wall opening where there once must have been a massive wooden gate.

"This rock has been vitrified," said Ali. "You can see the mica and magnetite in the stone has turned to glass, formed by extreme heat. It would take over a thousand degrees of sustained heat to alter the stone into this glassy state, as if wooden ramparts blazed for days to cook the stone."

"Do you think it was the attackers?" asked Donnie. "Maybe the people themselves burnt the stone walls to make them shiny or hard for more protection."

"No one knows. There are no histories to read. Maybe when they were attacked they started fires along the walls, and added timber from houses to the pyre to keep the attackers away. If the whole city gave up their houses to burn fires along the walls, they would be safe as long as the fires burned. I can't imagine that they did that though because it would destroy their city."

Angus touched the vitrified stones, as if they could tell their secrets. "There are settlements all over Portugal just like this one, and all seem to have been abandoned around the same time. Perhaps Scota's report of grave drought ended this civilization. With the advance of Iron Age weaponry, and a drought, perhaps the people themselves did destroy their cities by burning all the timbers of the homes. What we see here is the end of a culture, with the Romans soon to come."

They walked freely among the ruined houses and streets, quietly listening to the treeless landscape. It was hot and humid on the hilltop fortress, eerily vacant of animals other than birds overhead. Perhaps the dirt was a bit discolored there, but Donnie stubbed his shoe purposefully at a little mound in the corner of one enclosure. Sure enough a bit of linen string emerged from his stubbing, and as the compacted dirt fell away a tiny linen bag was revealed. Ali grasped his pant leg to stop Donnie's kicking, and Angus bent down to blow on the earth.

"How are you so lucky, my boy," said Angus, "that in all this expanse of ruin to find a little spot worth digging!" With a little tug on the bag, it came free. Coins clinked out into Angus' palm. He held them out for Donnie to see.

"Silver drachma. Three Roman coins," said Donnie.

"Should we put them back?" asked Ali.

"Not necessary," came a female voice behind them, as a tour docent speaking English came up behind them. A little name tag in both Portuguese and English was attached to her red guide's vest. She held out her small hand to retrieve the artifacts.

"We find things like that occasionally, but the major finds have already been excavated by sonar and metal detectors. The recent rains have dislodged a few small finds such as these and we put them in the museum."

"Thank you," said Ali, "we would not have kept them. These men are archaeologists and my brother is just pure lucky. We're glad you are monitoring the site."

"Yes, this was my Fall Semester, said the young woman. I'm an exchange student from Chicago, just volunteering here while the tourist season winds down. My name is Valerie Belshaw." She straightened her name tag for emphasis, trying to look more official. She was barely five feet tall, her freckles and red hair made her look like a diminutive "Strawberry Shortcake" in a short red vest.

"Pleased to meet you," said Donnie, offering his hand. "I just stubbed my toe there, and the bag came out."

"No worries," said Valerie. "I need to mark this spot on our diagram of the ruins to record their provenance. These are Roman coins, not especially valuable. I'll turn them in for you. Have a nice visit in Portugal, and do visit the museum."

Everyone nodded their good-byes and as the day was spent, Angus suggested the museum as their next stop. "Bus to the museum in fifteen minutes," he said as he looked at his watch. "Ley's see Penafiel Museum before we call it a day."

Along a busy street, the Penafiel Museum was a two story building housed in an old row of buildings, whitewashed like all the other houses on the street. Inside were three well lighted rooms containing glass covered cases. Arched windows set into exposed brickwork filtered sunlight onto the polished terrazzo tile floors which had been hardened by years to a waxed sheen. Displays held the regional artifacts of Galician culture for all to see. Everywhere the motif of the three armed triskelion blazed its symbol of "life, death, rebirth." Other spirals and obvious Celtic motifs were carved on small statues, stone bowls, and wooden implements. Wooden oars for stirring wine in vats had carved handles with the same design, and were on display with many other wooden implements for the kitchen use. Few weapons or metalwork of any kind were in the museum but one case had a display of coins, mostly Carthaginian, some Roman. In the last room was a display of textiles, scraps of linen undergarments and one wool cloak.

"This is a tartan weave," said Angus, pointing to the cloak. "The colors are muted but the weave is a definite tartan twill. It might even be plaid though since the colors have faded, it's hard to tell a pattern. Still, the type of weave is only found in true tartan cloth."

"Like what's found in Scotland?" Ali asked.

"Weaving like this came to the British Isles from here, to be sure," said Angus. "And the dye formulas for the colors have been traced to here, and Spain. They used vegetable dyes from moss and lichens, and certain berries for the brighter colors, mostly browns and blues. Then the dye was set with a mordant, usually urine."

"I know about "waulking the wool" in Scotland," said Ali. I saw a demonstration of ladies singing and working the wool at a Celtic festival back home. They sang songs, mostly call and repeat, and moved the wool in a circle around the table with their hands."

"Yes, they still do that on Lewis," said Angus. "Maybe when we get there you'll get a live demonstration. Mostly now that they have electricity they just use a washing machine."

Donnie laughed. "Well, ladies these days have better use of their time. I'm hungry now though, let's find a place to eat!" Ali smiled, seeing that at least her brother's stomach remembered his true nature, always hungry and able to eat huge amounts of food, while never gaining an ounce of fat.

They settled on a nearby restaurant, ordered a bottle of red wine, and selected entrees from the menu.

"May I join you?" said that voice with a Chicago accent. It was Valerie, smiling at the coincidence of finding the American tourists. Petite and red haired, Valerie had a smile that opened up to easy conversation. Gregarious and unassuming, Valerie found it easy to make friends with perfect strangers anywhere.

"I'm done for the semester, and you people were my only American visitors at Mozinho this last week. Did you enjoy the ruins?"

"Please do join us," said Angus. "I think we did enjoy our side trip to Portugal, though the museum was pretty minimal."

Ali and Donnie nodded in agreement as they shifted over in the booth to make room for Valerie.

"May we treat you to dinner?" said Donnie. "I don't think we were really introduced. My name is Donald Cameron, and this is my sister, Alison, and Professor Angus Morrisson."

"That would be lovely," said Valerie, accepting the menu Donnie handed her. "Just call me Val." The waitress brought over another wine glass and water for Valerie.

"I'm a Junior at Northwestern," said Val, "interested in field work, mainly. I've been on digs in the U.S., "mound builder" culture mostly."

"Mound builders," murmured Donnie. "I guess I don't know much about that culture. They didn't use written language. . .maybe some pictographs or petroglyphs?"

"Yeah, but the mounds are amazing, like trying to build a pyramid with just earth. The mounds are so huge people thought they were just mountains. They were ceremonial burials, though."

"So Portugal is really different," said Ali. "We're on our way to Ireland and then Scotland. Dr. Morrisson is from Lewis. And Donnie has been excavating finds in Spain."

"I had an accident there, kind of serious, lost my memory," Donnie explained. "We're on the trail of an Egyptian princess named Scota. Ever heard of her?"

"Nope. Fill me in though, sounds like a nice fairytale," said Valerie. Soon they all became fast friends, a table of geeks exchanging stories of lost cultures. Ali talked about the rocks, vitrification and frost heave, while Valerie chimed in with burial practices and what she'd learned in Portugal about Celts. The men talked about Egypt. Any observer would have thought they had been friends for a long time.

As they attended to their food of fish and octopus, conversations trailed away with the evening sun. Valerie seemed to be watching the door as newcomers came in, and Donnie saw her furtive glances, as if she were waiting for someone in particular. Valerie was rather hunched over her food, but watched the door even with her head bowed.

"Are you expecting someone?" asked Donnie. He remembered being in the day room of the hospital, and how he would hunch over, watching the attendants come and go, waiting for a recognizable person, and how it felt to be so alone and lost.

Valerie straightened up with a jerk. She tried to put on a calm face, but there was something wrong, and everyone could sense it.

"Maybe it's silly, but I've been concerned that someone is following me, at least at nighttime. I felt safe out at the ruins but every night as I went to my flat in the city, I felt that I was being followed. You know how the hairs on your neck can tingle for no apparent reason?"

"That's your autonomic response to fear," said Ali. "Have you got any reason to think someone is stalking you? Or, anyone angry with you?"

Valerie gave a little shrug, "It's probably just nothing. I did have a little run in at the museum one day, as I thought some finds were not being catalogued. I thought some relics were being sold or smuggled instead of being put on display. At least I couldn't find some of the artifacts that were turned in, and that happened three times. Your little bag of Roman coins were the last ones. You know they don't have a lot of value, except that they should have been catalogued."

"What else was missing?" asked Angus

"There was a small votive statue of a lady, maybe a foot tall, that never made it into the display. It was colorfully painted, and had unusual features. The hairstyle was like round doughnuts over each ear, and the carver put lots of jewelry and big earrings on her. I think it was Carthaginian, but that was wrong really, since those cultures should not have come this far north."

"What else?" asked Angus.

"Some beads from a broken necklace had been found. They were scattered and not found together, as if the necklace broke and the person didn't realize they had dropped. Sometimes the rains uncover things even when the site director thought everything had been found. They finished excavating the site at least ten years ago."

"What were the beads like?" asked Donnie.

"Don't laugh. They were blue faience, really faded, but the blue color was what revealed them. A friend of mine found them and I turned them in. Guess some wayward Egyptian got lost there," Valerie sighed.

"Those things have some value," said Angus, "so what you're telling us may be clues to a wider smuggling ring or thievery. If you were the only one to notice, did you report it?"

"Well, I did ask about the little statue. They ignored me, and my Portuguese isn't that good. I thought they would pursue it, but they didn't. The Director seemed miffed at me for even reporting it. His voice was carefully modulated and he told me their museum was extremely careful with artifacts, and nothing was missing. I got the message and dropped it. But I got the feeling later that I was being shunned a bit, like a snitch. Maybe there is something going on. I'm just glad to be leaving, because of it. I had a great time here, at least until the last week or so. But it's not like I know something or have any real evidence of wrong doing."

"There may be other motives," said Ali. "I've noticed something odd about archaeologists, I mean, not only with them, but people in general. It's kinda like if you find an anomalous artifact that doesn't fit your frame of reference, you want to get rid of it. It's like ignoring the "outliers" or denying things that don't fit the accepted chain of events, or what you believe. Do you know what I mean?"

"It's like a murder investigation by the police who discount certain clues because they don't lead to the guy they've arrested," said Donnie. "It ties things up in a neat package if you leave out the stuff that doesn't fit."

Valerie nodded, "Yes, it's like only excavating the main fields, and only putting artifacts that fit the paradigm into the museum. Then not having the money or space to put in or excavate the "less important" areas, or leaving artifacts in drawers hidden away. When we were excavating the mounds back in the States, one of my friends found some human bones that looked abnormally large. I mean it must have been like a giant. I saw the jawbone he found. But it never was catalogued for some weird reason. Of course, the Native Americans around there said the mounds were built by giants. And nobody in academia believes in giants!"

"So, if your team found evidence of Egyptian artifacts, they might lose them on purpose?" asked Donnie. "At least the Roman coins would be easy enough to explain, as coins do travel well. This is like racial pride?"

"Perhaps these things will sort themselves oot," said Angus. "DNA research will eventually rewrite our history books, at least as far as major migrations of people in antiquity. The "Out of Africa" theory will find new meaning if we are open to the possibilities and truth found in the artifacts as well."

The waitress brought the check, and they made ready to leave. Donnie helped Valerie with her jacket while Angus paid the bill. Valerie seemed to hesitate, not wanting to go off by herself, so she naturally became part of the little American party and they walked out as a group.

"What are your plans?" Donnie asked, as Valerie continued to walk alongside them. "Are you heading back to the States now?"

Valerie hesitated a bit, then replied, "Actually I had thought of visiting Ireland rather than leaving from Portugal. The airfares were substantially less if I leave from Ireland. I really am free to stay longer, as I have this semester abroad and no real timetables to meet. My family name is Irish, I think, but my mom's side was Greek. Lots of red-heads from Thrace, I guess. But I have no family at home now, just collage friends, and no one knows of my plans. You must think I'm pretty brave to go over here alone, but I'm used to being alone."

"Yeah, I would have been lost forever without my sister coming to find me,"said Donnie. "There's a sense of belonging with her that I guess you don't have...no one to worry about you at least." Donnie was truly grateful for having a sister to look out for him, even though as a child they mostly teased each other. That sibling bond had proven to be his salvation. Without Alison in his life, Donnie would still be in the St. Bernard Hospital day room, staring at the ocean. He thought some more about Valerie's bravery, and wanted to assert himself for a change. Then he asked her this question.

"Valerie, would you consider exploring Ireland with us, for a few days at least? We have no set plans, but I think we are going to see the main touristy things, like Blarney Castle, before we go to visit Dr. Morrisson's sister on Lewis. It would be extra nice to have another archaeologist with us."

Valerie couldn't believe her good luck. She had hoped to find companionship on her travels, safety in numbers so to speak, and was thrilled at Donnie's suggestion.

"I would like to see the various Mesolithic and Bronze Age settlements, and all the mounds," said Valerie. "What's so nifty about Blarney Castle? I mean, I know it's a tourist stop."

"Well, Blarney Castle is supposed to have a piece of the Scottish "Stone of Destiny." said Angus. "And Ali here is a geologist. We'd like to get a close look at it."

"Where is the stone?" asked Val.

"It's cemented into the side wall of the castle, part of a "machiolation," said Angus. "That's an opening high up on the wall where defenders could pour boiling oil down on invaders. It's part of the parapet, and to see the stone, someone has to hold your ankles while they lower you down."

"And you're supposed to kiss it?"

"Yes, that gives you the 'gift of gab' according to legends. Somehow the 'talking' stone imparts eloquent words. But maybe the stone itself has something to say," said Angus.

"Well, if only stones could talk," said Val, "we'd have lots more to put in our history books, wouldn't we?"

"Stones can talk," said Angus, "if there's a bit o' writin' on 'em. It's worth a good close look. And a good geologist can at least identify the type of stone. I've heard that the stone doesn't match any quarried around the castle in Ireland, at least."

Donnie was listening intently, thinking about what he'd written in translation a lifetime ago. His natural inquisitiveness was coming to the fore, and this bit of a puzzle began to form even more questions.

"How did that piece get to Ireland, anyway?" asked Donnie.

"Ach, to be sure, here comes a history lesson for you," said Angus, with a funny Irish lilt in his inflection. "At our Battle o' Bannockburn, back in the fourteenth century, our King Robert the Bruce gave the piece to the Irish for their support in the rebellion against the English. "Tis a legend, o' course, but it's a gesture that would have a lot o' meaning to the Irish back then."

That bit of Irish lilt superimposed onto Angus' Broad Scots made everyone giggle. Donnie listened, thought some more about symbolism and the efforts that some Egyptian princess had made so many centuries ago. If her papyrus story proved true, they might be able to trace the stone's history all the way to the British Isles.

"Where is the real "Stone of Destiny" supposed to be now?" asked Donnie.

"Don't laugh," replied Angus. "It's in the English throne room at Westminster Abbey in London. At least right now it is. But the English just made another offer to placate the Scots. They are planning to give the Stone back to Scotland in November. They've kept it since Edward I stole it back in 1296. Funny thing though, they've offered to give it back several times, but somehow it never happened. It's like the Scots themselves didn't care about it anymore. Still, there's a big ceremony being planned for its trip back to Edinburgh. That would be brilliant to see!"

"Well, I have the time, if not the money, to stay that long," said Valerie. "Let's see some sights in Ireland. I can't wait to get where the people speak English!"

Angus and Ali chimed in, and soon they had tickets in hand for Erin's Green Isle.

TWENTY SEVEN

Invasion of Ireland 303BCE

Freezing cold wind and icy rain pelted the sails and the shoulders of Prince Amergin as he bent to the till to turn his ship. Gale force winds threatened to scuttle the craft as its timbers heaved and creaked against massive waves. The sons of Scota and Gamal Miledh believed it was their destiny to invade this new land, whatever the cost. The storm had come out of nowhere, so suddenly, as if some ancient sea god had been angrily awakened by the tickle of their oars. Amergin recognized fury in the waves, their swells were like mountains of angry dark death. Turn they must, away from the sea maw threatening to swallow them. Amergin called out the signal, repeated three times by the hornblower at the prow. Above the thunderclaps, the dragon headed carnyx bellowed Amergin's signal to turn south. Other horns answered above the wind, for the Milesian horn trumpeted notes the wind could not match. Amergin turned his ship to the right, knowing this would take them south, even though the darkness and cloud-filled storm obscured any chance of seeing a star.

But the storm brought more than sheets of ice clinging to sails. The bone-chilling cold brought disease in its wind, as it singled out a weakness on Prince Donn's ship. Many there became feverish, heated to crazed behavior, for though they were freezing, their foreheads burned like iron pokers left in the coals. Some of Donn's men sought the cool water overboard in their need for fever's relief. Donn, too, was struck with some pestilence, as he sought to climb the mast to reach the icy rain. Through the sheets of rain, Amergin saw this strange aberration of warriors losing control of their volition. The carnyx horns sounded again and again, ordering mastery over the storm's insanity.

Amergin steered by the directions formed in his heart, hoping they had not blown too far east towards the shoreline. The ship immediately behind his, that of Prince Eremon's, turned left, and signaled with their horns to the ships following, so that by alternating turns they fell back into their formation. But the gale winds were fierce, too fierce for the right turns of some ships. In the fury of the storm, Donn had climbed the mast of his ship, challenging the lightning to strike him. Then the charm-raised storm foundered his ship and all who rode within it. The extreme winds shredded sails and scuttled the ships turning right, and in an instant, hulls presented their curves to the black night sky. Warning horns sounded the distress, and warriors were pulled from the waters if they were heard calling above the crash of the waves. But many were lost, for the storm would have its way with them. The dark sea swallowed as many as ten ships, and those below decks met cold water and endless sleep.

Below deck, Scota knew the turn had been sharp, and quick, for she was thrown from her berth like a sack of wheat. Sceine, Amergin's wife, was on the floor as well. Though neither were injured from the fall, Scota saw that Amergin's wife was no longer breathing! She lay in a heap like discarded linens, sightless eyes and mouth agape revealed her valiant fight against the invasive pestilence. The sickness had struck in the dark, sent by unseen forces to cruelly take the most loved. Scota raised a cry of alarm, which brought Amergin to her side. Though he sensed the pestilence on the winds, he had not foreseen the loss of Sceine. Like black fingers it sought out its prey, and chose those hearts that would be greatly missed. His evasive moves had not been soon enough.

Warriors struggled to regain their footing in the dark of the hold. Some stores had shifted, but not into dangerous balance, and all around people were righting themselves and taking up responsibilities. On Amergin's ship only Sceine had died, and not from the storm. Why had Amergin turned the ship so suddenly, and at night? In this gale of destruction? Only he knew the answer.

Scota threw on her cloak and struggled up to the outside air with handholds and ropes for balance against the heaving waves. Gale force icy rain bit at her cheeks, even her eyelashes felt frozen with icy crusts. She made her way to the stern, and saw that Amergin had lashed himself to the tiller as he fought the winds. The waves threatened to take them to rocky shores illuminated by crashes of lightning. But his face was calm, and his teeth were clamped shut with determination. This Prince of Miledh would not accept defeat.

"If we had not turned now, the northward cold would have frozen our mast ropes and we would not have had even a chance to turn," yelled Amergin. "It nearly took us all! The death that came with the winds could not be evaded." His voice rose in an angry scream, above the storm, as if screaming could change the course of the destiny he had foreseen. It was all he could do.

In her heart, Scota understood, but heard the horns bellowing in the night as ship after ship attempted the turn. Those that turned left into the gale fared better than those turning right, so signals were sent which saved many. After what seemed like a lifetime of being pelted by stones of frozen rain, the ships broke free of the storm winds and were suddenly becalmed. As dawn broke, Scota could see shredded sails and beleaguered sailors lying in disarray on the deck. They had controlled their oars beyond endurance, and they had survived.

Some ships that were not so far north as Amergin's were able to avoid much of the storm, and with morning's light they found some survivors floating, buoyed by cargo torn from decks. But weapons and supplies of at least ten ships had been lost, as well as lives of those below decks. Heavy mist surrounded the armada, so they carefully sailed closer to whatever shores they could make out. At last a quiet cove appeared, and the Milesians of Amergin's ship made shore to assess their losses. Horn signals brought the fleet to this western cove, anchorage was found, and the invaders were able to rest and reorganize their assault. But first they set to burying their dead.

Donn's body was found. His body, burnt by lightning and torn by the jagged rocks, was found floating in the surf. Some thought it was a pestilence that drove Donn to climb the mast to his death. They believed his body should not be allowed to touch the shore. So these remains were taken to a rocky cairn which they named Tech Duinn. It was constructed with massive rocks to become the resting place of departed souls from the storm. Amergin called souls of the other dead to attend him there, where they would greet fallen warriors from the battle to come. If the pestilence was the first cause of Donn's death, this would be a safe place of internment, for these huge rocks would hold back the sea. Tech Duinn would hold many souls, of many future dead, a sacred place for fallen warriors. Then the survivors attended to the others.

Amergin's wife was lain in a cove, her cairn constructed of massive rocks. They named it Inver Sceine, a safe harbor for those who have lost their love. Anger against the pestilence replaced any sadness, for taking her life in such a cowardly way only made the warriors more determined to secure their victory. Death is but parting breath, and all knew her soul would be with them in the attack to come. Many others were interred there. She would not be lonely.

Then, after attending to injuries, they replenished stores of water and firewood. They repaired sails and rigging. Bowmen went into the forest. They easily brought down an unsuspecting buck whose antlers now graced the ship's prow. Soon braziers were feeding all with venison and honey cakes. Netted fish filled bellies, for all were exhausted and hungry. A perimeter watch was set for defense. If the trees sheltered any spies that hid in their dark recesses, the Milesians did not see them. All was quiet so they rested and prepared.

Scota's chieftains and sons of Gamal Miledh, met to assess their losses. Of the Princes, only Amergin, Eber Finn, and Eremon had survived the migration. Their force of a thousand warriors had been reduced to seven hundred, and sorrow for lost children threatened to defeat them before they even approached Inver Sceine. Within hours other bodies had washed to shore, the smoke of funeral pyres signaled their presence there. Still, there was no sign of the island's people. Amergin had sent two ships northward to find any shipwreck, but only pieces of ships were found, no hulls intact, no weapons could be gleaned from the seas. What had been lost, was lost. Thus, the Milesians assembled for their final trip south, and celebrated for the victory to come. There were no questions in their hearts, for somehow they believed the storm had been the real battle. Now, only a skirmish remained. No opposition met them at the sunny harbor landing.

TWENTY EIGHT

At their mountainous barrow, the beleaguered De Danann met in a great conclave. Their wars of long ago had defeated the Fomorians, the Fir Bolgs, and lesser tribes, now contained in the area of Leinster, until the lands were peaceful. The Tuatha de Danann built harmony, their enclaves open to all. Prosperity flourished. They did not fear immigrants, for an island open on all sides must, by nature, invite newcomers. Yet, they strove to keep their honor, displaying courage before the defeat they knew was coming. Nine waves were granted, giving the Dananns time to hide their treasures, many of their people, and their way of life. Some elders consigned themselves to the barrows, the hills, and the mountain mists, never to be seen again.

The princes of the Tuatha de Danann then made preparations, not with heaps of weapons that were beyond their skill, but with the mists of their land. They called upon Dagda and Lugh. From Manannan mac Lir came control of the seas, to guide the storm to the moorage of the invaders. They called upon Oengus, Ogma, and Goibniu, until the heavens broke open with rain. Dain Cecht opened her pool of solace for the wounded, and prepared healing waters for the fallen. High winds swirled in the causeway as the people chanted. Their pitched voices rose higher and higher until they were heard. Misty rain turned to sleet, then to hail, and this was sent northwards with gale strength. Nor did the people cower there, but turned their bodies openly to the skies. The storm winds flew to Teach Doinn, meeting the invader's fleet in the dark of a moonless night. Cold, cold water greeted warriors to their death, the storm raged at the bidding of those who had cared for their lands for so long.

Dawn of the ninth wave came with more rain. Hoped for sunlight glinting from swords gave way to sheets of sleet, and the sandy meadow where the armies met became a morass, sucking boots and bodies into immovable positions. Reminded of the marshes of Kemet, Scota's thoughts turned to Persians trapped in their chariots long ago. But the Milesians came in an onslaught, never wavering, but helping each other through sheets of rain to firmer ground. The sandy spit for landing had turned to quicksand, so they looked for rocks and firmer ground. It was morning, but dark clouds threatened to never show the sun again.

Inver Sceine opened its bay at Kenmare to receive ships of the invaders. The high lords of the Tuatha de Danann met them there, the Slieve Mish Mountain watched with anticipation and accepted human blood as payment. The people of Dan fought with fire-hardened spears, surrounding isolated warriors who had thrown off their leather body armor because of the rain. The Danann swarmed like enraged bees, attacking splintered forces of Milesians. For some time the battle went their way.

Lughaid, son of Eber, was one such Milesian, cut off from his group as a sheepdog singles out a chosen leader. Scota saw this happening and went to his aid, screaming her ululation. With her bronze edged shield she strove to protect his body from spear thrusts, but there were too many. He lay gravely wounded. Scota rested her head on the chest of her grandson and, with a smooth motion of her arm, brought her shield up, covering them both. One cruel point caught her below the armpit, fatally piercing her heart in one great lunge. Scota fell there, with Lughaid, near a huge boulder. Their eyes met in silence as the battle raged around them.

They no longer heard the world around them. "I see light breaking, the sun will come soon," he said. His last words.

It is all right now, Lughaid. We are home. Gamal? I see you! You are coming to me, Ir and Heber follow behind? Lughaid? You glow in the sunlight. Oh, Gamal, I see the golden hair curl at the nape of your neck as you bend to kiss me. I have missed you for so long.

Sweet roses scent the air, like petals under my feet of old. I hear the call of marsh birds, and voices of children singing. A breeze caresses harp strings and offers aeolian sounds to a song I have played all my life. We glide to our palace home, hand in hand All is golden. . . It is Amenti. I am at peace. Love fills my heart. . . I am home.

TWENTY NINE

At Tailteann, three princes of the Dananns fell, and the tall pines gave boughs and limbs for their pyre. The Milesian invaders then spread throughout the land, sometimes finding resistance, sometimes not. Between Navan and Dunshaughlin the rocky fields were spattered with the blood of many invaders, but the battle had been won. The Danann seemed to melt away with the misty rain. As the clouds parted, bodies began to warm in the sunlight. The Milesians retrieved their battle dead, and at the grey stone boulder they found their Queen. The rock knows who died there, and remembers, for she gave her life willingly for the new home of her people, who had wandered far and wide for so long.

It fell to Siobhan, Amergin's daughter, to wash the body of Scota, which she did lovingly. Perfumed oils caressed Scota's weary skin, and a burial shroud embroidered with Kemet's glyphs covered her body. A burial mound was constructed and named Glen Scohene, for Scota's body was not consigned to flames. Her golden torque and heart scarab were safely wrapped with her. No sarcophagus, only a reed mat served for her final bed. Her harp was given to Siobhan, her cedar chest and wooden key to Amergin.

Thus began the Kingdom of Midhe. The harpers and bards of the land recorded all in the Lebor Gabala Erren, for those who want to hear the history of this green island. Sons of the Milesians listen even now to the stories, and hear with their hearts, of a Queen who gave her life for her people. Her name will never be lost, for her cartouche is engraved on that ancient stone.

The invaders, these sons of Miledh, made Tralee their first home. They buried their Queen at Glenn Scohene, and set up their kingdom with Scota's stone, which rested ceremoniously under the palace throne. The "Lia Fail," this talking stone, bestowed authenticity to each new ruler invested there at Tara. And though none could read the writing on it, the stone was a symbol of royalty and an unbroken lineage of their queen. The whole of the island was named for Scota's first born son, Ir, who died with his father battling barbarians in their drought plagued land far away. The island itself was divided into lands named for each surviving prince. Eber Finn the musician, took lands to the south, while Eremon was granted lands in the north. Amergin governed the west, but gave all powers to his sons, that they would learn to rule justly. Sometimes the new king was from Connacht, sometimes from Leister, but lastly, after many generations of Milesians, the king was from Ulster, the far north part of the island of Ir.

With each coronation, Scota's carved stone would travel to the new palace, and be ensconced there in ceremony. Primogeniture was never the law of these people. Instead, they chose the most able and just person to be their new king. The Lia Fail traveled with them always, to grace each new king with protection. The stone itself would give three groans under the weight of each new king chosen by the people. Now weathered and beaten, the bluish grey stone had lost some of the ancient glyphs. New words had been added, in a language all could read. Thus it traveled with the Dal Riada, for one last sea voyage, to a new land named for their Queen.

THIRTY

Battle of Bannockburn, Scotland June 24, 1314

Robert the Bruce addresses his forces:

"This day of 24 June, 1314, by the Grace of God, we are victorious against Edward's hundred thousand men! Our great Stirling castle still guards the gateway to the North, and Scotland is united under my Kingship. Furthermore, the Kingship of the Isles is guaranteed under my brother Edward Bruce, and together we shall make a new Nation of Gaels. No longer will our people feel the yoke of tyranny and privation by the English!"

Mighty cheers arose from the throngs of soldiers before him. The archers, the pikes-men, the infantry and cavalry, all attended the words of their recently ordained king. Robert Bruce, Lord of Annandale and Earl of Carrick, had become Scotland's King Robert I, just seven years past.

"We do not forget Balliol stripped of his royalty! We do not forget Longshanks' stripping the Abbeys of Arbroath, Aberdeen, or Fyvie! Nor do we forget his sacking of Glastonbury! He has sacked the Cistercian Monks at Deer Abbey, and the Red Friars at Dundee! There is no limit to his greed and arrogance. But as he searched at Melrose, Dunferline, Pluscarden, and Crosnaguel, his powers fell short of finding our greatest relic that stands here before you, our "Stone of Destiny"!

At these words, pages on either side removed the royal velvet cover from the stone that lay before King Robert the Bruce.

"You see before you that holy relic carried across the seas, across the Western Isles, and here to Alba. It is not the privy stone Edward I stole from Balliol, nor is it either red sandstone nor white limestone. It stands here before you as the Black Galala, with its carvings and holy signs. Our great King Mac Bethad mac Findlaig, descended from the house of Loarn, and Kings of Dal Riata, nearly three hundred years past, added those holy words you now see, to signify that it is our right to keep and hold until the mountains crumble to the sea. Look here the words added by that noble king."

Ni fallat fatum, Scoti quocunque locatum
Invenient lapidiem regnasse tenetur ibiden[1]

"My fellow countrymen! Our victory here at Bannockburn was won by our stout hearts and strong arms. Edward II's ten thousand men could not prevail over Justice! Even with the help of our friends from the west, when we were outnumbered three to one, we could not be defeated! Valiant heroes and forces provided by Oengus Og and Cormac McCarthy have come to our aide. You see them among us! They have our heartfelt thanks, and will receive payment, both in goods and treasure, from the mighty retinue of that defeated king. We have captured Edward's raiment, his crowns, his treasury, verily his whole entourage, and it shall be parceled out in its entirety. Furthermore, as a token of his fealty towards me, I hereby give a portion of our Tanist Stone to Cormac McCarthy, so that those of the Isles know of our unity."

Then the Bruce brought down his heavy axe, the selfsame axe that had split the head of de Bohun, down upon one corner of the stone. With a mighty whack, he knocked off a hefty corner, which he handed ceremoniously to the waiting Irishman.

---

1 "If Destiny prove true, then the Scots are known to have been Kings wherever men find this stone."

"With this stone, I declare unity between Scotland and Ireland from this day forth!"

Cormac McCarthy rose from kneeling and accepted the chunk of stone. He cradled it in his arms as if it were an infant, knowing the symbolism it engendered. The stone was greyish-black, and had curious markings on one side, but they were aged such that nothing was really legible. He wondered if the markings were runes, or Latin letters, or carvings by some long ago Druid. The small piece was still very heavy, and he laid it with reverence into a wooden chest, part of Edward II's captured booty.

Cormac knew the Stone's mythic reputation, of being a "talking stone." The seat of Kingship was said to groan or speak if the new king was acceptable to the people. And though he had not attended the coronation of the Bruce, he knew this smaller piece would grant sovereignty to those in his homeland across the western sea. McCarthy himself had been to Tara, and seen the "Lia Fail" standing silently on the hill. Centuries of stories told how the original Stone of Destiny had been taken across the sea, and then to the Hebrides, with the Scotti, who had hoped to form a nation between the Isles and western Scottish lands. This piece of dark stone, chopped from Bruce's stone, would find it's home in Eire.

All these thoughts blossomed in Cormac's face as he received the relic from the hands of Robert the Bruce. The sun shown down on his tear streaked face as a tremendous cheer rose around him.

"Long live our King Robert! Long live the King!"

"Let lips be sealed this day among us," called the Bruce. "We will send our Coronation Stone north to Dunsinnan, far enough away from further invasions of those English. It shall be hidden there, among monks who have been sworn to secrecy. Let no one repeat my orders. Let Edward II believe his father found the true relic."

Soldiers thumped their right breasts in promise to their new king. All who heard his words obeyed, and were satisfied. Providence would guard their every forward step in forming a new Celtic Nation of Scotland and the Western Isles.

THIRTY ONE

Kenilworth Castle, 1575, Elizabeth's Castle

"Odds Bodkins! Does he take Us for a wig?!"

The parchment-like skin on the white powdered breast began to turn as bloody red as her jewel encrusted necklace. Rubies graced the long white neck of Elizabeth I, swollen veins were near to bursting. Her cheeks grew redder and redder as if blood itself boiled up from her most regal heart. She heard the report and the outside world fell away. Her patience and queenly demeanor had turned to a furious rage.

"It's all blither, blather, and blarney! We are not amused!"

Lord Dudley, Earl of Leicester, favorite of our good queen, had nothing better to report than a pleasantly worded unending list of excuses from Cormac McCarthy, Lord of Blarney Castle. The oath of fealty was demanded of him, otherwise he would lose the occupation of his land and titles. But surrendering his castle, as proof of loyalty, was replaced by tactics that might delay his predicament long enough to see the death of the Virgin Queen.

The gaiety of Elizabeth's court, the musicians, and the dances, had come to an abrupt halt with the news Lord Dudley conveyed to his queen. She sat in regal splendor, stiff collared and pristine, while her ladies in attendance tried to fan the heat from her brow.

"He could entirely talk the noose off his head! Such fair words in soft speech that signify not a twit! I have sent Robert Devereaux, Earl of Essex, to put down that rebellion of Papists, and now you also, Lord Dudley, report only failure!"

Elizabeth was near screaming now, as excuses, one after another, became solidified in the air. "Must we send the armada to bow his head?" Her eyes burned into Robert as he gave obeisance to resist her wrath.

"I am but her majesty's messenger, good Queen," replied Dudley, "though it is well known I would do much more for Your Grace."

At this, Elizabeth softened. Regaining her composure, she allowed a wisp of a smile to form as her skin began to return to its arsenic whiteness. There was quiet for a space as all eyes focused on the throne, anticipated a royal decree. Her supercilious voice sliced the waiting air.

"We must expect that our subjects love and revere Us, for who can stand for them before God but Myself? We shall demonstrate the "patience of Job" for all under Our dominion, as We are known for our Justice and Love. Thank you sir, for your honest report. Let the music ensue."

With a wave of her jeweled hand, Queen Elizabeth returned to the gaiety of the dance before her. She would deal with the Irishman in her own time, not his, but the deadline would be hardened by threat of sword and scaffold, or the castle walls brought down!

I have some power, she thought. *After all, We are the most revered Queen!*.

THIRTY TWO

Ireland, November, 1996

The flight to Cork Airport arrived mid-afternoon as the quartet of Americans found a pleasant B&B for the evening. Blarney Castle was a mere ten miles from Cork, and from there they planned to take a short flight to Dublin. Auburn House had all the amenities, if not an excess of Irish lace everywhere, and the intrepid American adventurers settled in for the evening. Mrs. O'Flarherty gave them two rooms, and Ali and Val had the opportunity to became better acquainted.

Their room had two twin beds with soft duvet covers, embroidered with Irish shamrocks. Pillow shams were of Irish lace, that matched the lace curtains. There was a folding rack for a suitcase and two chairs, otherwise the room was devoid of furniture. The walls were of soft green wallpaper, which sported a large map of Ireland. Major cities had gold stars, and each of the five provinces was clearly outlined. They were in County Cork. Nearby was another framed chart that showed a list of cathedrals and their townships. *Buildings* thought Ali, no interest here in the land itself. The girls flopped onto their beds and began to talk.

"My brother is suffering from severe amnesia," she told Val. "The doctor in Gibraltar thought it might reverse itself, and he does seem to be better lately. He still seems to have regular severe nightmares, though."

"He seems alright to me," said Val. "I think he's real cute. Is there anything we can do to help him get better?"

"Well, maybe we just won't plan any boat rides. I think he fell overboard outside of Gibraltar which is the cause of the nightmares. My plan is to build up his memory with photos of our childhood, it's just that those things are all back home. Eventually, I hope he will regain enough of his past that he can get his career back on track. He is an Egyptologist. We've been tracing the migration of some ancient people through Spain and Portugal. I think the best thing is to try having him talk more.

"I don't get the connection between Spain and Egypt. But I can talk to him about the culture at Penafiel."

"How did you find the job at Penafiel?" asked Ali.

"That was a student exchange program, and there were some longer internships available. I don't know much about Egyptology, certainly not here in Spain. I'm sure Donnie would qualify for something like what I did in Spain but they aren't really paid things, just room and board plus day work. It's tough to find a good job in this area. I think you'd do better as a geologist."

"Yeah, I can always work for some highway department when they have to put in a new road through Indian burials. I've been thinking of teaching, too, might go get some hours in education just in case."

"Who knows? Maybe the two of you will make some great find and rewrite the history books! You never know. I do like Angus too, he has such a caring attitude, are you related?"

"Goodness no! He just offered to come and help me when Donnie was missing. He is interested in the finds that Donnie made in Spain. I think we told you that we are following the trail of an Egyptian princess if you can believe that."

"What's that got to do with Blarney Castle?" asked Val.

"There are some artifacts there that may have come with an invasion back in 300BC. It's worth checking out, anyway. We are really on an adventure now, just trying to jog Donnie's memory before we have to go home. Blarney Castle is supposed to have a piece of rock that gives you speaking skills. Weird, I know. The piece of rock is supposedly from Scotland though, and according to Angus, it was given to the owner of the castle by Robert the Bruce. Problem is, it has been described as marble, sandstone, or even granite. What I want to do is to get a close look at it."

"What's so special about the rock? I don't believe the rock has magic or can make you talk. That's a bunch of Irish superstition like leprechauns and shamrock clovers."

"Yeah, I agree. I think the only way a rock can make you talk is if it has writing on it. Or at least the strata and age it came from. The legend is more about lots of evasive letters to the first Queen Elizabeth. The Irish lord was supposed to pledge allegiance or send taxes I guess, but he just kept beating around the bush as long as he could. The Queen said he was full of "blarney.""

"Oh, I can imagine how frustrated she must have been," said Val, "everyone jokes about Irish stories and how long they are. Usually a good twist in the end though."

"Let's get some sleep. Hopefully the rain will lift tomorrow or we'll all be wet."

Then they turned in for the night. Ali was excited about going to Blarney Castle in the morning, and wasn't the least bit nervous about being lowered by her ankles to kiss some old piece of rock. Her dreams were filled with rocks, as usual, with an occasional scene of a movie set in Egypt. She, too, was infected with the migration myths.

In their room, Angus and Donnie were having the same sort of conversation. Angus explained how Robert the Bruce had managed to unite the Scots and Irish under his new kingship, and had placed his brother as King of Ireland. The piece of rock was supposed to unite the islands into a strong force against the

English domination. Donnie easily remembered the movie called "Braveheart" with the love story and William Wallace.

"There was some problem with Robert the Bruce becoming king?" said Donnie.

"Yes, the Scots believed in "tanistry" which is different than primogeniture, though both the Bruce and Balliol were descended from the Scottish royal lineage. Tanistry means the new king could be chosen from great men who may or may not have "royal" lineage. Edward Longshanks had chosen Balliol as the Scottish King, but he was deposed, leaving the Bruce to take over. There are lots of stories about Robert the Bruce's rise to prominence. Do you know the story of the "spider"?

Donnie thought a bit, then said, "Yeah, something about watching a spider that kept weaving a web, and not giving up."

"You've got it!" quipped Angus. "And the "Saltire"?"

"The Saltire is St. Andrew's cross, the cloud formation that appeared over the battlefield when Bruce won at Bannockburn."

Angus was so pleased he began to dance a little jig. "Your memory is coming back just fine, my boy. Soon you'll be right as rain! Perhaps come home with me to UCLA and start a doc program? Writing up what we've learned on this trip would make a worthwhile dissertation. Think about that, my lad. Now, off to sleep wi' ye!"

Dream Angus has dreams to sell, went the song in Donnie's head. Every night he practiced his list of memories, filling in gaps until he had a more complete sequence of events of his life. The new adventures were added into this narrative of experiences. His travels were beginning to make sense. He knew that Princess Scota had brought treasures on her journey to Ireland, and now they were hot on the trail. Could a piece of the Stone of Destiny be identified at Blarney Castle tomorrow? They would need to compare it to the stone housed in Westminster Abbey, and Ali had the expertise to do it. Donnie was full of anticipation as he too drifted off to dreamland.

THIRTY THREE

A light drizzle greeted the misty Irish morning as the Americans settled into their breakfast. Irish soda bread with currants and strong black tea complimented the eggs and sausage. Ali asked for an extra piece of lemon, but instead of squeezing it into her tea she surreptitiously folded it into her paper napkin. Mrs. O'Flaherty might have noticed that both milk and lemon in tea make for a rather ill concoction but she didn't remark about it. Val noticed the conflict, had a quizzical look on her face for a fleeting moment, then attended to her scrambled eggs. Ali carefully put the lemon wedge into her purse. She had plans for it when they got to the castle.

Donnie was excited as he had been thinking about the "history review" he'd gotten last night from Angus. He was eager to talk about the implications of the Blarney Stone.

"So Sis, do you know what you're in for today?"

"Yeah, you guys are going to hold my ankles and lower me down the outside of the castle wall. The picture I have in the travel brochure shows a dark triangular stone cemented into the wall. I know it's darned high. You won't let me slip down in this rain, right?"

"No worries, my dear. The rain is supposed to burn off by mid-morning, and we should have a sunny day for it," said Angus.

"So, what's your plan?" asked Donnie.

Ali kept her voice low, not wanting to be overheard. There were other travelers in the B&B, but they looked Asian, and were speaking Korean or possibly Japanese. Since it was November, the tourist season was virtually over, and travelers to Blarney Castle were sparse at best. At least there shouldn't be an impossible queue at the castle.

Ali stirred her tea, then spoke. "Well, I'll visually inspect the rock, its grain appearance, etc. I will let go of the rail on one side, maybe both rails, unless there's a guard or something. I'm going to check its hardness, of course, then do a little test."

The ten mile bus ride to Blarney Castle gave tourists a good look at the Irish countryside. Green rolling hills and whitewashed cottages with their attentive sheep on the hillsides seemed to lull the passengers into midmorning naps, but not the Americans. They bounded off the bus, and were first in line for the tour, and the chance to get the "gift of gab."

Like most fourteenth century castles, this one had very thick walls, the typical ramparts and fortifications seen in storybooks, as well as the McCarthy coat of arms on the front pillar. Inside the castle the guests were shown beautiful parquet floors polished like mirrors, ancient solid oak furniture, and huge paintings of the castle's family members from long ago. Plush Persian carpets had perfectly arranged fringe, and Irish lace draped over velvet upholstered chairs. Everywhere lead glass crystal from Waterford glistened from light falling through high narrow windows. After the grand tour of room after room full of statuary, armored knights, and walls decorated with weaponry of old, the tourists were led up to the ramparts of the castle.

"This is called a 'machiolation,'" said the guide as he showed them the framework of stone that allowed defenders of the castle to look over the walls to the invaders below. "In olden times, burning oil could be dropped through these openings, with the cauldron being supported by the structure. It is here on the high wall that our famous stone is encased. Anyone here brave enough to kiss it?"

The small crowd of late-season tourists had several brave takers. Their hands went up, and the Americans waited patiently for each visitor to take their turn at being lowered down against the wall. Photographers were on hand to record the special moment, though most people did their own photos instead of paying a fee. When all the others were finished, Ali stepped up for her turn. The attendant gave Donnie and Angus strict instructions with the safety harnesses, and Ali signed the waiver of responsibility for participating in the stunt.

Ali placed the lemon wedge into her cheek carefully, so as not to squeeze it, gritted her teeth, and then Angus and Donnie carefully lowered her down. The stone was a good four or more feet below the top of the rampart, low enough to be seen by someone on the ground. Ali held the side railings and eased herself into position.

When she was directly level with the stone, she placed her right hand on its shiny surface. She knew if it were soft gypsum or alabaster she would be able to scratch it with a fingernail. She looked for the obvious sand layers that would reveal sandstone, but she could only see metamorphic rock. *Calcareous*, she thought, not granite. She again scratched at the stone, and since it was very hard, no tiny grains could be scratched off. It wasn't as hard as granite, nor did it have the fragility of closely bonded sand grains. So, this was not kin to the reddish sandstone rock in pictures of the stone in Westminster Abbey. Satisfied that it wasn't sandstone or granite, Ali carefully retrieved the lemon wedge, and positioned her mouth to kiss the stone. Instead, she gave it a good squirt of lemon juice, and watched intently as tiny bubbles formed over the surface. The minuscule fizz told her this rock was limestone. Moh's hardness scale of three or four, but still very heavy and hard. Perfect rock for carving inscriptions or statues. Then Ali ate her lemon wedge, gave the stone a good sloppy kiss, and motioned for the guys to pull her up.

"Are you gabby, now?" asked Donnie

"You betcha!"

The Americans moved out of earshot from the other tourists, and took photos of the gardens below. Soon they gathered around Ali to hear more.

"I've got lots to say! It's as we suspected, this bit of rock sure doesn't look like the pictured stone in the throne room at Westminster. Either this stone is false or Edward I must have taken a fake rock!" she whispered.

"The monks surely expected him to steal all their treasures," said Angus. "And we're no but canny folks! They would have hidden the real stone away somewhere's safe. But we're relying on legends that this piece was given to the Irish by The Bruce. That could have been a fake piece too."

"In the 'history review' Angus gave me last night,"said Donnie, "there was a mention that the stone in Westminster had been identified as the same type of sandstone found at Scone. All the rocks around there were of the same reddish sandstone, so I guess it would be easy enough to switch it out with something lying nearby. Edward wouldn't have known." Everyone nodded thoughtfully. Then Donnie added another thought.

"And I remember once when Mom lost her keys, that I found them. But they weren't the right keys. Had to look for more keys before she could lock the house."

Ali had the most pleasant smile, hugged her brother for that bit of news. He was remembering bits and pieces of child-hood memories.

"Do you remember the house we had, or the furniture?"

"Yes, I remember sunny yellow kitchen curtains, and the windowsill where the keys were. The other keys were on the floor by the living room couch. Was it brown?"

Ali gave her brother another good hug. "That's right! You were our "Donnie Detective" those days. You could find anything! And Mom was always misplacing her keys. Can you remember her face?"

Donnie closed his eyes, and thought a bit. Yes, I think so. And I remember we were always late for stuff because she would misplace her keys."

Everyone was thrilled to know that Donnie was getting past the memory block from his near death in the waves. And, happy to know about Ali's examination of the Blarney Stone. Finally, her studies had become useful on their adventure. Now they would be off to Dublin, to see the Hill of Tara, and that chunk of the "Lia Fail," Ireland's coronation stone.

The bus ride back was nearly empty of tourists. They were wanting a good dinner back in town. Off in the distance a double rainbow appeared over the faraway hills. "Sure, tis an Irish blessing," lilted an elderly lady on the bus. And everyone laughed.

THIRTY FOUR

Morning Chronicle, **2 January 1819.**

On the 19th of November, the servants belonging to the West Mains of Dunsinane-house were employed in carrying away stones from the excavation made among the ruins that point out the site of Macbeth's castle. Part of the ground they stood on suddenly gave way, and sank down about six feet, revealing a regularly built vault, about six feet long and four wide. None of the men were injured, so curiosity induced them to clear out the subterranean recess. There they discovered among the ruins a large stone, weighing about 500l [230 kg]. which is pronounced to be of the meteoric or semi-metallic kind. This stone must have lain here during the long series of ages since Macbeth's reign. Besides it were also found two round tablets, of a composition resembling bronze. On one of these two, lines are engraved, which a gentleman has thus deciphered.— 'The sconce (or shadow) of kingdom come, until Sylphs in air carry me again to Bethel.' These plates exhibit the figures of targets for the arms. From time immemorial it has been believed among us here, that unseen hands brought Jacob's pillow from Bethel and dropped it on the site where the palace of Scoon now stands.

A strong belief is also entertained by many in this part of the country that it was only a representation of this Jacob's pillow that Edward sent to Westminster, the sacred stone not having been found by him. The curious here, aware of such traditions, and who have viewed these venerable remains of antiquity, agree that Macbeth may, or rather must, have deposited the stone in question at the bottom of his Castle, on the hill of Dunsinane (from the trouble of the times), where it has been found by the workmen. This curious stone has been shipped for London for the inspection of the scientific amateur, in order to discover its real quality.

THIRTY FIVE

Dec. 26, 1950. Midnight, Westminster Abbey, London

"Fash, it's too tight! It won't budge!" said Ian Hamilton. "Even pushing from the rear won't move it!" The Stone was just too heavy in its confines under the regal wooden throne. They hadn't wanted to destroy the wood snugly holding it, but there was no other way.

"Use the jimmy," whispered Gavin Vernon, the young engineer who could open a beer bottle with his teeth. He was not hesitant about using the pry bar on the Throne before them. So Ian broke off the old oak front and side panels and soundlessly laid them on the Abbey floor. This exposed the iron chain. He gave a pull, and the Stone began to slide forward. And then, it broke!

"Och nooo! We've broken it! Wouldn'a thought it was so mouldy!"said Gavin.

A large piece, maybe less than a hundred pounds but still a good-sized chunk, had separated from the majority of the Stone.

"That can fit in Kay's car, easy enough to hide in the back." said Ian.

The rest of the Stone weighed about three-hundred pounds or more. What to do? Ian threw his coat on the floor and the young men rolled the Stone onto the coat for dragging. Crunch! A cracking sound came from the plaque that had proclaimed "Coronation Stone," now broken in the coat pocket. Also, Ian's watchband had caught on the wooden throne side, and it broke off in their haste.

"My graduation watch!" moaned Ian. It had been repaired, but never kept good time. Now he didn't have a free hand to even retrieve it. Anyhow, it wasn't worth worrying about, as their caper was already at the height of excitement. Once the stone was moving there was no turning back. They dragged the heavy sandstone across the Abbey floor by pulling on the coat sleeves. Finally they emerged into the pre-dawn air.

It was now three a.m. and unbelievably cold-- negative ten degrees-- as Ian retrieved his now ragged coat to his shoulders. Alan Stewart, the civil engineer of the bunch, was along for the heist because he was the only one with a car, a Ford Anglia. As they hefted the stone, they realized it wouldn't fit in the boot, so they removed the passenger seat, and put it there. The car suspension groaned under the weight. Then the car wouldn't start! Persistence and faith finally got it started. What else could go wrong?How many weird coincidences would happen this night! Their luck was unbelievable. Still, things were not as flawed as their previous effort to steal the stone.

That first plan had been for Ian to hide inside Westminster Abbey at closing time, then let the others in when the guards had left to celebrate Christmas. Big Ben had struck six so after waiting a few minutes and not hearing any noises, Ian crept out from under the service cart in the hallway. The bright light from the guard's flashlight lit up his face as he tried to hide behind a statue. He was caught almost immediately! All the plans they'd made became useless. Instead of calling the police, the guard took him to the door.

"What do you think you're doing?"

"I'm lost...um, got left behind...didn't know I'd be locked in," Ian said.

"You should have called out!"

"I was too scared. And I feel pretty stupid."Ian made a feeble attempt to act like a lost child. He acted embarrassed, and the guard had a kind heart, didn't brain him with his nightstick.

Wonder of wonders, the guard believed that thin story and took Ian outside. Brutal cold wind whipped the overcoat in which he'd tried so hard to hide behind the statue. So now they were done for, or so he thought. They had no money for a hotel in London, penniless students that they were. But when he met his co-conspirators they unanimously decided against giving up. Instead they tried to sleep in the car. Keeping warm was a major problem on such a cold night outside of Westminster Abbey, no amount of blankets or woolens would keep them from frostbite. It was that cold. There was no going back.

So, they tried again in the wee hours of Christmas Day, when no guards were scheduled to watch the Abbey. Breaking in was easy, so was breaking out. Later, every time they were questioned by police, as to where they were going or what they were doing out on the roads, their excuses were met with plausible belief. It was as if Obi wan Kenobi was telling the storm trouper "these are not the droids you want." There were so many opportunities for the authorities to catch them, yet they had gotten away "Scot free." Their luck was unbelievable!

Since the rock wouldn't fit in the boot, they removed the front passenger seat and put the Stone there in its stead. Alan sat on it with his legs straight out, covered with a blanket. Stopped by the police, when asked about the automobile seat now stowed in the back seat, they told the policeman they intended to sell the extra seat. The Bobbie even believed that! They then took the Stone 200 hundred miles north, at twenty-five miles per hour, on ice-covered slippery roads, barely managing with so much weight to climb the hills. The puny Ford Anglia certainly did not have the suspension required to do the job, but somehow they managed to cross the border. The Stone was now returned to Scotland.

At the height of this irony, the young men had no idea of what to do next. They had fully expected to be caught red-handed and marched to the tollbooth. But, as they had managed to escape the formidable Scotland Yard, now they had no plan. So, for the time being, they left it in a field, letting it toboggan down the frost covered hillside. It came to rest in what later would be an encampment of gypsies!

The whole escapade probably started with Ian's mother's stories told at bedside when he was a wee lad. Stories of Scottish history and legends stirred nationalistic fervor. Dreams of Robert the Bruce, of the great Wallace, and other famous figures in Scottish history provided a pride of country that Scots of the world take to heart. But the Scots were a subjugated nation, controlled by English laws and English money. The "Stone of Destiny" was the one central artifact that could stir their patriotic soul. Wasn't it time to return it to Scotland? Ian's friends agreed, and it would be carried out on Christmas Eve, just to restore their sense of Scottish pride!

Ian, a poor student, had neither money nor car for this adventure. He befriended the President of the Student Union on the Rectorial Committee for funds named Bill Craig, and another man, John MacCormick advanced him L10. Ian's other friends, Alan Stewart and Gavin Vernon were keen to give the escapade a try, and Alan had a car. Bill Craig, the fourth student, was not so confident. But Kay Mathieson, their patriotic gaidhlig speaker, was braver than the lot of the young men. Like Flora MacDonald of ages past, had more courage and composure than any of the men would have believed possible. Once during a sudden halt the car lurched forward and her small piece of the stone actually popped out of the boot onto the road. She calmly hefted the stone back into the boot, and no one noticed the slight lassie picking up a rock that no doubt weighed as much as she did.

Perhaps recovering the Stone of Destiny had been Ian's reason d'etre. The men had discussed stealing the stone for months. How could they do it? First, they took a trip to a cemetery to get an idea of the stone's weight. Ian posed as someone needing to order a headstone.

"How much does something that size weigh?" he asked the stone mason.

"'Round three hundred or so,"says he, "but we deliver," said Bertie Gray.

"Oh, that's heavy. Is it like the 'Stone o' Scone', that weight?" Ian asked

"Verra close. We have a 'Destiny Stone' replica over here, as a comparison," said the man. We made it for the tourists who want to see the size o' it."

Bertie Gray showed Ian the replica that he had made in 1928. Ian gave it a shove, and felt it's mass. He was convinced that with help, they could carry it to a car.

"Thanks kindly for your help, sir. We'll be in touch."

That had been their first issue, to estimate the size and weight of the stone. Ian found the accurate dimensions in a description of the stone, but it was even better to see the replica at the headstone shop.

Now they had an idea of the weight and size, and were confident it would fit in the back of the car, if only they were strong enough to heft it. Later, as it turned out, the stone couldn't fit in the boot after all. Instead they had to remove the front seat, throw a blanket over it, and had Alan sit on it, concealing it with his legs and a blanket.

After passing through several roadblocks, Alan said, "So here's a toast to the myth of the "unbeatable Scotland Yard"'! They were stopped many times, as the police were looking for "four young Scots" who had stolen the "Coronation Stone" from Westminster Abbey. They were stopped and questioned as to their purpose on the road, where were they going, and so on, but never searched.

Once, when seen loitering in the alley, Kay and Ian kissed and pretended to be lovers out at a late night. The officers believed that ruse as well, not noticing the torn coat or the terrible night cold.

Another incident of possible interception had happened with Kay when she was driving alone back to Scotland. Motoring at her slow crawl, she saw a roadblock some distance ahead. She calmly turned off into a side road, took another route, and was able to evade capture easily again. The theft was a true comedy of police errors! They were looking for the owner of the broken watch, with a photo of it splashed in all the papers. But the authorities were not looking for a pretty young girl driving alone on the road to Scotland.

Finally, when the young men slowly crossed into Scotland at the car's excruciatingly slow pace, they looked for a place to hide the stone. They pulled to the side of the road when they saw a likely memorable place. But the earth was covered with sheets of ice, some muddy patches, and it really was a nondescript area. The ice and snow helped them slide it down a hillside. Here in this lowly spot by the side of the road, the Stone of Destiny nestled into some other rocks, amongst a few thistles. They made sure it was obscured, then went home. They were certain they could find it again later, when the authorities arrested them. They were absolutely sure they would eventually be caught.

The papers were full of odd descriptions of the brazen Scots who had ransacked England's holiest throne room. When Ian finally made it home his parents were surprised to see him, as he hadn't been home all summer.

"Where have you been?" mother asked.

"I've lost my watch ....in Westminster Abbey," Ian said.

Ian's mother had a shocked look on her face but said, "Was it you who took the Stone? We thought you might have a hand in it!"

Then Ian turned to his father, the stern Presbyter that he was. A broad grin spread over the elder man's face.

"Well done, laddie. Well done. I haven't been so proud of anything for a very long time."

Though he'd expected the worst, Ian received his very first blessing of parental pride. What's more, his parents agreed to lie to the authorities if asked, for Ian had no alibi for his whereabouts on Christmas Eve. It was an unheard of gift to him that his unco guid father could tell a lie on his behalf. On behalf of Scotland, really. They went over the alibi version until it sounded plausible, then Ian went to meet the others. His parents told him they supported him whatever the penalty might be, if he were caught.

The problem was, what to do next? The conspirators hadn't been found, the broken watch couldn't be traced, and the stone lay in a field somewhere in Scotland. Both Ian and Gavin thought the best thing would be to return the stone to Scone Abbey, or at least present it to the Earl of Mansfield. But this had to be done in such a way that the Earl would not be implicated in the theft. After some serious discussion it was decided that Ian would approach the aristocrat by himself.

Ian made an appointment to meet with the Earl of Mansfield and Mansfield at Logie House. Mungo David William Murray was the 7th Earl of Mansfield, and had been a member of Parliament for the Scottish Unionist Party, and was now a member of the House of Lords. He was Governor of Edinburgh and East Scotland, and had all the forces of law and order on his side. At fifty years of age, the Lord had acquired all the benefits of peerage, educated at Eton and Oxford, and yet was obliged to meet with this miscreant who had stolen the stone. And Ian was late! The roads were difficult even on a good day, and Ian was beside himself wondering whether the Earl would even admit him, he was so late. The Earl's dinner party was being delayed, and he should have been furious at Ian's rude tardiness. Yet he received him with the cultured dignity and patience of his aristocratic station.

"Don't tell me your name," said the Earl. "It's better that I shouldn't know it. But let me congratulate you on one of the most brilliant exploits in Scottish history!"

Ian was relieved to know he was not thought of as some scoundrel or communist, or wild republican. He held his breath as the Earl continued:

"I understand that you wish to return the Stone to Scotland. However, it cannot be delivered here to Scone Abbey, or I might be implicated. I will not have a hand in this, however noble and patriotic your efforts have been. You must return the stone to the authorities. Did you dump it in the river?"

"No m'Lord, it is safe. And I fully understand your position. It was an impulsive act that I have done, and I wish to make things right."

After assuring the Earl that the stone was not dumped in the Serpentine, or lost in some other impossible to recover place, they worked out a method for Ian to propose returning the stone. It would be returned to the police station in Glasgow, as if they had "found" it. The conspirators would not be arrested, but thanked for its return. Ian wanted the return to be coupled with a petition to the sovereign, a petition that would explain the reasons for the theft in the first place.

This could not come directly from the Earl of Mansfield of course, as he was the King's representative and he had done nothing to apprehend Ian. The Earl was confident that the Stone would be returned, so Ian returned to the flat in Glasgow and meet with Bill, Gavin, and John MacCormick, the other young man who had given money for the prank. It was decided that rather than typing the petition, Ian should write it in longhand so that a typed page couldn't be traced to the typewriter in their flat. It would be given to a Glasgow newspaper.

When Ian got back to Glasgow, Alan expressed further concerns. The stone had been lying unattended for several months, out in the damp of the Scottish hillside. It had occurred to him that a piece of Scottish sandstone that had laid securely for six centuries in a dry palace, would suddenly start to crumble with moisture. Like in a nightmare, the stone might suck up water like blotting paper and break into fragments, never to be assembled again. And then there was the broken piece that Kay still had.

After talking it over, they were able to consult Stuart and Stuart, a reputable engineering company, about the health of the stone. Mr. Stuart was terribly concerned about the safety of the Stone, and wanted it retrieved as soon as possible. At least Kay's piece was still safely in the boot of the car, in a safe, dry garage, and not exposed to the elements. And though the roads were still being patrolled they had to get the pieces safely back together. This meant another long road trip, with all its hazards. It fell to Bill to bring the petition to the newspaper office, and Ian to retrieve the stone.

Bill, Ian, Alan, and Gavin drove out of Glasgow, and finally came to the environs where they had left the Stone of Destiny. Ahead they saw the gleam of two bonfires lighting up a gypsy camp. There were two caravans, and brightly clothed gypsies were cooking their dinner by the fire. How to approach them?

Then a gypsy lady invited them to sit by the fire. Bill began to talk about the countryside, about Scotland, about freedoms, and things these people felt in their hearts as wanderers. Tramps and tinkers all, they too believed in freedoms that existed outside the law. And as he spoke about liberty, and the challenges ahead, a gypsy spoke up:

"You can't get it just now," he said.

Bill wondered how long the gypsies had been camping there. How did they know the Stone of Destiny was there? A gypsy spoke up.

"You can't get it because there's a local man at the other fire, and you can't trust him." We all sat and pretended to stare at the fire, just as the gypsies were doing. After a long while, the gypsy came to Ian and said, "It's all right now. That man has left."

The gypsies managed their little diversion around the fire while the four young Scots went to retrieve the stone. Litter and weeds had frozen a stiff layer of protection over it, which came off in a sheet when they lifted the stone from the frozen ground. How long had the gypsies camped there? Did they know the Stone of Destiny was there? Yes, of course. They were lovers of liberty and freedom, as much as any young patriotic Scotsman. Ian thought they had been guarding it all these months, until it would be taken to its rightful place in Scotland.

The men parted ways, Bill and Gavin caught a train to Newcastle, and Ian and Alan drove the Stone back to Longtown. The Stone was finally back in Scotland, and though the newspapers read "Stone to be Found Soon" or "L1000 Reward for Information" only the four Scots knew where the Stone really was. Ian and Alan were stopped several times more at roadblocks, once the policeman actually asked if they had the Stone of Destiny.

"Ach aye,, it's in the boot," Ian quipped, and the officer laughed, sending them through the roadblock. Soon they met with Kay and retrieved her piece. Bertie Gray, the stonemason, repaired the stone seamlessly. And then the Stone of Destiny was put into a large carton to wait for the authorities. Ian called the police and told them where to find it.

The Stone was soon taken back to London, loaded up in the dark of night, and whisked away from Scotland without notice or fanfare. Ian's petition was published in the newspapers, along with the description of his broken watch. The surprise most worthwhile was that the young conspirators were never charged with a crime, nor were they apprehended. The English simply ignored the whole escapade, perhaps to hide their own shame and ineptitude at not being able to catch the perpetrators red-handed. And the fact that the perpetrators could have stolen relics of much more obvious value, even the throne itself, was completely ignored.

So, Westminster Abbey recaptured its royal Stone of Destiny with no pomp or circumstance. It suffered no apparent worse or wear. The English never mentioned that the Stone had been broken. The wooden throne was easily repaired, and Ian received a new watch from his proud father. But the time for the stone's rightful place in Scotland had not yet come.

THIRTY SIX

Petition by Ian Hamilton

Despite the lack of evidence, it was believed that it was stolen by persons having sympathy with the Scottish Nationalist movement. A week after the theft a letter was handed into the office of a Glasgow newspaper, the Daily Record, asking that one copy of the Petition accompanying the letter should go to the police and the other to the press. The Petition stated:

"The petition of certain of his Majesty's most loyal and obedient subjects to his Majesty King George the Sixth humbly sheweth:

That his Majesty's petitioners are the persons who removed the Stone of Destiny from Westminster Abbey:

That, in removing the Stone of Destiny, they have no desire to injure his Majesty's property, nor to pay disrespect to the Church of which he is the temporal head:

That the Stone of Destiny is, however, the most ancient symbol of Scottish nationality and, having been removed from Scotland by force and retained in England in breach of the pledge of his Majesty's predecessor, King Edward III of England, and its proper place of retention is among his Majesty's Scottish people who, above all, hold this symbol dear:

That therefore his Majesty's petitioners will most readily return the stone to the safe keeping of his

Majesty's officers if his Majesty will but graciously assure them that in all time coming the Stone will remain in Scotland in such of his Majesty's properties or otherwise as shall be deemed fitting by him:

That such an assurance will in no way preclude the use of the Stone in any coronation of any of his Majesty's successors whether in England or Scotland:

That his Majesty's humble petitioners are prepared to submit to his Majesty's Ministers or their representatives proof that they are the people able, willing, and eager to restore the Stone of Destiny to the keeping of his Majesty's officers:

That his Majesty's petitioners, who have served him in peril and peace, pledge again their loyalty to him, saving always their right and duty to protest against the actions of his Ministers if such actions are contrary to the wishes of the spirit of his Majesty's people:

In witness of the good faith of his Majesty's petitioners the following information concerning a watch left in Westminster Abbey on December 25, 1950, is appended: (1) The mainspring of the watch was recently repaired; (2) The bar holding the right-hand wrist strap to the watch had recently been broken and soldered:

This information is given in lieu of signature by his Majesty's petitioners, being in fear of apprehension:"

(Scottish Daily Express, Dec.30, 1950).

THIRTY SEVEN

Ireland, 1996 The Rocky Road to Dublin

"My reservations were for a flight from Dublin next week," said Val. "I was amazed at how much cheaper it was to fly home from Ireland than from Portugal. But perhaps this can be changed, if you'd allow me to come with to Scotland? I had planned to see Tara, and then head home. But now I'm infected with your mystery stone!"

Everyone responded in unison, and Donnie was especially exuberant.

"We'd love to have you with me. I mean I'd like you with us, Val!"

So Val made some calls to the airline, got her tickets postponed for several more weeks, and they headed off to see the Mound of the Hostages and Tara.

" I know it used to be the high seat of Irish kings," said Val, "but that's about all I know. There is a standing stone there, too."

"That's purported to be the Irish "Lia Fail." Angus went on to explain the myth and everyone listened. "The stone supposedly makes a noise or sigh when the chosen king touches it. Like an oracle. There's another myth in England about a sword in a stone. It's like the ancients revered the truth of stone, as if stones had unseen powers."

"I have always had an affinity with stones, " said Ali. "I sure wish they could talk! At least with a microscope we can tell their composition and find out their origins. Every mineral has its own crystalline structure. They're like fingerprints."

"That's how the scientists determined that the stone in Westminster is very much like the stones from Perth?" said Val.

"It would be a lot easier if someone wrote on the rock, or had inscribed it with words," said Donnie. "Seems like I remember that Robert the Bruce had it inscribed with Latin?"

Angus smiled, seeing that Donnie still had the archaeologist's need for connections. "If so, the letters no longer remain, at least not on the stone in Westminster. Maybe the English chiseled 'em off. Would'na be too surprised wi' that," said Angus. Then he continued:

"But the Tara site is a huge mound, constructed by the people of ancient Ireland. There are two standing stones at the summit. Supposedly there were trials or contests in choosing the new king, and the applicant had to race his chariot between the two stones. As the chariot sides hit the stones, the stones would scream if he was the chosen king."

As the intrepid adventurers made their way to Tara, Val was exuberant. She had found all of her companions to be interesting people, and that particularly handsome man named Donnie was pulling at her heart strings. He seemed so vulnerable, a lost puppy really. But Val liked Ali, too, and especially admired the strength of family bonds that had saved Donnie. She was a bit envious of having such a sister. It had been many years since Val had felt the security of family, or anyone who cared.

" I've really enjoyed your company and friendship," said Val. "Perhaps meeting you all is "written in the stars" laughed Val.

"Well, the feeling is certainly mutual," said Ali.

"Who knows, maybe I should try another grad program in Chicago." said Donnie.

Valerie began to blush, but gave Donnie a hug. "We could be a good team digging in the mounds, for sure. Though that's a far cry from digging in Egypt."

"I think my Egypt days are over," said Donnie. "The more I think about trying to regain my lost memory, it makes me sad. I'm thinking maybe just start over with my life, do something new and different. But I am really hungry, right now."

"Hunger is the best kitchen," quipped Angus. "The lad will repair himself with something good to eat...and a good draft of ale."

They quickly found a nice pub and filled their bellies with tasty Irish food. Musicians in one corner provided a "ceilidhe, and everyone in the pub was singing traditional songs. Ali moved over to talk with them, and soon they let her sit in on harp. She had plenty of O'Carolan tunes in her fingers, and everyone applauded the youthful American lass. It was the highlight of the evening, and perhaps they stayed too late. The B&B was a welcome sight in the wee hours of the morning. Tomorrow they would be at Tara.

The Mound of Tara loomed in the distance. It was a sunny day to view the Irish surroundings, and soon the Americans heard all the history involved with the "hostages" and the Irish myths. Angus was perturbed to hear that the 'Lia Fail' was not in its original position, that it had been moved to its present location about 600 feet to the south. It was now in "Cormac's House" a circular rath, and shares its space with a huge monument to IRA fighters who died in 1938. So nothing in the area was of particular interest, certainly of no geologic importance to Ali. The mound itself had not even been excavated, and though the earthworks were many, nothing really made any sense to Val either. The stone itself was sandstone, in the shape of a pillar, about four feet high. Not much was said among the group, their travels together had come to a rather unremarkable end in Ireland, except for the budding relationship between Val and Donnie. For the extra time together had proven a real gift to Donnie's self-confidence. He felt much better than the washed up and out of work archaeologist he was, and in Valerie's eyes he saw admiration and what he hoped would turn into real emotional support.

THIRTY EIGHT

A wee bit of Scottish history

In 1292, John Balliol was solemnly crowned in the Church of the Canons Regular at Scone. The King took the oath that he would protect Holy Mother Church and his subjects, by ruling justly. He would establish good laws and continue the customs of the nation of Scotland. This was the last time that a King of Scots sat on the Royal Coronation Stone at Scone, for according to history, Edward 1 took the stone to London in 1296. He purportedly also took the Scottish royal regalia, the scepter and crown, and sixty-five boxes of relics. It is believed that thereafter the Stone was in Westminster Abbey in London.

In the Treaty of Northampton, 1328, between the Kingdom of Scotland and the Kingdom of England, it was agreed that the captured Stone would be returned to Scotland. However, riotous crowds prevented it from being removed from Westminster Abbey. The Stone remained in England for another six centuries, even after James VI of Scotland assumed the English throne as James the First of England. For the next century, the Stuart Kings and Queens of Scotland once again sat on the stone, but at their coronation as Kings and Queens of England.

THIRTY NINE

Isle of Lewis, Scotland, November 1996

The flight from Edinburgh to Stornoway had been delayed several hours, as a force ten gale did not provide for a safe landing. Sadie Morrison, Angus' sister, met the group of Americans, the only foreigners on the small plane. "Where do you stay when you're not here at home?" she asked as she sized up the red-haired Americans who looked every bit Scottish. After proper greetings all around, she put everyone in her Land Rover and treated them to a boisterous drive down the one lane road to Tolsta Chaolais.

Angus had told them that the village of Tolsta Chaolais had about forty homes, though its people were employed on the mainland. The daily ferry at Stornoway brought provisions and tourists, but Lewis was a lonely, barren, and bleak place to live, where peat, flowers, and bracken grew. There were no indigenous trees. could grow. This far north, a mere five hours of true daylight could be had at this time of year.

The ride through the treeless landscape was embellished by conversation in the car as Angus gave his sister the short version of their travels and sights they had seen. Soon enough they came upon Sadie's B & B, the "Black Hoose," and soon were made comfortable inside.

"Lang may yer lum reek," said Angus, "'tis well to be at hame." The common Scottish expression for having smoke in the chimney made Sadie laugh. He gave Sadie an expressive bear hug, twirling her around until they nearly lost their balance. The Black House had a rather low ceiling of thatch and timber. The walls were of stone and peat, thick enough to keep out the continual winds. It was black, not only from years of peat fire smoke, but for the fact that there were no windows.

"What are you doing coming at this time of year?" jibed Sadie. "The tourist season is lang spent, and the darkness of winter is upon us. The hearth will warm ye up. Tea is soon ready."

"We're havin' a bit o' adventure," replied Angus, "as I told you we've gone to search oot the 'Stone o' Scone.'"

"The news has been full o' it," said Sadie with a wee chuckle. "The Sachenachs will return oor Stone on 30 November. You'll be wanting to be in Edinburgh for it, for sure. So at least I'll have a few days with my emigrant brother!"

"The Sachenachs will do their huge ceremony, full of pomp and circumstance, but I fear little improvement for our people. They pretend to make reparations for all their sins, and their Parliament can vote all they want. They'll ne'er be able to really repay us," said Angus.

"What happened?" asked Donnie. Both Val and Ali had quizzical expressions too.

Angus scowled at the history he told. "Well, in 1707 the Scottish Parliament was dissolved and the country was unified with England. This was decided by aristocrats, not the common people. At least not by the people who truly loved Scotland. The people were taxed into poverty, then evicted, whole villages at a time. It was called the "Clearances." Scotland lost nearly half its population during those hundred years! The English can never undo what they've done." Then his voice rose, "They can return our Stone, but not our people."

"Enough of old politics!" said Sadie. "I'll treat our Americans to our ancient ruins, things they would be more interested in, for sure. You've a few days before 30 November."

"I want to show them the Carloway Broch, see the main Calanais site, and maybe even spend some time on the beach if the weather holds. Just some sight seein' for these folks," said Angus.

"Well, I can loan ye torches for some sight seein'," said Sadie. "There's no much light to be had this time o' year. Maybe by midday the standing stones will greet ye wi' some strong daylight. I hope yer people here ha' warm cleids. But, I've been knittin' up quite a store. The ladies at least can ha' a jumper or twa."

Sadie showed Ali and Val to a huge wicker basket filled with thick wool sweaters, mostly heather grey or sienna brown. An intricate Celtic knotwork pattern was knitted in rows down the front and back, and along the length of sleeves.

"I work my own yarn here, too," Sadie said. "My spinning wheel and spindle are here, if you'd like a lesson a' times."

"These sweaters, I guess you call them 'jumpers,' are so heavy and warm. How long does it take you to make just one?" asked Val.

"Best part o' a month, mostly, considering if I have to stop and spindle more yarn. I prefer makin' child sizes these days though. They do sell very well at a shop in Stornoway. They're nice to me there, too, don't take much o' commission. There's a historical movement to keep the old ways, so they support my craft. But so much has been lost."

Ali and Val were thrilled to pick out two sweaters, finding that though they were a bit large, they would then fit over their other layers. Val was so short her sweater hung way past her hipline.

"'Tis almost a dress on you," said Sadie, "but that's the style these days. Now let's get you all some supper."

The Black House had a cooking area built into the central fireplace. Soon curls of smoke went up through the ceiling vent and Sadie put some covered iron pots into the coals. It was warm and cozy in the vicinity of the heated fireplace, but the stone and sod walls were cold to the touch. At sleep time bedding would be moved closer to the central fireplace, although the coldest part of winter had not yet come. Angus explained the "but and ben" of having a house with rooms for the livestock, though Sadie kept no sheep. The wool she used was a gift from a neighbor's sheep, who supplied all of the crafters in the village.

Sadie brought out a fine dinner. Slices of black and white puddings for the Americans to taste, plus a hearty lamb stew. Tatties n' neeps and buttery bannock buns filled everyone's bellies, and soon after came a dessert of fruit trifle. Sadie explained that she kept the Black House true to tradition, but an out building held toilets and a refrigerator. Though electricity had come thirty years ago, she had signed an agreement with the Sottish Tourist Board to keep the house as a living museum. Any modern advances were kept out of sight. Most food was cooked over the open fire, a cast-iron covered skillet provided an oven for short-bread and other baking. Light inside during the day, and for dark winters, was provided by kerosene lanterns, candles, and the peat fire flame. It was a cozy existence for the elderly matron. Sadie still had hopes of being like "Kate Dalrymple" in the song, but she'd never be an heiress to any fortune, and eligible bachelors on Lewis were as scarce as palm trees.

"On the morrow I'll drive ye over to Calanais and the Carloway Broch, at least by midmorning there should be enough daylight to see the landscape. I'll call ahead and get permission for the Broch. If there's not a force ten gale we can have a picnic!" Sadie had plenty of thermoses to pack hot tea, and though they might have to eat inside the Land Rover, it would be an interesting excursion.

Dawn broke just before nine AM and the hardy travelers went off to see the sights on Lewis. Carloway Broch, called Doune Broch by the locals, was just two miles or so from Sadie's house. The Broch stood prominently like some ancient guard tower, open to the sky. Two concentric walls circled each other forty feet into the air. A low door had a small enclosure just inside, enough room for one person to stand guard.

"This is all dry stone construction," said Angus. "The stone stairway between the walls spirals up to what would have been several floors. Look at the masonry here, and you can see where the stones would have supported a floor. We think the lower section would have housed the animals, though the door is only large enough for sheep. The broch is probably two thousand years old, considering the building methods, and though it would provide shelter, it would be of little use as a castle keep."

"Yes, the two windows are looking into the interior rather than outside," said Donnie. "Maybe this isn't a defensive tower at all. Could it be for production of something, like tanning leather or making ceramics?"

"I don't find any vitrification of the stones," said Ali, "but you're right. This isn't a tower for withstanding any siege. If there were wooden floors above at various levels, there's really no evidence of them except that the stone protrusions could support a floor. Maybe they were smoking fish? Like suspended poles that crossed the open space, just supported at the ends by the protrusion of rocks. That would make this thing something more useful."

"It's a bit like the Toreon in Portugal I've seen," said Val. "But you're right, having the concentric walls and but a few interior windows makes me think they were producing something here. Maybe even drying peat for fuel. Perhaps in ancient times there was a lot of rain, and this at least could hold a fire to dry something. The stone construction is as amazing as any I've seen. They were masters of dry stone construction to have this height of tower without any buttressing or internal support. The one wall that has partially collapsed at the top is still tight as the day they raised it."

As it was now lunch time, Sadie brought out her picnic basket of savories. The peat was dry on the sunnier side of the hill, so Sadie threw down a sturdy blanket, and the group had a filling lunch. Thermoses of hot tea, a flask of whisky, and hearty meat pies filled their bellies before the wind began to change. Angus and Sadie broke out in a Gaidhlig song about the Great Selkie of Skule Skerrie, then explained the verses in English.

"The Selkie is a seal man, who takes human form on land. He finds a willing maiden to mate with, then comes back later to collect his baby son," said Angus.

"The legend says, he gives her a 'bag o' gold' for the wee bairnie, then takes him out to 'swim the foam'."

"Doesn't the mother protest?" asked Val.

Sadie said, "Och aye! She doesn't even know who the bairnie's father is. It's like she's hypnotized. But she has no choice. It's not hard to see how the song excuses an out of wedlock bairnie, and its disappearance. And seals do look very human when they poke their noses up to watch those on shore."

"The light here is spooky enough, too," said Donnie. "I know it's around noon but it isn't really sunny. Soon we'll be "in the gloamin' I guess."

Sounds of the surf and ocean birds contributed to the lonely peat covered hills. The sunlight provided little warmth, the skies were low with clouds, and though they had plenty of food, there was a chill in the air that got them soon back into the Rover. They drove back the way they'd come, passed the village, and after another four miles north came upon the standing stone circle that was Calanais I.

The standing stone circle was one of four sites, each one a bit further north. Thousands of years had passed since their erection. Only a century ago a sheep farmer discovered the circle because he had tried to move a stone protruding from the peat. After digging around to move the rock, he found that the stone went down another ten feet. Peat moss grows excruciatingly slowly, about a half-inch a year, so the original ground level was meters below his feet. Dating the stone circles correlated with the depth of peat covering them, and they were found to be thousands of years old.

Angus explained more to them, taking on his professorial demeanor as if he had a captive group of students in his lecture hall. The standing stone site was thousands of years older than the broch, and would have only a loose connection to Scota's people. But soon enough he broke into his gleeful love of the sites, touching and embracing the stones as if they were long lost cousins.

"Look here, everyone. The alignment is not only solar, but also lunar. Being so far north, nearly to the Arctic Circle, we could see the moon rising and setting in a straight line against the farther horizon. That mountain ridge is called the Sleeping Beauty, because the moon appears to stop and rest where the mountain dips. We're here on the wrong week for that, but just imagine how it must have looked to the ancients that constructed this stone circle."

"It must have taken several generations of observations," said Ali, "just like the circle at Penafiel. The similarities between those and Stonehenge, and all the others.....it must have been a major part of their civilization. And worldwide."

"There are even standing stone circles in Tyre, even some circles in Egypt, even some along the Silk Road into China," said Angus.

Donnie was listening, cataloging everything as usual, trying to fill gaps in his memory. "It's a wonder to me that so many megaliths are still standing in Scotland. I would think the Christians would have purposely taken them down."

"That's not an easy chore," said Angus, "for the stones are buried deeply in order to stay vertical. The people of later times probably just thought of them as road markers since so many of them are in line of sight from mountain to mountain, all across Scotland."

"How did they know where the ley lines were?" asked Val.

"No one knows," said Angus.

"Ach, You need a Druid," said Sadie. "And they're long gone! It's not a full moon this week, either, so although it will be dark in a few hours, you're not likely to see the moon do its rest stop. It is a very magical thing to see the moon move in a straight line over the stones, then appear to stop completely where the ridge dips. I've seen it dozens of times, and it still is very spiritual, even to a Christian like me."

Donnie held Val's hand and they walked a circle around the stones, weaving around each one, as each dolmen was different. The stones weren't shaped or worked smooth like the stones at Stonehenge, nor would any of them have supported a cross piece stone. Instead, the stones must have been chosen for their length, and the intricate swirls of gneiss granite caused in their formation. There was a central "altar" stone, but Angus explained that that rock may have been added later, by other people. There was no way to be sure about that.

The skies began to darken into the twilight, and though they could not see the ocean from this vantage point, they could hear the surf pounding in the distance. All was very quiet and still, and with the light fading, and the wind dancing through the stones, the group naturally met in the center of the site. They formed a little circle, embracing each other as if a ceremony would soon ensue.

"Give us strength and hope for the future of our Land. And bless us each with your guidance, to be kind and helpful to others, always," said Angus.

Sadie gave her brother a tight hug, then a pinch on the cheek.

"That's for the de'il in you, brother, for praying here and not in church!"

"Seemed like a good thing to say," said Angus. "Wasn't sacrilege."

"Just teasin'" said Sadie. "But we should be off soon, as it's a trek back to the Rover, and what's left of sunlight will cut out behind the rise all a'sudden."

"I'm cold," said Val. "even in my jumper."

Donnie again put his arm around Val as they all walked back down to the car. He liked the sensation of keeping her warm and close. It was as if she was part of the family now, his new family. And the feeling was mutual. Val smiled up at her tall laddie, and his face shone with a strong sense of new-found strength. They were walking "in the gloaming."

It had been an exceptional excursion on Lewis. Ali pocketed a small stone that would join her little collection of basalt, limestone from Tara, and sandstone from Portugal. Angus and Sadie led the way to the car, holding hands to steady their footing. Sadie was cautious, as long shadows hid their footsteps in the soft peat. They drove the four miles back to Sadie's, using headlights on the car as darkness was falling.

Safe back at her home, Sadie lit the lanterns and began warming the peat fire to life. Soon they were all warmed through. Angus suggested a farewell dinner at another place in Tolsta Chaolis, and soon they were off again to the four-star restaurant.

Lewis House had once been a private Gregorian style mansion, two stories with a clear view of the western ocean. There were no trees, but the proprietors had planted a lovely garden of hardy shrubs that would flower for some time in the summer. The ceaseless wind brought the smell of the sea, and the stone walls of the house had weathered many a strong gale. Upstairs were B&B rooms, while the first floor had been turned into a well renowned restaurant. Mainlanders would come on the ferry for an expensive dinner, stay the night, then catch the morning ferry back to Skye.

"In olden times," said Angus, "farmers would send their sheep flocks to the mainland on the ferry, with only their sheep-dog to control them. The dogs would be fed by other farmers on the route, then sent back alone to their masters. This way the farmer didn't have to make the trip on the ferry, but trusted the dog and people along the way to care for his sheep, all the way to market at Fort William. It worked this way for centuries."

"Amazing that they trusted the other villagers to not poach a sheep or two!" said Ali.

"And trust their dog to take the trip, care that none were lost, and remember his way alone," said Val.

"There's a lot o' pride in an owner for his dog," said Angus. "They were worth their weight in gold, for sure.'

The menu for the month of November sported a St. Andrew's Day Dinner of Bawd Bree, Haggis, and Howtowdie with Chappit tatties. Val was surprised to see the liver dumplings in the soup, as they reminded her of those served in a Bohemian restaurant back in Chicago. Donnie was asking for seconds of the soup, which the waitress was happy to give.

"What about haggis?" asked Val. "I'd like to know what that is before I eat it."

"The haggis is a steamed meat loaf, cooked in a sheep's stomach or paunch. It is lamb, oatmeal and lots of spicy pepper, really a peasant sort of dish." said Sadie. "It's oor national dish, well renowned by the poet laureate, Rabbie Burns."

"Aye, we'll toast the haggis when it arrives," said Angus. "But though everyone expects haggis for this meal, the second course will be salmon dressed with lemon and crabmeat. So if the haggis isn't tae yer likin, you will have more things to taste."

"I'll be happy to eat everything I'm served," said Val, "I've never been squeamish. Just wanted to know what's in it, since it seems to be some sort of joke."

"Aye, 'tis "hamely fare"," said Angus, "but well worth its reputation as 'king o' the puddin' race."

Before the dessert course was to be served, the restaurant brought out their fiddler, who played some slow airs as well as some strathspeys for dancing. Couples around the room joined arms and danced to the tunes. Angus danced with Sadie and put a sparkle in her eye as he dipped her at the end of one tune. Donnie asked Val to try a slow waltz with him, and she was delighted.

As he held her waist, Val put her head on Donnie's shoulder, and felt the strong leadership of his feet. She felt protected and safe in his arms, but he was still fragile. In many ways, Donnie was a lost soul, starting his life over. And Val was adrift in the world. Perhaps the two of them could make one intact person. Donnie looked down at her face and smiled. Val brushed her lips against his cheek. And then they kissed.

Still dancing, Donnie said, "Thank you for coming with us, Val. You have such an easy way among strangers, you seem so trusting of people you've barely met. Where does that come from?"

"I don't know," replied Val. "Some sort of fatalism, I guess. I tend to believe that what will be, will be, and don't question my future. People really are good hearted, for the most part. I guess that's why I was uneasy in Portugal at the museum. I just didn't want to believe that any harm would come to me. And, I like to think there's no such thing as a coincidence."

"You mean, our meeting was meant to be?"

"Yeah. We never know where our steps will lead. Just have to listen to the small voice in our head, and trust that the future will unfold as it's supposed to."

"That's determinism," said Donnie. "I don't believe in that stuff."

"Well, you asked. That's why I'm such a free spirit, I guess. I have this feeling that everything will come out the way it's supposed to happen. Felt that way all my life."

"It's okay, I understand. But, it's my choice for this dance. Hope you liked it." Then Donnie gave her a little twirl as the music ended, and they went back to their table for dessert.

The waitress brought out a large Drambuie souffle topped with orange whisky cream. There was sticky toffee pudding topped with raspberry and caramel sauce, and shortbread cookies piled high like an Egyptian pyramid, as each triangular cookie poked out like some buttery pine tree. After-dinner wines and Drambuie cordials were followed by hot black tea.

"We will be leavin' in the mornin' for Edinburgh," said Angus. I've made reservations not far from Old Town. We were lucky to find a place with the city full to the gunnels all getting ready for the Stone's arrival. We'll hae a few days to see the sights of Edinburgh, and then be in the crowds to see the Stone.

Ali looked at Sadie, half expecting her to say she'd join them on the flight. Instead, Sadie said, "I've certainly enjoyed your visit. Thank you all for bringing my brother hame. I won't go wi' you to the mainland as I don't like crowds. I'm so lost when I'm not in my wee hame, don't think I'll ever travel to America. But be sure to tell me all about Edinburgh when you can."
Sadie's voice trailed off, and she became wistful, knowing it might be the last she'd see of her brother. Each of them understood the ache of separation. How would they each go back to the normal separate lives they should lead? The emotion hung in the silent space over their empty plates. Angus would return to his position at UCLA, Ali would finish her degree. But Val? Back to Dublin and her flight back to Illinois. And Donnie? Should he go to Chicago, Los Angeles, or back to Boston? He did not know.

In the morning, Angus loaded their baggage into Sadie's Land Rover. Their flight from Stornoway would be short, much quicker than taking the daily ferry to the mainland. Even so, taking a ferry was out of the question for Donnie's frail foundations.

"I wish you enough," said Sadie as she embraced Angus at the airport.

"I wish you enough," echoed Angus as he kissed his little sister. Goodbye's were always hard, as an ocean would separate them soon. Donnie, Ali, and Val hugged Sadie in succession, and heard her say the same parting wish.

But then Sadie added, "Haste ye back!" And then no one wanted to leave.

FORTY

Edinburgh, 30 November, 1996

In July of 1996, Michael Forsyth, Conservative MP and Secretary of State for Scotland's Parliament, had risen to discuss the government papers from 1950 that said England would return the Coronation Stone. It had not yet been done, so demands were made, now to be fulfilled this St.Andrew's Day, 30 November, 1996. The Stone was to be enshrined in Edinburgh Castle.

There had been some controversy over this, as Viscount Stormont, the son of the Earl of Mansfield, had suggested that the Stone be brought to Scone Palace instead. After all, that should have been the official depository, historically speaking. But it was decided that Edinburgh Castle had the requisite security already in place for such a relic, and Edinburgh was Scotland's capital. The Honors of Scotland, the regalia of crown, sword, and scepter were already ensconced securely in the throne room of Edinburgh castle, which awaited its long delayed "Lia Fail."

Published words of Alex Salmond, the vociferous member of the Scottish Nationalist Party, proclaimed, "We'll take what he's giving us back, and then we'll ask for more." The underground movement for "devolution" had begun, and though no date for such a vote had been determined, MP Salmond knew the people of Scotland would someday be given a chance to vote for succession from the United Kingdom.

In preparation for this historic ceremony, the Stone had been removed from Westminster Abbey on the fifteenth of November, by the use of a block and tackle. Great care had been taken so as not to damage the throne, for the ancient wood was brittle and had already been broken previously by thieves. It took five hours to remove the stone, lower it into a fitted wooden box, then safely seal it for transport overnight under police escort to Coldstream Bridge, the historic border between England and Scotland.

A specially designed flatbed vehicle guarded by the Coldstream Guards, met the Secretary of State for Scotland and the Lord Lieutenant of Berwickshire, and a new escort was drawn from the Royal Scots and the King's Own Scottish Borderers. A military brass and pipe band wearing Stewart tartan played as the Stone was taken to the Conservation Centre for analysis and treatment. The Stone had survived the 400 mile journey without damage.

The massive Edinburgh castle complex, built on a basalt extrusion, had once been surrounded by a moat. After draining the loch, the Royal Mile was constructed with barrows of dirt that had been excavated in the building of "New Town." This dirt formed the slow incline up to the castle, so all in the crowd could see the parade advancing. Our intrepid adventurers stood in the throng of ten thousand people who watched the specially adapted Land Rover with bullet-proof glass come into view.

"There's one thing the English do well," said Angus. "They know how to make a parade! Those are the Lothian and Borders Police, and the Royal Scots Dragoon Guards."

"Who are those men in black velvet?" asked Val.

"Those are the Queen's archers. Their longbows aren't strung, they're just for show. As if six archers could protect the stone. But they get to use their velvet jackets," Angus quipped.

The stone itself rested on a wooden pallet atop a plush red velvet cloth, and all this was covered by armored glass. The spectacle was a vision of a sharp-angled glass sarcophagus protecting some dead symbol of a nation's regal past.

"Who is that ahead? He looks important," said Donnie.

"Oh, that's His Royal Highness Prince Andrew. His title is the Duke of York. And I see the Secretary of State for Scotland, The Commissioners of the Regalia, The Lord Lyon King of Arms, The Lord High Constable of Scotland, and the Gold Stick for Scotland. The Lord Lyon is the keeper of coats of arms, and he decides what's historic or authentic for the heraldry things. I think those men in blue are the Hereditary Bearers of the Royal Banner of Scotland. You see the Lion Rampant, and the Scottish Saltire? The English banned the use of the flag for the last hundred years or so, but now it's allowed."

"They sure have a lot of officials," said Ali. Angus pretended to organize his invisible medals and epaulets. He gave a little strut, imitating the officious manner of the English flamboyance, bowed and stomped his feet to attention.

Val giggled and said, "I do like the bagpipe music, it's loud and makes all those fancy costumes even more ostentatious! Donnie was laughing and really enjoying Angus' antics.

"Can we go into the cathedral?" asked Donnie.

"Ach aye! We'll have to scurry though. We'll be lucky if they'll let us commoners in, but let's try it," said Angus.

As the lorry with the stone was going at an excruciatingly slow pace, with the archers walking slowly beside it, the Americans were able to make it to the west door of St. Giles' Cathedral in time to see it enter. A fanfare of trumpeters played as the stone was escorted into the church, but a swarm of reporters from all the newspapers blocked the entrance after the stone went through. Inside the church service began, and loudspeakers presented the proceedings to the crowd beyond. There were quotations from the Old Testament about the lesson of Jacob and his pillow of stone (Genesis 28, 10-22) which was read in Gaidhlig, and more readings about St. Andrew and his brother Simon Peter as the Rock (St. John 1, 35-42). After the Rev. John MacInroe accepted the Stone from Prince Andrew, and it rested on the solid oak table in front of the grand fireplace in the great hall, the service was ended with more trumpeter's fanfare. The official dignitaries made their exit under security, and the populace was allowed to enter.

So there it sat, resting on its plush dark purple velvet bedding: a pinkish tan sandstone, worn on all corners, lumpy bulges, and only flat on the bottom. Iron rings, impaled at each rectangular end, carried a short length of heavy forged chain which now draped and touched the luxurious velvet. Incised lines on the top surface marked out a rectangle, as if some long ago mason had intended to cut the stone into a regular sized block for a monument, such as a tombstone. There were no apparent inscriptions on the naked stone, nor had the corners any straight angles. Corners were rounded and broken, perhaps from many rough travels over mountains, seas, and centuries.

But it was not Scota's stone.

FORTY ONE

Illinois, September 17, 2014

"Is it the PTSD?" asked Val in a soft voice, her forehead creased with worry. She lay next to her husband, caressing his shoulder as the morning sunlight filled their bedroom. "You thrashed around most of the night. Nearly kicked me. You've been good for such a long time. What is worrying you?"

"I remember dreaming," replied Donnie, "but most of it was a really good dream. I guess I'm surprised that I startled you. I'm not concerned about the baby. Maybe worried about you though. Childbirth stuff."

"The Lamaze classes will get us through OK. Don't worry. I'm not scared," said Val. Even small worries dredged up nightmares for Donnie. "We need to keep using the pen and pad by our bed, so you can write details every time. So, what do you remember?"

Donnie reached for a tube of lotion kept by their bed. The note pad had been replaced by Vitamin E cream, special for stretch marks on pregnant women. He warmed a dollop in his hand before reaching under her nightgown and caressing the belly of his wife and their soon to be born son.

"Cold ocean waves, and falling, like in my old dreams. But then I fell into a damp crypt, dark and mossy. At first the walls seemed slippery, wet, and cold. Cold stone was at every hand, but I didn't feel trapped. Dim light came from outside. It was like a mausoleum, but I felt safe."

Val purred from the smooth caress of Donnie's hand on her belly. The baby inside stirred, as if he too were relaxing with the massage.

"Did you have a sense of where you were? I mean like were we around here? Or far away?" asked Val.

Donnie closed his eyes and paused making circles of lotion with his hand. He tried to recall all the feelings in his dream, because it was different, somehow safe, not like his terror filled nightmares of being lost at sea.

"I remember a sort of glow in the room, like dawn coming through old windows. Oh my gosh, there was a person there with me. It wasn't you, but a woman with red hair. I think. It's weird, but I think I've dreamt of her before, like she has something to tell me. But I wanted to get out of there, so she pointed to a doorway. It was dark though. Then I woke up."

Val turned close to Donnie, caressing his face. "Don't worry yourself now, my love, I'm not jealous or insecure. Just next time tell her you're taken."

Val kissed Donnie on the chin and walked in her muumuu to the kitchen to make breakfast. She was eating for two now and had baked up a batch of apricot scones. She put the kettle to boil for tea, and had oatmeal bubbling in no time.

Donnie was eating for two also and had put some extra weight on his sparse frame. His usual appetite seemed dented by his recent dream. Val knew Donnie didn't want to go back on sleep meds, but there was a possibility of hurting her while they slept. At least he was not a sleep-walker. Donnie played with his oatmeal as he had done as a child, but he was smiling. It was made by his loving wife in their ranch house kitchen. It wasn't the hospital. The pastel kitchen had potted plants crowding the window sill. Fall colors painted the trees outside. Yellow wallflowers bloomed in clumps on swells that looked like waves, or the scenery in Scotland. Prairie grasses undulated with the morning breeze. Sunlight streamed through the kitchen sparking another beautiful autumn day in Illinois. Tall waving grass covered the prairie as it had for millennia, and Donnie had nothing to fear.

Outside, the jeep held their archaeology tools and a thoughtfully packed overnight case for the hospital, ready at a moment's notice. Val's baby was due any day now, and the hospital was only a ten minute drive from their dig, though the house was an hour away. Like Donnie, she had not wanted to leave their dig until the last minute and she had been feeling fine. Donnie was bemused that real civilization was built nearly on top of what had been a long-held settlement of native people.

The dig had been promising from the start. Donnie was almost psychic in finding where to look for artifacts, and soon the lab tent was littered with potsherds and broken implements. Their most interesting find had been an axe head. Not stone, but iron, rusted and pitted by corrosion. It had only a partial shank, no wooden handle remained. It was shaped like many found in ancient Scandinavia and the dulled cutting edge was well worn from use. As if some long lost Viking had hewn a tree or two, built a boat and sailed away on the nearby river.

Donnie was the head archaeologist now, working under a lucrative grant from the University of Chicago. He had not finished his dissertation, even with Dr. Morrisson's help. His paper was on migration patterns of Haplogroup X, comparing DNA evidence of Cherchan culture with that of Spanish Basques and the Mound Builders here in Illinois. But it wasn't Egyptology. He had never been able to pursue his Egyptian papyrus finds from Spain, since he couldn't remember the river or the territory where they were found, nor was there authority for that dig in Spain.

That thread was closed to him, tangled in ganglia that might never reopen.

Angus had been negotiating with the Spanish government for an exploration in the area near the Mediterranean that he felt was promising, but without any actual evidence, the officials were not inclined to grant permission for such a fishing trip. Still, Angus kept trying, researching the princess, and hoping Donnie would remember the original location of the secret papyrus. He had pored over that Egyptian papyrus from that long ago dig in Spain, but could find no clues to where it had been found There were well documented remains of Egyptian's mining concerns along many rivers in southeastern Spain. But which one? Those remains at least weren't controversial.

Now this axe-head was a different problem, both for its nature, and for Donnie's credibility. It shouldn't have been there. It was anachronistic, but its provenance was secure as it was dug from a layer far below the surface finds. Heavy iron could not have been blown in by wind or transported by water. Donnie considered leaving the artifact out of the inventory because it defied explanation.

This piece of five pound iron could make or break his career. He had to be prudent.

Using the internet, Donnie was able to find other references to iron axe heads in America. Several sources were cited, but the amateurs who had found the things had removed them, thus destroying their provenance. Val wanted the axe head to be published as a great find of Norse exploration. Donnie wanted to be more cautious.

After breakfast, they dressed and drove for an hour or so, then found the bumpy dirt road to the dig.

"Isn't it too bumpy for you?" Donnie asked. He was concerned when he saw her belly jiggle with the little bounces over the rutted dirt road.

"Nope. Those little jolts actually feel good," said Val. "But I'm tired of feeling so bloated and ungainly." The baby was due this week, but she'd take any day sooner. "It would be cool if our baby came into the world out here on our dig."

"No, not cool at all," said Donnie. "Your confidence scares the hell out of me."

Sunshine blazed on the prairie landscape as Donnie parked the Jeep under the shade of a scrubby tree. As they pulled to a stop, another archaeologist named Pete walked over. He and two others were camped out at the dig, to keep the site secure overnight. Pothunters had been known to ruin many promising finds, but as yet this midden had been undisturbed.

"Looks like good weather today," said Pete. He had long stringy blond hair pushed back with a headband, a torn t-shirt hung loosely over his dirty jeans. His face and arms were tanned like leather from many bright hours under hot sun. "Had some raccoons visit last night, nasty buggers! Seems like no matter how well we manage our stuff, they can get into it. They managed to open the metal tool box latch, didn't find any food of course. We've been keeping edibles locked in the camper. But it's spooky hearing them rummaging around in the dark."

"It's no use setting out traps," said Donnie. "Maybe play the radio all night? I hope you're up for the next grid today. Val wants her hand in it too, couldn't keep her away or leave her alone."

Pete nodded, grabbed the tool bag, and they strode along the string marked plots to the next grid. Molly and Tom were already easing their blunt shovels into the turf, waved "hello" and kept at their slow lift of prairie grass. The dirt was dry under the first foot or so of roots and pebbles, and soon they were at the layers they wanted. Donnie set to digging as well while Val sat on a big piece of cardboard while sketching the embankment, noting larger rocks for bearings. Soon they had exposed the ancient layers of a Native American midden. Broken pottery and seashells began to emerge from the dirt bank. Val cataloged each find with her drawing, measured and sketched each potsherd, and was happy in the sunshine for several hours until her ankles were met by a rush of water.

"My water broke!" called Val.

"Any contractions?" asked Molly.

"No, but I guess that will come next. The doctor told me it could be many hours before the baby really comes out. But I'd rather stay here, said Val.

"No way, lady," said Donnie. "I want clean sheets and sterile water for our baby! We're off to the birthing center. See the rest of you later."

No sooner had Donnie said those words when the embankment where Val was sitting began to slide out from under her. She was sliding feet first on her cardboard like a conveyor belt, into a gaping hole. The earth was moving slowly but there was nothing for Val to grab onto, so she just did her best to remain upright. Donnie jumped after her, hoping to catch her when the slide stopped. Luckily, the sinkhole formed by eroding limestone wasn't more than ten feet deep.

When the dirt came to a stop, Val was laughing. Donnie protected her with a bear hug, desperate to keep her safe. They were both covered in sand and dirt, but safe enough. Pete, Molly, and Tom made the easy slide down without falling, as rubble skittered under their feet.

Before their wondering eyes a series of small caverns were before them. Their Indian midden had been deposited over what looked like ancient burial grounds. Carved catacombs emerged from the limestone formation. Donnie and Val shook off the dust and dirt and stood there, embracing. Speechless at first, then everyone began cheering and hugging each other.

"You've got magic water!" yelled Molly. "Look what you did!"

Val and Donnie stood in disbelief. Even at this distance, they could see burial bundles, baskets, and intact pottery within easy reach. Val bent to retrieve her sketchbook when the first contraction hit, nearly doubling her over.

"Ooh, guess that's a contraction," she said. "How can we leave *now*?"

"Just like this," said Donnie. He encircled her waist and carefully guided her up the slope. In minutes he had her loaded into the Jeep. Donnie gave instructions to the others, but they knew not to disturb anything until proper precautions could be made. They would rope off the area and begin sketching, photographing and otherwise clearing the rubble. Donnie and Val drove off in a cloud of dust.

The ten minute drive seemed longer, but Val counted only two more contractions on their wild ride to the hospital. Soon she was properly washed and draped, and Donnie was washed and gowned for the delivery room. Their Lamaze training kicked in, with Donnie squeezing Val's palm through contractions until the baby's crown burst into the bright world. Another strong push, and Val delivered her new son, who gave a loud scream as he entered the world.

"Good job, Val," said the attending doctor. "You have a son. What do you want to name him?"

"His name is Andrew," they said in unison, "Drew for short."

"Andrew Angus Cameron," added Donnie.

After the baby was weighed and cleaned a bit he was put into Val's arms. He had a head full of reddish blonde hair, and the blue eyes of his father. The happy couple was wheeled into a recovery room blessed with subdued lighting and soft music. Donnie crept into the bed beside Val while she cradled their son to her breast. The warmth of the white sheets and smooth blanket warmed Val's tired muscles as the excitement of the day turned into quiet evening. They spoke of future plans for their son, but images of the collapsed dig surfaced into their reverie.

"What culture do you think we unearthed?" asked Val. "Native Americans don't make burials like that. I wanted the baby to come, but not right then!"

"We need to be really careful, do stuff right," said Donnie. "We'll get back there as soon as we can, but I want you to rest and put it out of your head for right now. I'm going to call Ali and Angus with our news. I expect Ali will want to see the cave-in when she comes out here. We'll know soon enough. Right now, get some sleep." He put his newborn son into the bassinet at Val's bedside, and watched them another moment or two while they drifted to sleep.

Donnie turned out the lights, slipped out of the hospital room, and went down to the waiting room to find a phone. He could have called from the room, but didn't want to interrupt the quiet of his wife and baby. Reporters on television were giving news about the "Devolution Vote" taking place in Scotland. In his excitement about the baby he had forgotten all about the upcoming vote for Scottish people who wanted to cancel their alliance with Britain. Tartan clad people, some with faces painted like the Scottish Saltire flag, were demonstrating for secession from the British Commonwealth. Big signs with the single word "Yes" were waving in crowds, while other crowds of people held signs that screamed "NO!" The demonstrations and speeches were all over the news, and it was St. Andrew's Day.

Donnie had forgotten the significance of 18 September, but it was the chosen day for the vote. Reporters were interviewing important aristocrats for their opinions as news sources flitted between Glasgow, Perth, or Aberdeen. Edinburgh seemed solidly "NO!" while the highland areas were decidedly "YES!" Scone Palace officials gave their opinions saying the vote should be "No" but if it were "Yes" their lands might be put into Scottish Trust rather than private ownership. So they were quite opposed to the SNP views. Various Scottish banks were threatening to make a move to London, as another threat against a "Yes' vote. And those connected with the North Sea oil fields wanted the "Yes" vote, saying Scotland should "ring its own till!" The hospital personnel were distracted by the TV screens. One nurse said maybe Texas could be its own country too. People were unusually lively for a late evening in September. It was not business as usual. The air was filled with excitement as Donnie dialed the number to his sister.

"It's a boy!" called Donnie on the phone to Ali. "And he has red hair like us! Can you come out? Stay with us for a while?"

Ali already had put in for a September vacation from her job at the Bureau of Reclamation, hoping the baby wouldn't be delayed. "Of course, you silly doofus, what do you think! My bags are packed," said Ali. "I'll be out to your place asap, whatever flight is cheapest. Don't forget to take some pictures!" She knew that Donnie relied on his photographic memory so much that he'd no doubt forgot that others wanted pictures. She could hear him making excuses already. "I'll bring my camera, see you soon!"

"Tell Angus for me, too," said Donnie. "He's eight pounds, six ounces, and a head full of red hair. And the appropriate fingers and toes. We named him Andrew Angus. Can't believe he's ours. We'll wrap him in some Cameron tartan for his first picture when you come."

Then Donnie headed back to Val's room, crept in as silently as a kitten, and slid back into bed with his wife. The hospital was quiet. Immediately, he fell into sleep.

Suddenly, Donnie realized he was back in that dank mausoleum and his recurrent dream of cold, wet, mossy stone. But this time he saw the room more clearly. It was not a crypt, but a chapel, and there was a candlelit meeting going on. Not a service. Aristocratic looking people in Prince Charlie jackets were gathered in discussion, holding hands, and with worried talk they were discussing the "vote."

The oldest gentlemen was asking his heirs to swear an oath. Donnie did not hear words at first, but the scene seemed taken from a movie called "Tunes of Glory", with British military seriousness. They swore an oath of secrecy, somehow dependent on the vote happening today. "Our fortunes, and our very way of life, are dependent on a vote of "No," the old man was clearly saying. Donnie felt like he was eavesdropping, even "distant viewing" something of monumental importance.

"You all know this!" said the aged man who stood supported by a cane. Our lands and future depend on the status quo as you well know. Heaven forbid those SNP scoundrels. If we win the day, and we must, then keep your promise and our family secret." Then the old man lowered his head as if in sorrow. "But if the vote is "Yes" we must reveal our treasure to the world, and make Scone Palace the pride of Scotland it once was."

"Father," said the young woman in the group, "we are each sworn to our family secret. Our family has held these lands for four hundred years. Let us pray that the vote be "No!" Let us each touch the Stone and so swear!" Then Donnie watched as each person solemnly laid their right hand on a stone fixed in the chapel wall. It seemed no different than others next to it, but all knew which stone to touch. They promised to keep it safe, and only reveal its true nature if Scotland became free of British rule. And then the old man, his son, and his grandchildren went to the chapel's door. Candlelight was snuffed out, the doors were bolted shut, and Donnie's dream ended. He awakened to find Val smiling at him, waiting to greet the new day.

AFTERWORD

Afterword, Scota's Harp

I wrote this novel to share my love of Scottish history and my intuitive feeling that many myths have origins in fact. History and scenes in the novel have been portrayed accurately to the best of my ability, with the exception of the last scenes where our intrepid adventurers view the return of the Stone of Scone to Edinburgh. In reality, the procession and parade happened several days before the actual entrance of the Stone to St. Giles' Cathedral. The public display of the Stone at the castle took quite some time before being open to the public. I have taken the liberty of compressing those events into a single day.

When I took up playing the Celtic harp, people often asked me where harps like mine came from. People are more accustomed to seeing symphonic pedal harps, large gilded machines that cost many thousands of dollars. My Celtic harp is wooden, about five feet tall, and is used for folk music and contemporary songs, not orchestral works. The earliest triangular-shaped harps date to very early China, and Egypt. Archaeological evidence shows no harps such as these in Europe until the Renaissance or later. Tracing the history of the folk harp led me to other legends and myths, until the idea for this novel took form. If the Celtic harp travelled across the Mediterranean, then why not the revered Stone of Scone!

—Sincerely, Michele Buchanan, Ph.D.

GLOSSARY

Scota's Harp Glossary

Apis Bull: In Late Period Egypt a religious cult flourished in what is now Alexandria. The Apis Bull is adored as a god incarnate, and as Hapi-Apis is worshipped for the Nile floods. These bulls were kept in luxury, and worshipped until their death, then mummified. Young calves were identified by their white forehead blaze and certain markings on the flanks, but they were a rare find, much celebrated. Their worship was to guarantee the fertile flood of the Nile, for without this nutritious flood, crops would fail.

Abyssinia: ancient name of Ethiopia. Legends say that Pharaoh Nectanebus escaped the Persians by going west into the desert, or then to Ethiopia, then to Macedonia, where he lived as a soothsayer and court magician.

Akra Leuke: Ancient name of modern Allicante, Spain. Statue called "Lady of Eiche" found near here.

Amergin Gluingel: third son of Scota. Called the "Poet" he had the "Sight" and could prophecy. His poetry is written from memory in the Lebar na Nuachongbala, called the Book of Leinster. His major work recalling the invasion of Eire (Ireland) is sometimes entitled "The Mystery". He is said to be buried under Millmount in Ireland.

Ankh: Egyptian symbol of mortality and life, as a rope strap from a sandal ties one to the earth. Also called "crux ansata", a cross with a circular or oval headpiece.

Articana: wife of Ptolemy I, marriage arranged by Alexander. Historically she had a Persian mother, so this union was for political alliance. Ptolemy I had two other wives, Eurdike, and then Bernice, whom he loved.

Bentreshyt: translates as Harp of Joy in Egyptian

Calbe: Ancient name of Gibraltar. Riddled with limestone caves, the waters off Gibraltar are filled with hundreds of carved scarabs, votive offerings for safe passage through the strait.

Calanais: One of four standing stone circles on the Isle of Lewis, pronounced Cal-an-ish.

Cartouche: Royal names in glyphs, encircled by an oval rope with knot at the bottom. Written name insures immortality. Circling the name separates it from other text.

Cruithe: Inhabitants of the western and northern parts of Scotland, the people the Romans named "Picts."

Dagda: Irish god with a magic club, also a magic harp of oak that puts the seasons in their right order. His music captivates the listener.

Djedhor: Egyptian spelling for Teos, the Pharaoh following Nectanebus I, the "Falcon," may have been a nephew. As Pharaoh was incapable as leader, found refuge with the Persians after losing his main battle.

Eber Finn. Son of Scota and Gamal Miledh, one of the three surviving sons of the invasion of Ireland. He was defeated in battle by Erimon after the island was divided.

Evagoras II: Grandson of famous Evagoras I, King of Salamis 410-360, succeeded his father Nicocles who was assassinated in

361BC. He was appointed Satrap of Sidon by Artaxerxes but revolted against the Persians. He invaded Cyprus 350BC, the attempt failed and he was executed in 346BC. Alliances with the Persians to control Cilicia, Caria, Salamis, etc. Ambition to be King like his grandfather led to many different alliances. He had an unique gold stater, a grounded, attacking lion with an eagle perched on its hindquarters.

Faience: a self-glazing paste that when fired turns a brilliant blue, or sometimes green or white. It can be molded into small amulets such as scarabs or swabtis, small statuettes such as the famous faience hippo. When fired it is hard as stone and can be set into jewelry.

Felluca: lightweight Egyptian boat for use on the river with a triangular sail, rowed by a tiller.

Gades: modern day Cadiz, Spain

Goibniu: Irish god of smelting and blacksmithing, he has the magical cow of abundance. He is clever and makes weapons of silver.

Hariesis: vizier in the court of Nectanebus II, chief assassin and controller of palace servants.

Heka: Egyptian word for magic

Inber Sceine: an estuary in Ireland named for Scene, wife of Amergin who died at sea.

Isleta del Banyets: Queen's bathing pools. An island near Gibraltar having an ancient city devoter to the Goddess Tanit, which means "Land of Neith" the war goddess.

Karkissa: Ancient name of Caria, Languages there belonged to Hittite-Luwian sub-family of Indo-European languages, but some spoke Greek. Herodotus' father was a Carian. Long tradition of mercenary warriors, Carians invented shields with handles, devices on shields, crested helmets. Most inscriptions in Carian language are found in Egypt, rather that the homeland. Halicarnassus was the capital, other cities such as Miletus. Ephesus. People prayed to Carian Zeus and Hecate. The name means "steep" or rocky land and the Persians called their warriors "cocks" because of their plumed helmets.

Kart-Hadasht: Carthage "New City" settled by Phoenicians or Sea Peoples 800BCE

Kemet: Ancient name of Egypt, from which we have the word "chemical" sometimes spelled KMT

Kurnos: Ancient name of Corsica, harbor Aptoucha, traded metals, minerals.

Lahaf: Egyptian word for shawl

"Lang may yer lum reek": old Scottish greeting, the lum is the chimney, implying a warm/cozy house of long life.

Lia Fail: Irish name for Stone of Destiny/Coronation stone. Found at Hill of Tara, Ireland

Lugh: Irish war god of light, "blacksmith" and makers of weapons, skilled in many arts. He wielded a magic spear that could attack with lightning.

maHat: tomb or cenotaph, stone sculpture or marker place of burial

Manannan mac Lir: Irish God of the Sea, has a sea-borne chariot and a cloak of invisibility. He brings sea mists and fogs, strikes with a magic sword called the "Answerer."

Massalia: Ancient name of Marseilles, under Carthaginian control

Mausoleus: King of Caria, husband of sister Artemisia, who built his famous grave enclosure called Mausoleum

Myrtale of Epirote: Princess of Epirus, Mother of Alexander the Great. She changed her name to Olympia when she became the fourth wife of Phillip II, King of Macedonia. Her reputation of shrew, murderess, and scheming, manipulating mastermind is deserved, as Phillip was murdered at the wedding of his daughter. She probably had this carried out.

nibit-pi: mistress of the palace, who controls the economy of the household, the servants, schedules, visitors, and any sort of petitions from commoners. menu for feasts, etc.

Oengus In Irish Mythology: Oengus is a son of Dagda. He is described as having singular strength, with singing birds circling his head. He represents a god of love, youth and poetic inspiration. Hi lands were the passage at Newgrange, near the mouth of the Boyne. He is credited as killer of his stepfather Elcmar (who killed Midir)

Og: Irish god, son of Etain, champion of Lugh. He recovers the harp of Uaitne, the Dagda's harper. He helps to overthrow the Fomorians.

Osirion: an underground labyrinth used for novitiates in Osiris mystery for passage into true understanding of Egyptian religion. Water flows through it, and possibly crocodiles lived there, at least it is a fearsome and treacherous construction of the underworld.

praA: Great House, the palace

Rekhyt: common people of Egypt

Rhakoti: Ancient name of Alexandria, now submerged, northern Nile Delta

Sardo: ancient name of Sardinia, the Sea People called Shardana lived there and built over 7,000 towers called Nuaghe, very similar to those in Spain and Scotland. Ancient port of Tharros had beautiful white sand beaches.

Sea Peoples: or the "Nine Bows" in Egyptian literature, a coalition of tribal warriors who behave like modern day pirates. They pillage and burn settlements all along the Mediterranean but can be used as mercenaries agains invading Persians. No records of their homeland exist, nor do we know their language. They sometimes used a Phoenician script. First hegemony of pirates.

Shay: Egyptian word for fate

Shobou: palm wine

Stela: flat surfaced monument stone inscribed with proclamation. Sometimes used as geographical markers, records of military campaigns, royal decrees, etc. plural stelae. The Rosetta Stone is an example.

TAty: Palace overseer or seneschal, head chamberlain to the Pharaoh

Stone of Scone: "Lia Fail," "Stone of Destiny" or talking stone upon which Celtic kings were crowned. It is rectangular, weighing about 200lbs, has metal handles on each end for carrying. The stone was taken to Westminster and put under the English throne by Edward I. The stone is sandstone and measures 30" x

15" high, rough hewn and has a corner missing. and an obvious repair through the center. Historically the stone was used to crown Scottish Kings since the time of Robert the Bruce, who gave a corner of the stone to Cormac McCarthy, King of Munster, for helping at the Battle of Bannockburn. This piece is displayed on the wall of Blarney Castle, and the legend says kissing the stone will give the person the "gift of gab". Queen Elizabeth I in frustration for not receiving taxes from Ireland's King, said his words were "bunch of blarney" words with no substance, as money was rarely paid. However, this piece of stone is bluish granite and does not match the stone in Westminster. The Stone of Scone was returned to Scotland on St.Anddrew's Day, Nov. 16, 1996.

Ta-Urit: Hippo goddess of fertility, portrayed with a ponderous pregnant belly, a metaphor for the fertility brought by the Nile River and its flood.

Tech Duinn: Cairn on Ireland where souls of the dead may visit to bless Donn on their journey. Righteous souls may see it from afar, and are not led astray on their trip to a heavenly reward.

Tuatha de Danann: "Northern People of Dannu" or sometimes thought to be worshippers of Diana, or sons of the tribe of Dan. Inhabitants of the Irish land who defeated the Fir-bolgs and the Formorians. At the time of the Milesian invasion, there were three kings whose wives names were Eriu, Banba, and Fodla, who made peace with the Milesians after their husbands were slain in the battle. The island was named after Eriu as a battle concesion.

Uadjet: Usually the left eye of Horus, stylized by a mathematical formula. The eye has tears, long eyebrow, and symbolizes protection from the evil eye, guides the wearer to right action. Part of the Osiris regeneration myth.

About the Author

Michele Lang Buchanan grew up in Los Alamos, NM, as her father was a scientist with the Manhattan Project. She enjoyed a fulfilling career as a special education teacher for the Albuquerque Public Schools, working mostly with behavior disordered and incarcerated students. After retiring, she immersed herself in learning to play the Celtic harp, and traveled the Renfaire and Celtic festival circuit with her hand-made costumes. That small business, called "Vestments," kept her very busy for another ten years.

Michele delivers lectures on Scottish history, harp history, and performs with "Celtic Singers of NM." She lives in Albuquerque with her husband Tom, and performs with harp for hospice, at Celtic festivals and various fairs. As a fiber artist, she has won acclaim for embroidery, quilts, and needlework of all types. Perhaps it's a love affair with strings!